20   EXT. POOL — MORNING   20   *

MED → MCU YOUNG SOON
MED YOUNG SOON → MED 2 SHOT   20R

20   *

Young Soon Choi, the giant young Korean woman sits in a tight   *
swimsuit on the other side of the pool. She is the only one
out here. She has schoolbooks spread out on the chairs around
her.

CLEVELAND: HEY

Young Soon sits up as Cleveland walks over.   *

YOUNG SOON: HEY (CHI)

                    CLEVELAND
         Got a l-lot of homework?

                    YOUNG SOON CHOI   *
         University gives many pages of
         reading. What they think? I have no
         social life?

Cleveland smiles at the giant woman.   *SIT*

                    YOUNG SOON CHOI
         I got more books for you.

Cleveland takes a seat with her on the pool chair.

RESHOOT: "ANCIENT"
TKS 1+2 HAVE
TKS 3+4 DO NOT

                    CLEVELAND
         Could you look up the w-word 'Narf'   *
         for me?

(ANCIENT)   *ADD "ANCIENT"*
TKS 3,6 → 10 (NOT 11)

                    YOUNG SOON CHOI   *
         It is Eastern bedtime story Mr.   *
         Heep. I do not remember it. My
         Great Grandmother used to tell it
         when she was alive.

She hands Cleveland a group of books.

                    CLEVELAND
         A bedttt-time story? What's the
         story?

                    YOUNG SOON CHOI   *
         I do not remember...

She sees his disappointed expression.

                    CLEVELAND
         How about your mother?

                                        CUT TO:

The
Man Who
Heard Voices

ALSO BY MICHAEL BAMBERGER

The Green Road Home

To the Linksland

Bart & Fay (a play)

Wonderland

This Golfing Life

The Man Who Heard Voices

Or, How M. Night Shyamalan
Risked His Career on a Fairy Tale

MICHAEL BAMBERGER

GOTHAM BOOKS

GOTHAM BOOKS
Published by Penguin Group (USA) Inc.
375 Hudson Street, New York, New York 10014, U.S.A.
Penguin Group (Canada), 90 Eglinton Avenue East, Suite 700, Toronto,
Ontario M4P 2Y3, Canada (a division of Pearson Penguin Canada Inc.);
Penguin Books Ltd, 80 Strand, London WC2R 0RL, England;
Penguin Ireland, 25 St Stephen's Green, Dublin 2, Ireland (a division of
Penguin Books Ltd); Penguin Group (Australia), 250 Camberwell Road, Camberwell,
Victoria 3124, Australia (a division of Pearson Australia Group Pty Ltd);
Penguin Books India Pvt Ltd, 11 Community Centre, Panchsheel Park,
New Delhi – 110 017, India; Penguin Group (NZ), cnr Airborne and Rosedale Roads,
Albany, Auckland 1310, New Zealand (a division of Pearson New Zealand Ltd);
Penguin Books (South Africa) (Pty) Ltd, 24 Sturdee Avenue, Rosebank,
Johannesburg 2196, South Africa

Penguin Books Ltd, Registered Offices: 80 Strand, London WC2R 0RL, England

Published by Gotham Books, a member of Penguin Group (USA) Inc.

First printing, July 2006
1 3 5 7 9 10 8 6 4 2

LIBRARY OF CONGRESS CATALOGING-IN-PUBLICATION DATA
Bamberger, Michael, 1960–
The man who heard voices, : or, how M. Night Shyamalan risked
his career on a fairy tale / by Michael Bamberger.
p. cm.
ISBN 1-592-40213-5 (hardcover)
1. Lady in the water (Motion picture) I. Shyamalan, M. Night. II. Title.
PN1997.2.L33B36 2006
791.43'72—dc22   2006014777

ISBN 1-592-40213-5

Printed in the United States of America
Set in Scala
Designed by Elke Sigal

For *Ellen Nalle* and *Jay Hass,*

ambassadors of love.

Trust thyself, and another shall not betray thee.

—BENJAMIN FRANKLIN

April 17, 2004

M y wife and I are movie buffs. We go to the movies regularly on Saturday nights, and every so often, when the kids are in school, we sneak off and see a matinee, when the prices are lower and you can sit wherever you like. A cup of hot coffee during the noon showing of *The Talented Mr. Ripley* on a cold and drizzly workday—it's an altogether pleasant thing. I am nothing like a movie expert. (Ingmar Bergman, man or woman? I don't know.) Mostly I just like the escape, the drift into a dreamworld. Christine's the same way. We have similar tastes.

There are, of course, Saturday evenings when we don't go to the movies, and the third Saturday of April 2004 was such a night. It was a balmy night, humid and breezy, odd for Philadelphia at that time of year. I remember the night well because of the dinner party we attended. Christine, if I may say this about my wife, improves any party, and because I'm a sportswriter, some hostesses confuse me with the witty scribes they remember from old TV shows, Oscar Madison in *The Odd Couple*, maybe. Anyway, we're invited to some nice gigs. I am not a party person, but sometimes you can't help yourself.

We were the guests of a sparkly couple, Bob and Susan Burch, we knew through friends. They live in one of the grand mansions still standing on the Main Line, the string of affluent Philadelphia suburbs. We had not been to their house before.

The walled driveway went on forever, and above the entrance road, in an apple orchard, one of the Burch children was riding a pony, no saddle, with war paint on his face and a quiver of arrows across his shirtless back. What we thought was the house was actually the guesthouse, so we kept going. Jim Courier, the tennis player, was with us. He saw the boy on his pony and the Philadelphia skyline ten miles beyond and interrupted himself in midsentence to say, "Where the hell are we?"

Bob Burch—a book reader, God bless him—got rich selling sweaters, and if he ever had a boss in his life, you cannot tell. When Susan recounted a cross-country family trip in a Winnebago, Mother Susan at the wheel and a goggled Bob almost keeping up on his latest bike, it sounded like a scene from an Albert Brooks movie. Her guest list comprised an unlikely hodgepodge of people. Brian Roberts, who runs a giant cable company, was there with his wife, Aileen, a Philadelphia do-gooder, visiting the Burches for the first time. Courier was there with a date, a former model and pianist, and there were five or six other people, including an investor/weekend poet and a futurist. Christine and I were the only poor people, relatively speaking, on hand that night—we have a nice collection of yard-sale art—but this was a crowd no longer worried about money. (Surely a lie, but it is the privilege of the city-dwelling working typist to romanticize such people.)

The guests of honor, a phrase I use casually here, were M. Night Shyamalan, the screenwriter and director, and his wife, Bhavna, then a doctoral candidate in psychology at Bryn Mawr College. The Burches and Shyamalans lived near each other and were involved in some of the same charities, and Susan had wanted to get Night and Bhavna over for some time. It was not easy, because the Shyamalans guarded their free time carefully, and Night was famous for being secretive and private. Susan knew they avoided parties in general, especially if the conversation was likely to run to old golf courses or new hedge funds. Susan's social IQ is at the genius level, and she laid out the guest list for Bhavna ahead of time; on that basis, she got the Shyamalans, as the salesmen say, "to yes." The Shyamalans didn't know the other guests, but in a manner of speaking, they had picked them.

I had read M. Night Shyamalan's surname a hundred times in *The Philadelphia Inquirer*—he had grown up in suburban Philadelphia and made his movies in and around the city—but I didn't know how to pronounce it (as it is spelled, except the y just sits there doing nothing: *SHA-ma-lon*). He was a Philadelphia celebrity in a low-key way, though Philadelphians are not much for hero worship. In the days of the Founding Fathers, the city claimed Benjamin Franklin; in the nineteenth century, the city's great industrialists were its stars, your Lippincotts (books), your Baldwins (locomotives), your Stetsons (hats), plus the Barrymores (actors). For most of the twentieth century, the Main Line bluebloods were still prominent, with their estates and their horses, plus Grace Kelly and Rocky Balboa, although you could argue that he was a movie character. In the new millennium, there was Allen Iverson, the elfin NBA basketball player; Donovan McNabb, the Philadelphia Eagles quarterback; and M. Night. Nobody I knew really talked about him. You just went to see his movies. I had seen his three big ones: *The Sixth Sense* (disturbing, in a good way); *Unbreakable* (didn't like it while watching it, but it stayed with me); and *Signs* (entertaining but didn't linger).

Christine and I had seen *The Sixth Sense* on a Saturday night, every seat taken, people murmuring about the streets they recognized. We were blown away by the surprise ending, like everybody else. You know the supermarket chain Trader Joe's? When I'm in it, I can never tell if it's a grocery store for foodies or a big-box discount place. I had the same kind of thing with *The Sixth Sense*. I didn't know if it was an especially entertaining movie—or something more momentous. I was curious to meet Night, but not in any crazy way. Meeting the famous and the faintly famous, it's an occupational hazard in my line of work. Barry Bonds did a whole verbal rage thing on me once. All part of the fun.

Before I get to Night, let me tell you about his wife, Bhavna. She is Indian, like Night, with traces of a British accent, from her Hong Kong childhood, and a quiet, poised manner. Listening to her, you knew she was an academic heavyweight, but she had the stillness and manners of a princess. She had a delicate beauty, like that of an idealized Miss India, with glossy lips and the figure of a swimsuit model. Night had coaxed her into his camp when they were undergraduates at New York University, when he was just another kid writing scripts and borrowing money to rent cameras and spotlights. He must have had some major mojo going, Austin Powers and then some. I'm sure he wasn't a total schlub, but please. He was a *writer*. I've been there. It's not easy.

And then there was Night, with his drooping earlobes, bug's-life eyes, curling lips, nasal voice. He was slender and boyish, with gym-built arms and jet-black hair that had a few silver strands hanging just over the tops of his ears. He was wearing high-fashion jeans and a short-sleeved, post-nerd untucked plaid shirt, wide open at the neck, and a leather necklace that held a Sanskrit prayer in a silver case, like a miniature mezuzah. He and Bhavna arrived last, holding hands as they made their way through the small Saturday-night-fever crowd. In almost no time, Night looked completely comfortable. He was warm, friendly, interesting—amazingly energetic. He laughed readily, as if you were saying funny things. He'd enter any debate without ever getting haughty about what he knew. I go down the New Age road skeptically, but I felt a powerful force coming off the guy.

Outside the big house and down a hill there was a giant te-pee and a roaring bonfire nearby that, late in the evening, was encircled by the menfolk. There was a Native American theme going on at the Burches', and it worked for Night. He talked about his next movie, *The Village,* and how at the start of the shoot, the main actors—William Hurt, Joaquin Phoenix, Sigour-ney Weaver, Bryce Howard (Ron Howard's daughter, he pointed out)—had gone into some sort of sweatbox built deep in the woods where an American Indian holy man led them in medi-tation. He was talking about big stuff—community, faith—with strangers, and we weren't looking at our shoes. It was all very 1967. Night's shirt was half open—Tom Jones in his prime. "It was my idea, as a bonding thing, but it was for the actors. What happened in there, what they wore, what they talked about, I don't know," Night said. "Pretty cool, right?" I was amazed at the effort he was making—that's not recom-mended in the celebrity handbook—and by how open he was and how trusting. Also, by how much he loved to talk.

Earlier, Night had asked Jim Courier about his tennis ca-reer, about his training methods, about the tennis academy he'd attended for high school. Night said he'd followed Courier's professional career as a player on his own high school tennis team. Night spoke of how he had disliked it when his oppo-nents came on the court with a stack of virgin rackets, alu-minum, titanium, whatever. "My feeling was always, *What did you do to deserve those rackets?*" Before long, Courier was asking Night about his days in junior tennis as if they were significant, and to Night, they were.

With Brian Roberts, Night was much the same. Brian's company, Comcast, was trying to buy Disney at the time. That was all over the papers day after day. Night had made three big movies for Disney, starting with *The Sixth Sense,* which had grossed close to $700 million in worldwide ticket sales. He had made *The Village,* not yet out, for Disney, too. The first two movies starred Bruce Willis and the third Mel Gibson, but *The Village* would be sold on its director. Brian asked Night a series of incisive questions about the movie business and its players, about Michael Eisner and Harvey Weinstein and Night's prediction for the future of movies in the movie house. Listening to Night's long, involved, articulate answers, you would have thought he was Michael Eisner's boss. Brian is an excellent reporter and listener, and you could say he was leading the whole thing, getting the information he wanted, but something else was happening, too. Night was having exactly the conversation he wanted to have with Brian, the man he'd be making movies for if the Disney deal went through.

Night didn't anoint himself the star of the evening. The rest of us did that for him. I had often seen Bob Burch or Brian Roberts or Jim Courier or Aileen Roberts in that role, but not this evening. Night told us excellent star-of-the-show stories, the kind you hear on late-night talk shows. One involved, as these stories often do, his parents, both doctors, both émigrés from India.

Night: I've got exciting news.

Mother: Yes?

Night: I'm gonna be on the cover of Newsweek.

Mother: That's nice.

Father: Not Time?

Night: No, not Time. *I'll be the first director ever on the cover of* Newsweek.

A beat.

Father: Doesn't Time *have a much bigger circulation?*

Night laughed and then everybody else did, too. The underlying burden implied by the story—his parents' titanic expectations—was ignored.

You could tell that Night—with his sagging ears and swollen eyes—heard and saw everything going on that night. I watched him watching a housekeeper remove a wineglass from a serving tray, hold it up to a light, and disqualify it for soap streaks. How Night read this simple act of professionalism, I do not know, because I did not ask. My thing as a reporter has always been to get to the bottom of something, ask the right questions of the right people. Night's methods, I guessed, were totally different. I got the feeling that he had some secret move up his sleeve, one that let him come up with a big idea, invent a killing phrase ("I see dead people"), and sell close to $700 million worth of movie tickets across the world. I wondered how he did it.

On the car ride home and on the phone the next day, I polled some of the other guests on the subject of Night. They used different words—smart, quick, fun, cocky, likable, boyish, odd, captivating—and had different impressions, but all had felt the force of his personality. They could remember what he was wearing, the phrases he used, the way he twisted his rings while talking.

I sent Night a letter saying that I'd be interested in writing a book about him, about his methods, about how his head worked. Through his assistant, he invited me to his office, in a farmhouse on an old horse farm. We talked for several hours and followed that with several lengthy telephone conversations. By then he had read a book of mine about a big public high school in the Philadelphia suburbs. In the book, an eleventh-grader dies after a night of drinking. A female teacher has a relationship with a male student. A senior boy and a junior girl have a baby. It's all real names and real events. A boy with cerebral palsy, a social outsider, makes it to the prom.

"If you wrote about me the way you wrote about the kids in that high school, I'd read that," Night said.

"You realize that nobody from the high school had any say about what went in the book, don't you?"

"Of course."

"I'd need the same thing from you."

"It would have to be that way. If it wasn't like that, the book would have no credibility. I want to see somebody else's take on what I do. I want to learn something."

On that basis—no contract, no lawyers, no agents, nothing but a handshake—I started hanging out with him.

For a long time afterward, I thought about that balmy April evening at the Burches'. I wondered: Was the whole thing some kind of movie? Did Night direct us—without saying a word—on where to stand, what costumes to wear, what to say? Did he get Susan Burch, in some telepathic way, to put her son on a pony in their apple orchard as a magnificent piece of background scenery?

If he had these powers, where did they come from? Could another person develop them?

And if he could have that kind of power over a dinner party, what kind of power could he have over one of the largest entertainment companies in the world?

What kind of power could he have over me?

And what else could he do with his powers? Was there a great, good thing he could do?

Anyway, Night began as an intriguing subject. What he would turn into I could not then know.

1.

started making occasional visits to the farm, for lunch and a talk in the farmhouse. Everything was well-ordered: the hand towels, the water bottles in the refrigerator, the posters of Night's movies. There were six of them, now that *The Village* was out. There was a special shelf for books Night *hadn't* read. The floors and the walls and the furniture were pretty much all brown or beige. Near Night's office there was a secret room, with no doorknob on the door. You had to press on the right part of the wall to get in it. It was off-limits.

You might have said the whole setting was severe, but the sofas were plush and comfortable. You sank into them, but there was no chance of falling asleep. Night's voice—electric and squeaky, posing questions, pontificating about *something*—was always in the air. He was writing a new script and he'd break for lunch at noon—or thereabouts. He wasn't a total slave to ritual.

He had his own chef, and Night's assistant, Paula, and the man who ran his production company, Jose, ate lunch with him daily. If Paula talked about her upcoming honeymoon, Night might offer a theory about honeymoons as a predictor of married life. If Jose brought up Shaquille O'Neal's struggles as a free-throw shooter, Night might offer an analysis of the giant basketball player's arc problems. With Night, you didn't just sit there. There was no discussion of the weather.

He said his new script had been nothing but a struggle. He

hadn't wrestled so much with a screenplay since writing *The Sixth Sense.*

For the longest time, on that one, all he had was an idea. Night had gone to a funeral. A boy there was talking to himself. Night wondered what the boy was thinking. He went home and wrote down four words: *I see dead people.*

It was a start, but that's all it was. He began writing from the perspective of a ten-year-old boy. As a kicker, he had the boy say, "I see dead people." He reread the line. It didn't work. *I see dead people*, it sounded too young for a smart ten-year-old. It sounded like something a six-year-old might say. He drew a line through it.

"And then the voices came," Night told me.

"The voices?"

"The voices told me to put it back."

"What did they say?"

" 'Put it back.' "

It was interesting, but I really didn't know what he was talking about. I mean, we've all taken multiple-choice tests where you fill in one circle, erase it, fill in another circle, erase it, and go back to what you had the first time, right? What was different here?

"I had faith in the voices. I was just then learning the power of listening to the voices."

I asked, "Do you think everybody has these voices?"

Over $1 billion dollars, that's what *The Sixth Sense* did in worldwide ticket sales and DVD sales and in the sale of broadcast rights. It was an entertaining movie and a phenomenon. The movie came out and before you knew it "I see dead people" was on T-shirts, in commercials, in *Saturday Night Live* skits, in reference books. People would come up to Night in restaurants and whisper, "I see dead people, too."

There's a joke in movie marketing: when that greetings-from-God voiceover comes on during the trailer, deepened by a lifetime of smoking, and says, "This Christmas, the heart-warming story for anybody who's ever been in love—or wanted to fall in love." In other words, a movie for the population of the world, or that segment who can afford a $10 ticket. That's what *The Sixth Sense* was: *This summer, the spooky story for anybody who ever wanted to know what the hereafter is like—or for anybody who thought they did.*

Night wrote it, directed it, produced it. He appeared in it. After one good movie, people were calling Night the next Hitchcock, with the cameos and the smart creepiness, and he wasn't even thirty. He was praised as a director who loved actors—witness the understated performance he drew from the action hero Bruce Willis. It was 1999, and Night was like a rock star.

Night's three following movies all made lots of money. There were people who loved them, and of course people who didn't, but they were successful movies by nearly any definition. They weren't, though, phenomena. Night had the idea that the new one could be.

He had started writing it in the spring of 2004, when he was putting the finishing touches on *The Village*. He stayed with it through the summer and the fall. It was resistant to paper, *way* off-kilter, but he kept writing. That's what the voices were telling him to do, embrace a strange, beautiful, audacious idea. Late at night, he'd sit in the basement of his home in the suburbs of Philadelphia, his wife and two young daughters in their beds fast asleep, and stare into his red notebook, his skin tingling with anxiety.

He'd get down a good half page here, and a couple of worthless pages after it. There were scenes that sounded good when he talked to himself—which he often did, his lips actually moving—but not when his characters did the talking.

There were family vacations where he went through the motions of cheerful beach lounger, distracted all the time. The occasional party, where everyone thought he was in charge. Good acting. Always, somewhere in his mind, was his next movie.

There was an architect in his kitchen then, looking to move a wall to accommodate a larger kitchen. He was ready to spend more of Night's money.

"How's the new screenplay coming?" he asked. It was a little joke, as if the project's budget was tied to Night's next paycheck.

"Awful," Night said.

He paused. In a screenplay he'd call it *a beat*.

"But it's gonna be great."

For inspiration, he'd think of Michael Jordan. Night was awed by how much Jordan believed in himself, and how, right through his final game, everybody knew it. You could see it in the sweat on his shaved head, in his wagging tongue, in his backward canter after holing another long jump shot. Night could have made calls and arranged to meet him, but he didn't. What he knew from a distance was all he needed.

"He's playing his last game in Philadelphia," Night told his agent. "That's got to mean something. That's got to be some kind of sign, right?"

"Only to you and the other twenty thousand people," said the agent, Jeremy Zimmer.

"Bullshit."

Night went to the game and snapped pictures. Twenty thousand other people did, too.

Night knew there was something telepathic going on between him and Michael Jordan, him and Bob Dylan, him and Walt Disney.

While writing his new script, he read the David Halberstam

book about Jordan. He studied it. The hours "Michael" (as Night referred to him) logged in the weight room and at the free-throw line, long after everybody else had left. That image helped keep Night at it. Bhavna had once shown Night a book, a study of prodigies. The most common trait among prodigies was the sheer number of hours they devoted to their talent. Night took notice.

Night knew that Jordan not only made more game-winning shots than any other player, he missed more potential game winners than anybody else, too. Night liked that. He was ready to fail, to fall on his face, as long as it was spectacular. (For all he knew, he was doing so right then, with his new script.) Jordan came up at odd times of the day, unconnected to anything. "With the game on the line, he *wanted* the ball," Night said to me one day. It was early in the morning and he was already preaching. "He always believed he'd make the next one."

When he was starting out, before *The Sixth Sense*, Night was meeting with some businesspeople from Apple, the computer company, at Jeremy Zimmer's office in Los Angeles. The conversation turned to basketball.

"I believe if I had unlimited time to practice, after two years, I'd be able to shoot with any NBA player," Night said. The room went quiet.

Who is this guy? Who thinks that way? Who says these things to strangers?

The meeting ended, the room cleared, and Jeremy Zimmer said, "You can't say stuff like that." He knew how it sounded: grandiose, unrealistic, egotistical.

Night was unfazed. What he had said was true. That is, he believed it.

As a kid, Night once gathered his cousins around a table and cleared everything off it except a cup.

"Okay, if everybody stares at the cup, stares at it hard and really believes that we can make the cup move, it'll move."

A half-minute passed.

"It's not moving."

"C'mon, man, concentrate, *concentrate*. Think, *We can move the cup!*"

Another half-minute.

"Hey, I think I saw it move!"

"You see? See? *That's* what I'm talking about!"

The goddamn script! It was giving him panic attacks. There were sleepless nights, cold sweats, bouts of uncontrollable crying, odd dreams. In the movies, the image of the writer up in the middle of the night, tapping away while the rest of the world sleeps, is romanticized. For Night it was hell. One day, as he was describing his struggling self, I said, "But your life's good, isn't it? You're healthy, you're rich, your wife's getting her doctorate, your children . . ." His girls were a delight—little pixies.

"These movies I make?" he said. "They're who I am."

Every school day was the same. Get up with Bhavna and the girls, put on jeans and a T-shirt and work boots, drop his daughters off at school, and drive to his office at the farm, where a blinking cursor would greet him and mock him for the next nine hours. He didn't go out for lunch. He didn't schmooze with friends on the phone. He'd sit at the keyboard and write a line. Look at it. Hit the backspace button. Write a line. Look at it. Hit the backspace button. Write a line. Look at it. Not hit the backspace button. Another chip.

He had a title: *Lady in the Water*. He had the names of the two main characters, a woman named Story and a man named Cleveland. He knew who would play Story: Bryce Dallas Howard, his lead actress in *The Village*, in which she played a blind woman. He knew the story he wanted to tell. The themes were so broad, he had no idea how he'd fit them on a movie poster. It was about a secretive building superintendent who falls in love with a sort of angel—a "sea nymph," Night was calling her—who lives under the super's pool. It was about strangers coming together. It was a recipe for the repair of the world. It was a comedy. It was a horror movie. It was a bedtime story, one he had invented for his daughters, one he had told them night after night. He wondered why he was struggling so to get it to work in the form of a screenplay, the writing form that defined his life. And then he figured it out. This movie was more personal to him than anything he had ever written. It carried all his prayers. It was a self-portrait.

When he finally got a first draft done, he read it with no pleasure at all. His notes in the margins were slaps to himself.

Bad writing.

Makes no sense.

Common!

That last one stung particularly. His parents had escaped the Indian caste system, which bound them to the worn-shoe life of the working class; they had become, despite the pull of their family histories, medical doctors living in America. They had a backyard swimming pool. They were leading the good life. In the Shyamalan family, *common* was a loaded word. To be ordinary, how perfectly awful. His parents were loving, spiritual, engaged people—and strivers of the highest order. A certain kind of traditional American immigrant. They valued education intensely and sent their daughter and son to the best private schools. Night was the only Hindu at his all-boys coat-and-tie Catholic grammar school, Waldron Academy, and everybody there knew him by his given name, Manoj. The parents chose the school for its discipline. The students there were required to work.

For high school, his parents sent him to Episcopal Academy,

a private school loaded with high achievers, athletic, social, and academic. Night was scrawny and dark, and only academically was he a notable. He was a good HORSE player on the playground basketball court but had no chance of making a varsity team that included a future NBA player. His lone social triumph came late in his senior year. A pretty girl needed to retrieve something from a baseball player's car. The ballplayer tossed her the keys.

"I'll come with you," Night said, suddenly bold.

"Okay," the girl said, cooing.

The athlete glared at Night and said, "Whoa—I don't know about that. I don't know if I can trust you two."

The girl tittered. Night found the moment intoxicating.

He applied to New York University, to its Tisch School of the Arts, Martin Scorsese's alma mater. Night applied early decision. If he was accepted, he'd have to commit right away. The letter came back thick.

"Dad, I got in to NYU," Night said that evening. "That's where I'm going to go."

His father, an internist with a specialty in cardiology, had hoped movies would be a passing interest for Manoj, and that at some point he'd follow his parents into medicine or the law—some real profession. With Night's verbal scores and his extreme fluency, it was easy to imagine him becoming a high-profile trial lawyer, an F. Lee Bailey, somebody like that.

Dr. Shyamalan was watching a hockey game, and he was silent for a long moment. They were close, but the father could be tough with his son, comically so at times. When Night was young, his stomach was often upset. "Eat more toast, you'll feel better," his father said. Toast was his panacea for everything.

Dad, I think I broke my knee.

Eat more toast!

Dr. Shyamalan knew why kids enrolled in the film program

at NYU, the dreams they took there. He knew what the news meant for his son's future. He kept staring at the hockey game.

"It's not Princeton," he finally said.

Over the summer before he left for NYU, Manoj started thinking about a middle name for himself.

"Why don't I have a middle name?" he asked his parents.

"Manoj Shyamalan is a fine name," his mother said.

"I have no middle!" the son said. Not just a middle name but a middle, period.

His parents didn't know what he was talking about. That was often the case.

"Why don't you call yourself Jaya?" said his mother.

"Jaya? That's your name," Manoj said. "I'm gonna call myself by my mother's name?"

A lot of Indian immigrants in America, males especially, were using American names. Manoj knew there were many Indian Bobs and Mikes and Sams driving cabs and going to grad school and working at Wal-Mart. He wanted something distinctive. For a while, he used his father's first name, Nelliate, but it didn't fit. At the time, Manoj was developing what turned into a sustained interest in American Indians. The idea of finding God in the outdoors, worshiping nature, sounded better to him than anything else he was hearing. He admired the English versions of Indian names. (The author of *Blue Highways* was William Least Heat-Moon, to cite one prominent example.) Reading about the Lakota Indians, Manoj came across the name Night and liked it immediately. Adopting it took years. "Manoj had to go through the rituals of death," Night told me. "I had to earn the name Night."

In time, he did. In time, he came to own it. He took possession of one of the most common, essential basic words in the

English language, one of the first words infants learn. There's *mama, milk, baby, day,* and *night.* You might say *night,* what, thirty or forty times per day? It's everywhere. Genesis, Chapter 1, Verse 5: "And God called the light Day, and the darkness he called Night." Depending on when you Google it, *night* turns up around three million references. The first one I saw was the Elie Wiesel book. The second was an astronomy site named for the van Gogh painting. The third was *Saturday Night Live.* The fourth was M. Night Shyamalan.

He could have sold his screenplay for *Lady in the Water* without writing a single word. He was one of the highest-paid screen-writers in the business and any studio would have been happy to pay him upfront, like a ballplayer getting paid on the expec-tation of future home runs. But Night didn't want that sense of security. He worried that it would make him lazy and satisfied. He wanted to write his screenplays, then sell them. He called the draft he'd send off his sale script.

It was a mind game for Night. He knew he was writing *Lady in the Water* for the Walt Disney Studios, the company founded by one of his heroes. Disney was Night's artistic home. He had made *The Sixth Sense* there and his three following movies. There was never idle speculation in *The Hollywood Reporter* about what studio would pay the bills for Night's next movie. Technically, *The Sixth Sense* was released by Hollywood Pic-tures, and the three next movies were made by Touchstone Pictures, both divisions of Disney. Those four movies were too edgy—too scary—to go out under the Disney name. Still, Dis-ney was his studio. Not since Mr. Walt Disney himself had any one director been so associated with Disney.

Michael Eisner, the Disney chairman, came to the screen-ings and openings of Night's movies. He had stood with Night in the parking lot of a suburban multiplex after a test screening of *Unbreakable* and, without the benefit of a single test score, said, "The best Disney movie in twenty-five years." Eisner's praise meant the world to Night. He liked the idea of pleasing the boss.

Night wanted to make *Lady* under the Disney name, see it stamped in the opening credits by the tidy cursive Disney signature, with the flittering Tinker Bell dotting the *i*. His daughters loved the magic of Disney. He could imagine their faces when they finally got to see it, the story that began in their beds.

Night made two movies before his Disney years. The first, *Praying with Anger*, was shot in India and paid for with money that Night, still a student at NYU, had borrowed from family and friends. It played on one screen for one week in 1992 and was never shown again.

His second movie, *Wide Awake*, was about a little boy trying to solve a big riddle: Where do we go when we die? (It's a preamble to *The Sixth Sense*.) *Wide Awake* was shot at Night's Catholic grammar school in 1995—Rosie O'Donnell played a nun—and released in '98 by Miramax Films, then a small, frugal independent production company founded and run by the brothers Harvey and Bob Weinstein and owned by Disney.

On *Wide Awake*'s first day of filming, Night stopped action, and the cast and crew watched Bhavna as she performed a ritual Hindu service in a colorful ceremonial skirt. It was a prayer for the camera. Her husband was making a union movie, his first, with name actors and a crew of seen-it-all movie pros, and they all just stopped and watched, perplexed and delighted. The idea that they were doing something odd never occurred to Night.

After Night shot the movie, Harvey took over. He was famously tyrannical, an enormous man who had a reputation for squashing careers. He didn't like the footage Night had shot and didn't trust him to turn it into a profitable movie in the editing room. He pushed Night aside.

Night asked one of Harvey's lieutenants, "Why is he doing this?"

"Because you're not an A-list director."

"But could I be?"

Night heard Harvey screaming in the silence: *You're not, and you never will be.*

The movie bombed, as it had to. It had been made in bad faith.

Night swore that no matter how desperate he ever became, he would never make another movie for Harvey. To anybody else, that sounded absurdly bold. After *Wide Awake*, nobody was beating down a path to Night. The truth was, Harvey *owned* Night. He had a contract with Night for two more movies. But in his mind, Night was firing Harvey. The conventional thing, the political thing, was for Night to try to smooth things over with Harvey, so he could get more work. But Night had another idea.

He'd write something spectacular, so spectacular that competing studios would outbid one another for the right to own it, at a price Harvey would not dream of spending. So spectacular that the winning studio would agree to Night's demand to direct his own script. So spectacular that the winning studio, the one that would buy Night's script and permit him to direct it, would work out the contractual problems with Harvey, spend big money on lawyers, if need be.

Night wrote *The Sixth Sense* out of ambition and desperation—to get out of Harvey Weinstein's suffocating grasp. He labored over it obsessively, day and night, rewriting scenes again and again, permitting no one to see the script until he had every detail worked out. He believed he could write his way out of his hole. All he had to do was put in the time, concentrate the right way, believe in the voices. He wrote the line "I see dead people." He took it out. He put it back in. The voices had spoken: *Sometimes what doesn't make sense works.*

Night asked Jeremy Zimmer to impose these conditions on the sale: He wanted a minimum bid of $1 million; the guarantee that he would direct the movie; and for the auction to begin and end on the same day. All the scripts were sent by messenger and delivered at the same time, except for one: Harvey's, which went out by U.S. mail. Night could do that because the Weinsteins owned him as a director but not as a writer. The conditions would have been preposterous, except that Jeremy believed in the script as much as Night did, and he hadn't even read it. He could hear Night's belief in the script in his voice, so Zimmer ran with it. He called up one executive after another and said, "I'm going to send you a script, and I think you're going to want to clear everything and read it right away. It's that good." Night wasn't an unknown. His script for *Stuart Little* had been widely praised, as was an unproduced script called *Labor of Love.* But Zimmer was talking like he was about to send them *Psycho.* What Night had engineered was a study in chutzpah but also self-protection. He wasn't going to let Harvey Weinstein subvert his career and his life.

Four studios passed on the script within hours of receiving it. Nina Jacobson at DreamWorks read it and loved it. So did Michael Lynne at New Line; he put in an extraordinary bid, $2 million. Zimmer convinced David Vogel, the president of Disney Pictures, to cancel his lunch plans, read the script, and get in. Vogel did so. He thought it was the kind of over-the-transom script that a movie executive might read once in a career. Zimmer encouraged Vogel to better the New Line offer. Vogel wanted to end the auction immediately. He offered an astonishing amount for the script, $3 million, and added another $500,000 for Night to direct. A done deal.

Harvey was fine with it, as Night suspected he would be all along. Harvey was a bargain shopper who didn't spend one tenth that on a script, especially if a mediocrity (Night's take on Harvey's take) like M. Night Shyamalan was demanding to shoot it. Harvey insisted on a piece of the profits, on the off chance that the project would make any money. In the end, for Harvey, it was money for nothing.

Night's moves were spectacular. With no business experience, with no training, he had engineered a complex and lucrative deal. In 1998 he was a young outsider, twenty-eight years old and from suburban Philadelphia, and he had found a way to get a trio of powerful and experienced Hollywood men—David Vogel and Harvey Weinstein and Jeremy Zimmer—to do exactly what he wanted them to do. The experience was empowering.

Less than a year later, during the first test screening of *The Sixth Sense*, something was wrong with the projector. The reels were wobbling and so was the picture on the screen.

"You better stop the screening," Night's editor, sitting next to him, said. He knew a wobbly picture would not endear the movie to the audience.

But Night was at peace. All he said was, "It's okay—let it go." He could feel how the audience was responding to his movie, he could feel it in his tingly fingers, moist eyes, dry throat, and pounding heart.

When the movie was over, there were gasps. There was wild applause. In the lobby, Night was mobbed by people who hadn't known his name three hours earlier.

Hey, there's the guy who wrote it.

He didn't write it, he directed it.

I heard he did both!

With one movie, Night's status had changed. For the foreseeable future, or for as long as his movies made piles of money, he'd have the right to final cut, the last word in how his movies would look upon release. From then on, Night would also have a significant say in when a movie would be released in the United States and overseas, which actors would be hired, what the poster and the trailer would look like, and where he'd shoot. The list of big-budget directors who have that kind of say is short. There's George Lucas, Steven Spielberg, Peter Jackson, Quentin Tarantino, Robert Zemeckis, James Cameron, Ron Howard, maybe ten others. *The Sixth Sense* got Night on that list not because he had directed it but because he had written it *and* directed it. He had come up with an original idea and brought a whole world to life. He got people to think about his movie long after they left the theater.

After *The Sixth Sense,* Night no longer had to move the chess pieces himself. Others would do that for him. All he had to do was write and direct movies people wanted to see. Such power and freedom can corrupt, of course. But Night was lucky. He didn't want a harem, a mansion in Bel-Air, his picture in *Us Weekly*. All he wanted to do was keep making movies.

By the standard of his Disney debut, Night's next three movies were lesser events. But viewed collectively, Disney, from the accountants right up to Michael Eisner, had no reason to be anything but happy. *Unbreakable,* with Bruce Willis as the unscratched lone survivor of a train wreck, earned $249 million in worldwide ticket sales. *Signs,* with Mel Gibson as a lost minister/farmer trying to figure out the mystery of the crop circles appearing in his fields, grossed $405 million in ticket sales. *The Village,* the weird and dark one, marketed as a movie written and directed by M. Night Shyamalan, grossed $256 million.

Then there was the sale of DVDs and broadcast rights generating tens of millions more. The movies made enormous amounts of money, for Disney shareholders and for Night.

There was murmuring. There always is when somebody's getting rich fast. There were people saying Night had peaked early with *The Sixth Sense*. There were people—Disney executives, moviegoers, reviewers—who had him in a box: the writer-director who makes dark, creepy movies with surprise endings. Each time out, there were big pens who were kind to him, but even more taking free swings.

Kenneth Turan of the *Los Angeles Times* on *Unbreakable:* "Copycat films are a fact of life in Hollywood, and once writer-director M. Night Shyamalan's *The Sixth Sense* grossed more than $600 million worldwide and earned six Oscar nominations, it was inevitable that someone would use all the same elements to produce an inferior version. *Unbreakable* is the knockoff we've been expecting, but what's surprising is that it's Shyamalan himself who's at the helm."

A. O. Scott of *The New York Times* on *Signs:* "Mr. Shyamalan never gives us anything to believe in, other than his own power to solve problems of his own posing, and his command of a narrative logic is as circular—and as empty—as those bare patches out in the cornfield."

Then there was Roger Ebert, with his famous thumb pointing movies toward oblivion or fame. His contempt for *The Village* was outsized. In the *Chicago Sun-Times,* he wrote: "A colossal miscalculation, a movie based on a premise that cannot support it, a premise so transparent it would be laughable were the movie not so deadly solemn."

You read that stuff about yourself, it takes a toll. It seeps in. The movie Night was writing then, was *it* a colossal miscalculation? *Lady in the Water* wasn't like anything playing in his neighborhood multiplex. It had no conventional three-act structure, no turning point, no dramatic love scene or fight. It was a story in which the characters don't know if what they're doing or saying is real. There were times when Night felt he was making an artistic breakthrough, as Steven Spielberg did with *E.T.* (an alien with a heart), as Quentin Tarantino did with *Pulp Fiction* (killers double as wry social commentators), as William Friedkin did with *The Exorcist* (coexistence of good and evil in one young girl). And there were times when the script made no sense even to him.

Night was walking a plank. *The Village* had been a departure for him. *The Sixth Sense* and *Unbreakable* and *Signs* were about faith. *The Village* asked you to question authority. (To me, it was his most interesting picture.) *The Village* was a movie for heretics, and the fact that it exists at all is a testament to Night's powers of persuasion. Disney would have been delighted to see Night forever make reruns of *The Sixth Sense,* or even *Signs.* (The headline for the review of *Signs* in the *New York Post* was telling and funny: I SEE GREEN PEOPLE.) By any normal measure of a movie's success, *The Village* did extremely well. For a movie from an original script—not from a TV show or a game or a best-selling book or another movie—without any sex or guns or car chases, its success was stunning. But because of *The Sixth Sense* and *Signs,* Disney had spectacular financial expectations for Night's movies. The profits of *The Village* showed him going in the wrong direction. The movie did not represent onward and upward.

And now Night was writing something weirder still, an original fable. If he could make it work, worlds would open, for him, for other writers and directors, for people who saw the movie, for anybody who just wanted once in his life to say to the boss, *Haven't I earned your trust? Let me try to do my own thing here, okay?* For anybody dealing with his own Harvey Weinstein.

If *Lady* failed, Night knew what it would mean: The Disney bosses would push him back in his box. And there was no air left in that box. Night felt the Disney executives had never embraced *The Village*, never gotten its darkness or why it had no movie stars, though they had let Night make it. And it was not, to them, a home run. It was not another *Signs*. Night understood that whatever he did after *The Village* could not be in a minor key. On his good days, he knew that the script he was writing would be nothing like minor, if he could get it to work. *If, if, if.* If it came together, it would be like Dylan and Clapton and Springsteen and Eminem and Kanye West and Miles Davis and Bonnie Raitt and Joan Armatrading and Jerry Garcia and every musician you've ever loved joining George Harrison and belting out the opening chord of "A Hard Day's Night" at the same time. But how often in your life—your life, my life, Night's life, anybody's life—do you hear that chord?

Night was trying to write this ambitious, crazy, inspired, inspiring screenplay, and a lot of the time he had no idea what he was doing. Which meant that, at age thirty-four, with his Oscar nominations and his money and his farm and his beautiful wife and his adorable girls and his party invitations for which he controlled the guest list, Night was feeling more desperate than he ever had. More desperate, even, than when he was starting out.

He knew that if he wrote the wrong words, if he screwed the thing up, he could be viewed as a kook or worse. The forces of the industry would require him to become an assembly-line director, or to retreat to the art houses, and once you've had a taste of feeding the masses, you don't want to do that. It was the most powerful kind of drug, and he was addicted to it. With Woody Allen, you get the idea that if he's playing big in Duluth, he thinks he's doing something wrong. Night was just the opposite. He *had* to reach Duluth. He had to connect, to win you over. The world population was growing all the time, so there were always more people to reach. He wanted to get in your head. Making money was great as long as he was being true to the story he wanted to tell. His feeling was that if he wasn't constantly trying something new, moving ahead—then a piece of him, the liveliest piece, would die. He would no longer be the person his wife had married.

He felt like he was writing through a fever. This time he wasn't writing out of ambition. He was writing out of inspiration. He was writing for his daughters, and he was writing for himself. He'd create an artificial deadline for a new draft and pull an all-nighter to meet it. Every day he was a wreck, delirious and moody, but no one who saw him would have known. His secretary, his office manager, his cook, his driver, his daughters' nanny, the housekeeper, the farm's caretaker, the guys he played basketball with on Tuesday nights, his architect, his daughters, the guests at the Burch dinner, we all saw someone ready to laugh at anything. He could turn any little nothing—the pretentiousness of the phrase *take a meeting*—into a comic bit that would last for days. Only Bhavna saw her husband's desperation, his underlying sadness, his resolve.

Lady in the Water started to work. He put in the hours, day after day, night after night, carting around the script, physically and mentally, wherever he went. He got through a first draft, a second, third, fourth, all of them for his eyes only. The fifth he liked. He gave it to twenty-three carefully selected readers, including Bhavna, their nanny, the editor of *Signs,* and one of his basketball buddies. Each reader was given a numbered script, a strict due-back date, and a pointed questionnaire that he had used for his other scripts as well.

Night turned their responses into numeric scores on a ten-point scale, then compared them to the scores his other scripts had received. He chose readers who would give him what he wanted. Some would give him candor. Others would hold his hand. He'd use all of it.

The nanny, a bright young woman who had taught at his kids' school until Night and Bhavna hired her away, told Night she thought the script was strange, illogical, sacrilegious for Christians. The power of Night's myth overwhelmed her own religious values. "I love it!" Night told her. He didn't view her as a critic but as a sparring partner, somebody who could help make him better.

One reader thought it was too scary for children. Another said the script did not make her cry. Jeremy Zimmer thought the dialogue of one key character, Lin Lao Choi, was "stilted," but his feedback was positive in most every other regard. Night gave his agent's response a hand-holding 8.75. The composer who scored Night's movies, James Newton Howard, said it was "amazing, very cool, masterful, laugh-out-loud funny." Night graded his response a 9.5, and it made him feel better.

Night picked up on an odd pattern: Men liked it more than women. Usually, women liked his scripts and his movies more than men. Night theorized that women are more comfortable with believing in the supernatural, and they brought men to Night's movies. But for *Lady in the Water,* many of the first female readers found the humor too coarse and said it distracted from the underlying message. He knew what he had to work on. One more draft and he'd send it to Disney. Draft 6 would be his sale script.

He began work on Draft 6 on February 1, 2005. He wanted the movie to come out in the early summer of 2006, maybe even by Memorial Day, so that it could be sold as a summer "event" movie. For that to happen, he had to start shooting by August 2005. Which meant Disney had to have the sale script in February.

Night, who thrived on tension, chose a date: The three key

Disney executives would get the script on Sunday, February 13. Paula, Night's assistant, would fly from Philadelphia to Los Angeles that morning with copies of the script and hand-deliver them to the homes of Dick Cook, the chairman of the Walt Disney Motion Picture Group; Oren Aviv, the head of marketing (Disney did not make movies that it didn't know how to sell); and, most significantly, Nina Jacobson, the Disney president, who had moved from DreamWorks to Disney specifically to work on *The Sixth Sense*. Nina's tastes largely dictated what kinds of movies Disney made. Later that evening, on an itinerary established weeks earlier, Paula would collect Cook's script, then Aviv's the next morning. Night wanted to know where his scripts were at all times. Nobody kept them for very long.

Except for Nina. She could keep them. She had worked intimately with Night on all four of his movies for Disney. She was described to me as a quirky, opinionated woman, skinny with worry, which she expressed in a fast-talking squeaky voice. Her personal habits were amusing: biting her knuckles or applying lip balm while making an important point, which she did with a great torrent of words, like water from an open hydrant. She was like Night that way; they were both talkers. She used *fuck* so often it became gratuitous, little more than an affectation. At other times her language was out of the corporate manual; she spoke of certain movies being "Disney-branded." But she was not an empty suit. She was smart. You could tell her punk sensibilities were being thwarted by her job. When she wore Prada, it came off as sarcastic. Because she had worked with Night from what Disney saw as the start—*The Sixth Sense*—Night granted her one special dispensation. She could keep the script. Night trusted her.

Six o'clock, Saturday night, February 12. The date and time was embedded in his head. That was when Night would give Paula a disk with the sale script on it. He and Bhavna would go out for the night while Paula went to the basement copier at the farmhouse and made copies. Draft 6 needed every minute he could give it, and he had already given away so many minutes. His schedule was a mess. Why had he agreed to talk to a group of film students at NYU? That would cost him most of a day. Why had he agreed to fly with his father to Jacksonville, Florida, to watch the Philadelphia Eagles play in the Super Bowl? He doesn't like to fly (turbulence makes his stomach queasy, and toast does not help); he's afraid of large unruly crowds; he didn't think the Eagles would win (they didn't); and it would cost him a day and a half. Why had he agreed to go to the twentieth reunion of his graduating class from Waldron Academy, being held on the Saturday night before Paula would fly to Los Angeles? He could have been working that Saturday night. And then there was his other life, the one at home. He had always been involved in the lives of his girls—the new script had started in their bedrooms, after all—but now he was needed more. Bhavna was writing her doctoral thesis, about cultural differences in emotional responses, and two afternoons a week, Night was needed at home when the girls returned from school.

The self-made Saturday-night deadline and the insistence on the secretive distribution of the sale script were adding to Night's burden. Because of the twist ending to *The Sixth Sense,* and the surprises in his other three movies, Night had to keep his scripts under tight control. The script for *Unbreakable* had been leaked on the Internet months before the movie came out. Night was determined that would not happen again, and it didn't. Secretiveness had become part of how he marketed himself. There were no public records of where he lived or worked. He gave few interviews. When Paula used the farmhouse copier that could handle only twenty pages at a time, each page was stamped with a name or a serial number superimposed in large light gray type over the text. If this established Night as untrusting, which it did, it also established him as mysterious and neurotic, and he was okay with that, because it was true and because it served him well.

There was another advantage to having Paula hand-deliver the new script on a Sunday. That turned its arrival into an event, just as Night had done when selling *The Sixth Sense*. It promised his script immediate and undivided attention on a day of the week when phones rang less, when time slowed down, when people were closer to their emotions. He was comfortable getting in the middle of people's weekends. He felt that the reading of his script should not be considered work. It should add to the weekend's pleasure.

It was a feverish twelve days. The changes from Draft 5 to Draft 6 were major and minor, but more than anything, they were shifts in tone. By Draft 6, the apartment building had become a character. For comic relief, he had an apartment of young smokers, five guys in their mid-twenties still tethered to their dorm-room bongs, trying to solve the riddles of the world. The film-critic tenant was deliciously pompous, too full of himself to realize the smokers were mocking him. When Night had read the role of Vick, the writer—a part he had reserved for himself—he felt weak and exposed, exactly how he wanted to feel. Lin Lao Choi, party girl/university student, was sounding more real. (And what a visual: Night had her at six feet, with rolls of fat and a Britney Spears wardrobe.) And then there was the enigmatic love between Story and Cleveland, the super who was in almost every scene of the movie. Some days they seemed like a potential couple, on others like father and daughter. Night didn't know, and it did not bother him.

It wasn't *The Village*. This one, Night said, had no cynicism. The more he worked on the script, the more the characters came together, as the story wanted them to. By Draft 6, they were a world. By Draft 6, there were no more notes like *Common!*

In a moment of euphoria, he called Jeremy Zimmer and said, "I want to put up half the budget."

Night and his agent had talked about this before, but only in theory. Night wanted to personally finance half the movie and therefore be in for half of the movie's profits. Night had been thinking about making such an investment for years, long before Mel Gibson had financed *The Passion of the Christ* himself. *Lady in the Water* would have at least a $60 million budget. Night figured he could put up $30 million without going to a bank, though it represented most of his liquid wealth. But if the movie grossed $300 million, Night would double his money, even after all the muddled Hollywood accounting. And if the movie turned into a phenomenon, as Night thought it could, his haul might be $100 million or more. He liked the idea of investing in something he could control.

And then the voices came just as he was about to hand the disk to Paula. In the past, the handing off of the floppy disk had always been momentous for him. He'd kiss the disk, give it to Paula, pop open a bottle of champagne, and make a toast: "To the sale script!" Not this time. As Night was handing the disk to Paula, the voices suddenly barged in, unannounced and unwelcome.

You don't have it.

Yeah, I do. I always have it when I send off the sale script.

Not this time you don't.

Maybe it'll need another pass. But Nina will see that it's all there.

No, she won't. There's a fundamental problem in the script that nobody will see until it plays in front of an audience.

Well, at least I don't have to write anymore. Not for now.

The last sound he heard before leaving the farmhouse for the night was Paula closing the door on her way to the copying room, converted from an old bathroom.

Night and Bhavna headed out to the reunion at Waldron. Everybody there still called him Manoj. His mood was manic and intense. Memories came flooding back. He was twelve, at a school social, the only dark-skinned person there. He asked a girl a half foot taller to dance. They did, clumsily, and then she ran off to her girlfriends. In their giggles he could hear everything they were saying and thinking, and he went home that night and prayed that he could turn off the voices, but that never happened.

At the reunion he was doing strange things. He apologized to a teammate from a long-ago kickball game, when Night had celebrated his teammate's game-winning kick with an excessive hug. (Feeling things too deeply once again!) He heard stories about himself that seemed to be about somebody else, the dark-skinned Hindu boy who was pushed into the smelly confessional by the fat nun and *ha, ha, ha; ha, ha, ha!* Night was giggling crazily at the stories, laughing so inordinately it made others envious and nervous. What his old classmates didn't realize was that he was on the verge of hysteria, on the verge of doing the one thing he did not do, losing all control. Writing *Lady in the Water* had taken something out of him.

He was asleep the next morning when Paula boarded an early flight from Philadelphia to LAX. She did not drink a thing the flight attendants were offering; she would not be using the plane lavatory. She would not leave the scripts unattended for even a moment, and she would not call attention to herself by hauling them into the cramped WC of an Airbus 321. She had a window seat because it was more secure, more private, more removed. The scripts stayed in their snug little case, zipped and locked. She didn't nap, she didn't read. For five hours, she kept her eyes on her feet and the scripts underneath them, her knees shaking up and down, up and down, up and down.

2.

Paula was early. She was always early. She arrived at Nina Jacobson's ranch house in the Brentwood section of Los Angeles at 1:35 P.M. and waited ten minutes for her appointed time on the appointed Sunday, then rang the doorbell to deliver the script to Nina. It had to go directly to Nina. That was one of Night's ground rules. The time had been established in a series of calls with Nina's assistants. Paula knew both assistants, she knew Nina, she knew Nina's partner, she had tickled the cheeks of their two young kids. Paula had every reason to think all would go smoothly. It always had. Nina had always been punctual. Dramatic but punctual. She knew Paula had a busy schedule to keep.

The plan was for Nina to get the script at 1:45 P.M., read it that afternoon, and call Night at his home before 6:30 Pacific time, 9:30 P.M. for him. She knew how anxious he would be.

There was something about Paula's personality that made people behave well in her presence and, by extension, made them follow Night's rules. She was discreet without being uptight, good-looking but not haughty about it, and she never confused her workaday world with the lives of the rich and super-rich with whom she was in daily contact. Her objective was to perform her job exactly the way her boss wanted it performed, which was with precision and without officiousness.

A Spanish-speaking housekeeper answered the door. Miss

Nina was not in, and the housekeeper did not know where she was. Paula was immediately suspicious. This was not Nina being dramatic. This was something else. She thought the way she knew her boss would want her to think.

What could Nina be doing that's more important than getting Night's new script?

Paula retreated to her car to call one of Nina's assistants, a woman named JJ, and explained her predicament.

"It's odd," Paula said. "Nina knew I was coming."

"Let me see if I can get her on her cell," JJ said.

"I've got to wait here."

"I'll call you back."

Night and Nina had had a productive relationship, but combative, too. Night had a good understanding of her life in the office on the second floor of a soulless building on the Disney lot in Burbank, a building where most of the art was by Walt Disney himself. Disney elves were carved into an outside wall, like gargoyles, their cheerfulness fabricated. Night found it all mildly depressing. The hallways and the atriums were sterile and quiet and the offices bizarrely tidy, like the front desk at a Hyatt hotel. The building was meant to pay homage to Walt Disney, but Night felt that the spirit of the man had been sucked right out of it, and out of the executives who worked in the building. Over the years, whenever Nina had tried to tell Night he was going too dark, he'd bring up the name of the company's patron saint.

"*Bambi*. One of the greatest movies ever made by Walt Disney, right? People still love it today. Bambi's mother dies," Night argued more than once, each time in nearly the same words. "Shot dead. One of the greatest children's movies ever."

"Night, we're not making *Bambi* here."

"All right. How about *Pinocchio*? Little Pinocchio gets drunk! In a Walt Disney production. What are you gonna say today?

'We've got some notes for you, Walt. Can you lose the drinking?' Walt Disney couldn't work at Walt Disney today!"

He'd get a dismissive look.

Nina had been helpful to him on *The Sixth Sense;* she had understood the intelligent tone Night was trying to achieve. She knew the movie would require its audience to think, and it had to be marketed accordingly. That had worried some of her colleagues. The obvious way to sell a scary movie to a mass audience is to highlight its fright factor. She carried Night's vision and his marketing ideas to her bosses. She didn't leave the room until they got it. The message, that watching *The Sixth Sense* required a brain, was captured in the movie's trailer and poster and in every bit of Oren Aviv's marketing campaign. From the start, you were asked a question: What *is* the sixth sense?

Still on the high of *The Sixth Sense,* Night and Nina had worked well together on *Unbreakable*—until the Monday after the movie's opening weekend, when it became clear that audiences were confused by it. The two had their differences over *Signs,* but the movie was always within the parameters of broad mainstream entertainment, and the disagreements never turned into fights. On *The Village,* they clashed. Night got Disney to say yes to a dark, political, rebellious movie with a brown look and a series of unsettling questions at the points in the movie where Night typically offered belief. Without having to ask for a thing, he got Disney to put up a $70 million budget for the movie, plus another $80 million in marketing, for a script they might have rejected from any other writer, for a movie that might have been headed straight to your neighborhood art house, if you have one, had any other director made it. All the while, Night felt Nina's nervousness.

She was particularly unconvinced by a scene near the opening credits when dates are shown on a tombstone, suggesting that the action takes place in the nineteenth century. The movie had a huge opening weekend, a time when people go to a movie because they like the star or, in this case, the director. But the movie did not have staying power. When interest sagged after the opening week, Nina, in her frustration, kept going back to the fatal tombstone shot.

"You lied to your audience," she said. "You didn't show respect for your audience."

Her words hurt Night. Showing respect for the audience was his highest aim as a writer and director.

Night was bewildered. The movie was *about* lying. The old generation lies, and the young innocent has to run away to live her life. Anyway, you can go to any old cemetery and see a nineteenth-century tombstone, no matter what year it is. Confusion about time was a critical element of the movie.

"You want to know the single biggest reason why this movie confused audiences?" Night said to Nina. He never tired of fighting for himself. "Because my other movies gave people a reason to believe in the supernatural. In this one, the supernatural is not real. Now people don't know what they're going to get when they come see my movies. You expand your audience that way, you don't contract it. I'm saying, 'You can't trust me at all—you don't know *where* I'm going.' People come to me to believe in things, and this time I told them, 'The magic's not real.' You know, you can say to the audience, 'You don't own me.' They'll respect that."

Nina had no idea what Night was talking about. Night could tell.

He could see what was happening to her since she had become the boss. She had adopted the values of the modern Walt Disney Company. He had witnessed the decay of her creative vision right before his own wide-open eyes. She didn't want iconoclastic directors. She wanted directors who made movies that made money; to her, *The Village* was a lost chance. Had Night only listened to her, it could have been another *Signs*— that's the message Night was getting. She was aiming to keep her job by trying to make sure the Disney stock price only went higher.

The lesson of Night's own thirty-four years was so clear to him: If you're a Bob Dylan, a Michael Jordan, a Walt Disney— if you're M. Night Shyamalan—and you have faith and a vision and something original to say, money will come. But if you're chasing money, the audience will see you for what you are. Night knew his ideas were no longer making an impact on Nina. He was losing her, losing the hold he once had on her. He blamed that on the culture of her corporation. Disney, he realized, in the blind final years of the Michael Eisner regime, had changed. It was now in the business of cloning.

And now, a half-year after *The Village* had run its course, Nina was not home at the appointed time to receive Night's new script.

JJ called Paula back and said, "I couldn't get her on her cell phone, but I'll e-mail her on her BlackBerry."

Paula waited in her car, stewing, wondering how this delay would affect her other appointments.

A few minutes later, JJ called again. "Nina's on her way. She should be there in ten to fifteen minutes. She's just coming back from a birthday party with her son."

Birthday party? Nobody said anything about a birthday party.

Nina arrived home at 2:15 with her young son. By way of apology, she offered Paula low-carb soup from the refrigerator and a ride to Philadelphia on the Disney jet. Nina had a Tuesday-night dinner meeting with Night at the farm, to talk about the new script and an overall strategy for *Lady in the Water*.

Paula passed on the soup and on the ride home. She didn't

think it was her place to fly on the Disney corporate jet, not if Night wasn't going to be on it.

"Hopefully I can read it now," Nina said, "if I can get the kids down for a nap."

Paula handed over the script and left, perplexed and disturbed.

She went to Oren Aviv's house. She was making plans to retrieve the script when Aviv started to say, "If Night doesn't trust us with the script—"

"Please," Paula said. "This has nothing to do with trust. It's just how Night likes to do this."

That was different.

And then with Dick Cook, another strained handoff. As Paula gave him the script, she detected no emotion from him, just corporate good manners. When Paula mentioned she was scheduled to pick up the script at 9:45 P.M., Cook said that he might be out at a screening. "If that's the case, I'll leave it with somebody here to give to you."

Somebody? You don't give Night's script to some unidentified person. What's going on here? These guys are not playing by the rules.

She said nothing. She was the personal assistant to M. Night Shyamalan, and he was Richard W. Cook, chairman of the Walt Disney Studios.

When she was done with her rounds, Paula called Night at home. She seldom did that, only when she was sure he'd want to hear from her. The answering machine came on. She said, "I just want you to know that everybody got the script and everybody seemed excited." She regretted her words immediately, but there was no re-record option. *Excited.* Everybody in Hollywood used that word. *Seemed.* She knew that would worry Night. The truth was, the script distribution had gone poorly.

At 6:30 P.M. Pacific time, Nina called Paula on her cell phone and said, "I wasn't able to get the kids down for a nap. Could you call Night and tell him I'll call tomorrow and tell him what I think of it?"

Now Paula was beyond shock. She felt like a pile of bricks had hit her. She wanted to throw up. She was accustomed to people treating Night with deference—with the respect he had earned—and now they weren't. She was accustomed to people doing what Night wanted them to do. It was part of his aura. Something had changed.

Nina read the sixth draft of *Lady in the Water*, the sale script, that Sunday night, after her kids had gone to sleep and the house was quiet. Whatever issues she'd had with Night and *The Village*, she was still intrigued. On four previous occasions she had sat down to read original M. Night Shyamalan scripts, and all four times the scripts had been well-crafted, unique, and interesting. The scripts didn't have typos and misspellings or any big plot holes. He always worked them over hard before sending them out. They typically contained little direction, or notes for the director—for himself—about how the scenes should be shot. There wasn't much exposition. The story was told through the dialogue, in what was said, and often in what was not said. Reading Night's scripts was like reading a play, just about. The scripts were literate and grown up. She knew *Lady in the Water*, whatever it was, wouldn't be a mess. Night couldn't write a mess. He was too talented, and he worked too hard.

She looked at the black cover page with the emblem of his company, Blinding Edge Pictures. It showed a diver in flight. She liked Night's sense of style.

The script began with a dedication page, which was literary and rare. She knew the story came from a bedtime tale he had told his children. It wasn't like Night to tell her much about a script before she received it, but he had told her that.

To my daughters,
I'll tell you this story one more time
But then go to bed.

There was an early, funny scene in Spanish, the fastest-growing language in America. Nina was fine with that. The protagonist, Cleveland Heep, the superintendent of the apartment building, had a stutter. She made a note of it—two hours of stuttering could make an audience insane. The beautiful wet pool creature, the role slated for Bryce Howard, showed up on page 15. Bryce was not a star, nobody would come to a movie because she was playing the female lead, but she was pretty, talented, inexpensive, and Night had loved working with her on *The Village*. There was a character named Reggie who worked out only the top half of his body, and Nina found him amusing.

And then she started to have problems. She wasn't yet on page 20 of a 136-page script.

There was a scary-looking creature, sort of a mutation between a dog and a hyena, with sharp wet teeth and spiky grass for fur.

And Night wants this to be a Disney-branded movie? Too scary.

There was a fivesome of smokers, and even though they smoked only cigarettes, it was clear they'd logged a lot of hours, if not years, with their mouths on bongs.

Not Disney.

The film critic in the movie, Mr. Farber, was attacked.

Not smart.

Then there was the role Night wanted to play himself, Vick Ran, a stymied writer with a cloudy future, living with his sister and carrying the movie's message. It was an enormous supporting role, the second-biggest male role in the movie, and Night had never had a role nearly this big.

Should the audience see that much of Night?

Then there was the enormous Korean party girl, Lin Lao Choi, who explained the mythic tale that was the backbone of the entire script. She did her explaining not through action, the holy grail of modern moviemaking, but with words.

Way too much exposition.

With Lin Lao and her invented language came Nina's biggest problem with the script. She didn't understand the myth.

Scrunt, narf, tartutic, the Great Etalon—what are these things?

And her size.

How are you going to cast a six-foot-tall Korean girl, with rolls of fat, who speaks English and Korean?

Nina read it once and then read it again. She picked up a phone and called her boss.

"I don't get it," she said.

"Neither do I," Dick Cook said.

Jeremy Zimmer's first call the next morning—Monday, February 14, 2005; Valentine's Day—was from Nina Jacobson. The agent and the Disney president knew each other well, not just because of Night but also through Zimmer's other clients. They saw each other at business meetings and movie openings in Los Angeles. That Monday, Zimmer was in Philadelphia.

Nina got right to the point: "We don't get it. We don't think it works."

Zimmer was not prepared to hear that. He knew the script was not perfect. He had told Night he had problems with Lin Lao Choi; he thought she was "stilted." But he liked the script. More to the point, he thought it represented Night, and because so many people liked the way Night thought, an audience, a big one, would undoubtedly find its way to the movie. He listened to a short version of Nina's problems with the script and drove out to Night's farm.

The farm was a refuge, Night's weekday office and his family's weekend retreat, neighboring the great estates made famous in the movie *The Philadelphia Story*. The writer and agent hugged. Night had no use for many Hollywood customs, including the overly sincere man-to-man Hollywood hug. He used the Philadelphia hug, the one he had learned playing in city basketball tournaments: traditional shake, soul shake, followed by a meeting of the right shoulders.

He saw the worry on Zimmer's face. "What's wrong?"

"Well, this is a Valentine's Day you're going to remember," the agent said. "They didn't, quote, get the script."

Zimmer summarized Nina's problems with the script. Night's mind raced. He rubbed his face with his skinny dark hand.

Could I have sabotaged myself because I don't want to make this movie for Disney?

Is there some major flaw I'm not seeing?

Zimmer was imagining what would happen if Disney rejected the script outright. Night would be free to go wherever he liked. "It would be like Michael Jordan becoming a free agent!" Zimmer said. He started to rattle off the names of the studios and studio heads who would love to be in business with Night. Of course, the use of Michael Jordan's name was a bit of salesmanship. Zimmer knew how Jordan, even in retirement, still moved Night.

Night could not imagine it coming to that. Disney wasn't going to let him leave.

"They're still coming here for dinner tomorrow night, right?" Night asked. Nina Jacobson was coming with her boss, Dick Cook, and Oren Aviv, the marketing man.

"Yeah."

So he had two days to work. Two days to think. All day Monday and all day Tuesday.

Night's chef, Michael Schultz, had been preparing the dinner for days: a four-course meal with roasted lamb and feta ravioli for the entrees, the right wines for the right courses. Michael was built like a college football player, but he made exceedingly delicate dishes. He collected balsamic vinegar as others do wine and drizzled it on fruit for dessert. Michael prepared lunch every day for Night and Paula and Jose Rodriguez, who ran Night's business affairs, and he cooked whenever Night was entertaining.

Zimmer didn't think dinner in the farmhouse made sense now, everyone cozy and sitting together in a dark room with low ceilings. "Let's do it at the hotel," he said.

He was staying, as the Disney people would be, at the Four Seasons, a hotel on the Benjamin Franklin Parkway in Center City Philadelphia, a short walk from the art museum steps used triumphantly in the first *Rocky* movie. Night has an abiding love for that movie, particularly because in the end, Rocky . . . *loses*. In his Filmmaker's Handbook, a series of private notebooks he had been keeping for years, Night had written, *But he hasn't really lost. He's still standing at the end. Apollo Creed, the heavyweight champion of the world, couldn't knock him down. In Rocky's mind, that's a victory.* Night imagined that if Sylvester Stallone were making *Rocky* for Disney today, Nina would require Rocky to beat Apollo Creed. *The hero's gonna lose? Don't get it. Not Disney.*

"The restaurant at the Four Seasons? That's a suit-jacket place," Night said. "Everybody's wearing ties in there."

Night liked wearing good suits if he was trying to sell something—arriving at a premiere, being interviewed by Jay Leno. But not for this meeting. When Nina and the others read the sale script, that was supposed to be the sell job. The dinner was supposed to be something else.

They decided to have the dinner at Lacroix, a restaurant on the second floor of an elegant, modern hotel, the Rittenhouse, in the heart of Philadelphia.

Dinnertime came. Night's driver, Franny Malseed, drove Night there.

Franny had been a union driver on most of Night's other movies. He had been a teamster official. He knew the city and how it worked, and people and how they worked. He was smart and discreet. After *The Village*, Night had hired him to drive for him and his family full-time.

They arrived at the hotel and Franny asked, "Should I put away my Mickey ears?"

Franny had owned no Mickey Mouse ears in his rough-and-tumble Philadelphia boyhood, and he was possibly the least likely person in the world to own them now. Night laughed nervously. His stomach felt all clumpy.

Franny drove up the hotel's cobblestone driveway and let Night out under the heat lamp. A uniformed doorman opened the door for Night and said, "Good evening, Mr. Shyamalan." He said it easily, too easily, as if they saw each other daily. The doorman's greeting confused Night. It made him feel paranoid.

What does he know that I don't know?

From the start, the dinner was a disaster. The tables were too close together; Night felt that other diners could hear their conversation. The service was slow. There were many courses with tiny portions. Night was not touching his food, and at one point the chef came out to ask if everything was all right, then laboriously explained the menu. The waiters hovered excessively. Nina and Night did most of the talking. They were sitting next to each other, with Zimmer on Night's left. Usually, Night found Nina's screechy voice amusing, but this night it was only grating. She sounded like the adults in the Charlie Brown TV movies: *wha-wha-wha-wha-wha*. Her problems with the script came spewing out of her without a filter. The boundary between candor and anger, Night couldn't identify it.

You said it was funny; I didn't laugh . . . You're going to let a critic get attacked? They'll kill you for that . . . Your part's too big; you'll get killed again . . . You've got a writer who wants to change the world but doesn't, but somebody reads the writer and does? Don't get it . . . What's with the names? Scrunt? Narf? Tartutic? Not working . . . What's with all these rules? Don't get it . . . Lin Lao Choi—and good luck finding a six-foot Korean girl—is going to explain all these rules and all these words? Not buying it. Not getting it. Not working.

She went on and on and on. Night was waiting for her to say she didn't like the font Paula had printed it in.

The attack left Night feeling euphoric. He felt like a boxer, adrenaline coursing through him after getting hit. He came out flailing. He started with a broad attack, then planned to go into a line-by-line defense and conclude with soaring praise for his own work. He didn't want to have to do it, but who else would? He went right into Johnnie Cochran mode, which suited him. He did an excellent and funny "if the glove don't fit, you must acquit" bit. He was a good actor.

He continued, "All right, you know Harriet Beecher Stowe, she wrote *Uncle Tom's Cabin*, right?"

Throughout high school, all Night did was watch movies. Play sports and watch movies. He learned about acting and lighting and beats and storytelling by watching movies, and by listening to his parents tell their stories. After college, he became a serious book reader.

There was a group nod. Night found it unconvincing.

"It made you feel for the slaves. It's an amazing, amazing book. But in and of itself, it didn't change the world."

More nodding.

"Abraham Lincoln read it, became president, and ended slavery. That's what's going on here. A writer writes, and years later, somebody reads the books and gets inspired. The writer doesn't know he's written something important. He's just writing because he believes. It's a big idea, my biggest ever. What aren't you getting?"

For a moment he felt sane and clear. He heard Zimmer chuckling, and Night knew what it meant: *You'll never beat Night in debate.*

He was just about to shift gears when he looked at them carefully, one by one. He looked at Nina, at Cook, at Aviv. He saw nothing. They weren't engaging him the way an opponent is supposed to. There was no boxing match going on. They were looking at him like he was on another team.

Suddenly, he knew. The problem was not Nina Jacobson or Dick Cook or Oren Aviv. He wasn't looking at three individuals. They had morphed into one, the embodiment of the company they worked for, and that company, the great Walt Disney Company, founded in 1926 by Walter Elias Disney, no longer valued individualism. It no longer valued fighters. Nina and Cook and Aviv wanted Night to be a cog. They had talked so much about Team Disney, about turning every employee into some kind of bland cheerleader, all with the same nose and hair and body type, that they had left no room on the roster for the star. They didn't want stars anymore. And as Night looked at them, he realized this wasn't a dinner meeting. It was an intervention, as if they were meeting with an alcoholic who needed to get into a treatment program. Their purpose was to talk some sense into him. *Get on the team, buddy—we can all make lots of money!*

Night felt sorry for them. They felt emboldened by *The Village,* by their belief that had Night only listened to them, that movie could have earned double or triple or quadruple the money it made.

47

"What are you saying, Nina? What are you saying the script needs? Three weeks? Three months?"

Nina said nothing. Her face said, *Not three weeks, not three months, not ever.*

"You're saying I've lost my mind."

"No, we're not."

"Yes, yes, you are."

Night went into a long monologue of everything he had written as an adult, as a writer-for-hire, as a ghostwriter, as the writer of four original screenplays for Disney. He cited dollar figures, how the movies had ranked for their studios. When he got to the four Disney movies he had made, it was *pow! whack! zoom! bop! The Sixth Sense, Unbreakable, Signs, The Village.*

"Seven for seven. Two of the four I made for Disney are among the largest-grossing movies of all time. But now—now I've written *Lady in the Water,* and I've lost my mind. Suddenly, I can't write anymore. I've lost my touch, gone crazy."

Nina wanted her child back, the one who wrote *The Sixth Sense.* She said, "You know we had our problems with *The Village.*"

That was true. But Night had always thought they let him do his thing, as a writer and a director, because he had earned the right to do so. Now he was hearing something different. He was hearing: *We didn't put our foot down last time, and we regret it; we're not going to make that mistake again.* Nina talked so often about the underlying lie of *The Village.* In Night's mind, he was successful *because* he was honest. He wrote the stories he wanted to show and tell, not the ones he thought others wanted to hear. When he was telling a lie—and he was, of course, a fiction writer—it was willful. It was for the good of the story.

Nina started talking about a Disney movie on the docket that Night could direct. It sounded to Night like a girls' movie, maybe about ice-skating or something. She seemed to not even know him. All he'd done for Disney was direct his own original scripts. Warner Bros. had approached him about directing the first Harry Potter movie. Night was a fan of the book, but he couldn't do it. He was making *Unbreakable* then, his own idea. It had to take precedence. Steven Spielberg had once approached Night about writing a sequel to *Raiders of the Lost Ark,* the movie that had made Night want to be a writer and director in the first place. He was tickled. But in the end he said no. He didn't see a way to improve upon the original. To Night, the challenge was to say something original, to reach other people with his own ideas. It was so basic. How could Nina not know that?

He had known these people for years. He had always liked them; he had always thought they were smart. He knew they were good people. But a different kind of group thinking had taken hold of them. All of a sudden they looked like strangers.

It seemed to Night that they didn't know how they wanted the meeting to end. He could not relate. He was always thinking about endings. He couldn't understand why they didn't come in and say, "Help us understand this movie." Had that been the first thing said at dinner, the whole night would have played differently.

Sadness washed over him. He wanted to please people, that was a big part of his personality. He knew he had a conventional streak a mile wide, that there was more Bobby Zimmerman in him than Bob Dylan. He knew Manoj still lived. Manoj wanted to make his parents proud. Make his wife proud, his children, his sister, her husband, his employees. Make them all proud. The doorman he didn't know at the Rittenhouse, make him proud. In high school, when he was still Manoj, he always wondered what it would be like to be popular, what it would be like to be the guy who says to the girl, "You wanna—?" and she says, "Sure," without knowing where they're going.

Nina was practically screaming at him: *You can be one of us!* And it was so inviting. It was easy. *Be on the team, get even richer, get even more famous!*

No, he didn't want to be on the team, not *that* team. To be on a team of actors, real actors, to be counted among the iconoclasts and the misfits? Yes, that was appealing. To be on a team of conformist executives? No. He wanted to be Dirty Harry, breaking rules to get results. He wanted to be Michael Jordan, taking the last shot, whether he made it or missed, whether the Bulls won or lost. He wanted to be Dylan, Picasso, Kubrick, William Hurt, Walt Disney. He wanted to be Night the day he said to himself, *I'd rather not make* The Sixth Sense *than make it for Harvey.* He dug deep and said something he didn't know he still had in him: "I'm going to have to decide whether I make this movie at all, or whether I make it elsewhere."

Nobody responded.

Finally, Zimmer said to the Disney trio, "We're thankful for the truthful response you've given us."

The agent knew the Disney people were in a difficult spot. If the movie turned into a big hit at another studio, these three smart people running the Disney movie division would not look good. It was a business filled with second-guessing. Zimmer didn't want to see them embarrassed. He didn't want to see them fail. He had good relationships with them. He took projects to them all the time.

Night didn't look at Zimmer. "I don't agree with that, I don't think it was a truthful response," he said.

He felt Nina had been preconditioned not to like the script, that she hadn't given it a truthful reading. He had put his heart into that script, he had put his soul and his dreams and his faith into it. It had more of a big idea behind it—more of *him*—than anything he had ever written. It deserved more than *we don't get it.* And even if they absolutely could not see what he was trying to do, he felt he merited a different tone. They didn't have a single question about the script. How could that be?

"There's a certain amount of space you have to give an artist, and the problem here is that you haven't given me that space. I don't have any room to move. You like the side of me that does conventional things that make money, and you don't like the side that does unconventional things."

Everything was out now, including Night's unhappiness. Night could see how they were seeing him, as a child not ready to leave home. And now the child was no longer running to tennis practice and saying, "Loveya!" before slamming the door. The child was saying, "I've got a driver's license now, and I'm outta here." Disney was on the verge of losing its most successful writer-director since Walt Disney himself.

Aviv and Cook were gasping for air. Aviv said, "As we say, 'We don't smell it, we sell it.' " The meeting had gone awry, and now they were winging it. Cook told Night he could still make the movie at Disney, even if the executives didn't understand it. He said, "Prove us wrong, Night."

But Night knew he could not do that. Spend a year of his life trying to prove them wrong? No. What a waste of energy. He could not make a movie for these three people. Their lack of faith in *Lady in the Water* would infect the whole project.

There was almost nothing to talk about, and the dinner came to a quiet close. Night tossed his spotless napkin on the table. The check came and Zimmer paid. The fivesome headed to the elevator, even though the lobby was only one flight below. Zimmer inspected the bleached-blond wood of the elevator door. The air smelled of fresh flowers, the way it does in expensive hotels. The doors opened.

"You three go down," Cook said. "I want to talk to Night for a minute."

Soon they were alone outside the elevator.

"Just make the movie for us," Cook said. "We'll give you sixty million and say, 'Do what you want with it.' We won't touch it. We'll see you at the premiere."

"I can't do that," Night answered.

"C'mon."

"I thought we were going to ride into the sunset together," Night said wistfully.

"We still can."

Night felt like the boy his parents had raised, the one who always knew to thank his mother's friend for bringing him to Chuck E. Cheese's, even though the big furry rodent scared the hell out of him.

"I want to thank you for six great years and four great movies," Night said. He could have added *Mr. Cook*.

An elevator came, and they rode down together in silence. There were no hugs and there were no *loveyas*. The three Disney people walked together past the doorman and out of the hotel and into a waiting car. They returned to their hotel still believing that Night would change his mind, that he would abandon *Lady in the Water* and make a movie for Disney that made much more sense for everybody—for the three of them, for Night, for the Disney shareholders. But as they left, Night was crying. He was crying because he liked them as people and he knew he would not see them again, not as his partners. He was crying because he was scared, because there was a big part of him that did want to simply get along with everybody, to do something safe, to be successful, whatever that meant. He was crying because he knew they could be right. He was crying because in rejecting that script, they were rejecting him.

That night was the beginning of the madness. Not mad like Vincent van Gogh was mad, but mad for Night, mad enough that he found himself saying something very unsafe, something imprudent, something he had never said before: *Keep your god-damn money—I'm going to make the movie I want to make.* He hadn't even known he had it in him.

Night sat down on a lobby sofa. He hugged his knees and lowered his chin on top of them. His mind was moving fast now.

He started talking to himself. The voices were a chorus, screaming at him, advising him, consoling him. "I've got the fatal flaw. It's Lin Lao Choi. She can't just spout off the rules on command. It's got to be funny. I could give her a mother. She could speak only Korean. Now there's a cultural divide, an age gap . . ."

Zimmer said to him, "Do you realize what's happening here? Your career is about to go off in some direction, and we have no idea what it is."

". . . so if the mother speaks only Korean, she represents the old country, the old way of doing things. She knows the rules because it's part of her lore."

"Look at you," Zimmer said. "This is really all about story for you, isn't it?"

Night looked up. He hadn't heard a word his agent had said.

The next morning Night drove to the farm quickly, peering into his rearview mirror for aggressive suburban cops. He was ready to go to work, ready to write a new character. He felt everything all at once. He was eager to work; he was tired of work. He was weak from the fight; he was empowered by the fight. He was euphoric that he had stood up; he was scared that he had stood up.

He knew people did that in the real world every once in a while. They got mad as hell, stood up, and changed the world. But the act of standing wasn't necessarily altruistic. It could be intensely selfish. Lance Armstrong had beaten cancer and gotten back on his bike for himself. The fight he inspired in others was a happy by-product. When Bob Dylan played electric at the Newport Folk Festival, that was for himself, but the ripple effect reached Francis Ford Coppola and Joe Namath and the Kingston Trio, who lost their neckties for good. *Lady in the Water,* the version in his head, was already inspiring Night. He could feel it at the Disney dinner. Whether the real movie, out of his head and compelled to film, ever inspired you or me or anybody else wouldn't be known until later, when anonymous strangers gathered in darkened rooms and fell into Night's dream state—or not. Night had told me early on that he didn't truly know his movies until he saw them for the first time with strangers, at a test screening, cards in their hands. He could tell from their silences and their gasps and their rustling. The voices were always working on those nights in a state of high alert. And then the ultimate confirmation would come—their report cards.

For months to come, at odd hours of the day and night, that dinner at Lacroix would get replayed in Night's head like the wake-up scene in *Groundhog Day. I got you, babe.* Sometimes Night would close his eyes and see little oval black-and-white head shots of Nina Jacobson and Oren Aviv and Dick Cook floating around in his head, unwanted house guests that would not leave.

Ever since *The Sixth Sense,* Night could always get people to do what he wanted them to do. But on that night at Lacroix, he could not. What he did not know, what he could not know, was that that night would start a year when he could no longer get people to do what he wanted. His mojo had taken a hit. The Disney people had gotten deep inside his head, interfering with the good work the voices were supposed to do—and it would be hell to get them out.

3.

I don't want you to shop the script," Night told his agent the morning after the Disney dinner.

This made no sense. Not to Jeremy. Not to Jeremy's partner, Peter Benedek. Not to Jose. This was the chance for Night to make a clean break, to sell himself to the highest bidder, to let other studios try to woo him, to get his best deal.

Zimmer knew he could bring the script to Warner Bros., to DreamWorks, to Paramount, to Fox, to New Line. Executives at Warner Bros. had called Zimmer often about Night. When Night was on the cover of *Newsweek,* under the headline THE NEW SPIELBERG, he had called Spielberg, an owner of Dream-Works, and said he knew better even if the headline writers did not. There was a relationship there. Paramount had a new boss, Fox owned Night's only unproduced script (*Labor of Love*), and New Line had wanted *The Sixth Sense* from the beginning. Zimmer could easily create a feeding frenzy for the script that the Disney people didn't get.

But Night didn't want to play one studio against another. He knew an auction could leave even the winner resentful of his purchase. It was the normal way of doing things, and Night didn't want normal.

"I want to take it to Warner Brothers," Night told his agent. Only to Warner Bros.

In baseball, that would be like a star player, able to sign

anywhere, telling his agent to make a deal only with the Boston Red Sox.

What if the Warner people didn't get it, either? First Disney, then Warner Bros. In the space of a month, Night could go from ridiculously bankable to tainted.

But Zimmer knew Night wanted to take that risk. The agent could hear it in Night's voice, just as he could when Night had said the minimum bid for *The Sixth Sense*'s script should be $1 million. Representing Night, you had to do things differently than you would for another client, and you had to think differently, too. At the Four Seasons on the morning after the blowup dinner, Zimmer had to collect the sale script from Nina. Night didn't want somebody who didn't "get it" to be in possession of the script. Nina didn't want to give it up. She still believed that Night would change his mind and stay at Disney. Returning the script would be like returning an engagement ring. But Zimmer coaxed the script out of her. He had to. Night was in a frail spot, and Zimmer had to show his client he still believed. Getting the script back from Nina, awkward though it was, would be a symbol.

And now Night wanted to offer the script to one studio.

"Okay," Zimmer said. "I'll call Alan Horn."

Horn was the president of Warner Bros. Entertainment. Night and Horn had met once or twice, but Horn was lodged in Night's mind. He had called Night shortly after *The Village* opened, when the response to the movie was weird and mixed. Night was in Paris for the European premiere of the movie, and Horn had tracked him down. "The movie really touched me," Horn told Night. "It was a reminder to me of why I'm in the business of making movies." Night heard yearning in Horn's voice, to make movies that dealt with something many filmmakers didn't want to talk about: the role of faith in our lives. Not in some preacher-on-TV, repent-or-go-to-hell way. Just true faith.

Night didn't want Zimmer to make the first call to the Warner Bros. president. "The first call should come from me," he told Zimmer.

That made no sense, either. Zimmer, far better than Night, could put an assured spin on the Valentine's Day Massacre, as the Disney divorce was being called in Night's office. Zimmer could play the next move coyly, leave the impression that Night would like to make *Lady* at Warner Bros. but would consider other places, too. That's what salesmen do. Night knew that game well. He had played it expertly when trying to evade Harvey Weinstein. But that was when Night was desperate to make his mark. Now he felt a different kind of desperation. He wanted to inspire the masses. He couldn't do it alone.

Night feared being alone, the parish priest on a windblown rural island, somewhere off the coast of Ireland, maybe, pre-telephone, a man who listens to confessions and offers faith to doubters day after day, but who has nobody to turn to for himself.

He didn't want to make movies only for himself. During the process, he couldn't think of his worldwide audience—that was far too broad to comprehend. He tried to imagine one idealized audience member, who got the movie exactly as Night had intended it, and in ways that he never did. So far, that idealized moviegoer was a fantasy. Night hadn't found that person on any of his previous movies, nor had he on *Lady*. The idea that that person might exist helped fight the loneliness. But that's all it did, help. The loneliness persisted.

Night had a plan for his first conversation with Horn. All he wanted to say was "I've wanted to make a movie for you for a long time, and this is the one I should be making first." Then he would turn the matter over to Jeremy Zimmer and Peter Benedek and Jose Rodriguez for the broad strokes and to his lawyers, Marc Glick and Steve Breimer, for the fine ones.

Night went over the conversation in his head again and

again. His plan was not to say the name Disney. He wouldn't say a thing about the problems the Disney people had with the script. He could imagine Horn's voice, resonant and subdued, saying the things he wanted to hear.

Then he picked up the phone.

"This is a really important call I'm making," Night said.

"I like this," Horn said. He had two daughters, too. Night felt a connection with him.

"I always felt like someday we would work together."

"As you know, we've wanted that, too."

"I won't be making my next movie for Disney."

Horn said nothing. The walls have ears in the entertainment business, but this should have been news to him.

"I'd like to make it for you."

That was where Night had intended to stop, but he couldn't. Horn must have heard Night's confusion and anxiety, because to that most inviting of comments, Horn said only, "Then we would like to be in the next round of conversations."

Night was hyperventilating, and Horn was assuming the role of statesman. Night was giving up everything and expecting Horn to do the same. And he didn't. It was unnerving.

Night filled the silence by rambling. He said the name Disney over and over. Night started going on and on about problems with the script. There was too much built up inside him.

. . . *but maybe they aren't really problems, or maybe they are but they're fixable problems—and what's a world without problems?— and maybe I sabotaged myself because maybe I didn't really want to make the movie for Disney, but you know I was always going to be a child to Disney, and I'm ready to be treated like a man, but more than that, I just wanted them to show respect for me as an artist, as you did, Alan, when you called me in Paris that time—it was on August first, 2004, my daughter's birthday; we were on a rowboat in the Seine, and I had just lost a bracelet in the water, and then you*

*called, amazing timing, don't you—are you there, Alan? Hello? Is
any of this making any sense?*

Horn's diplomatic tone never changed.

"Yes, of course," he said evenly. "It all makes sense."

It turned out that Horn was the one to never mention Disney by name, the way a good college recruiter doesn't mention the other schools he knows the star athlete is considering.

"We'd like to read the script whenever you're ready for us to read it," Horn said.

"I'm going to come out to L.A. on March twenty-first," Night said.

The date was calculated. He knew Horn would be in town. Night's plan was to finish the second version of the sale script on March 20 and fly out the next day and deliver it himself.

Night knew he'd need to clear his head to finish the revisions. After the breakup dinner, the rewriting had been a slog. Every time Night sat down to write, the little oval head shots—the trio of Disneyites, Nina in particular—descended upon him. He'd try to chase them out, but he couldn't.

Horn looked at his calendar. "The twenty-first. Good. If you like, we could have dinner that night."

"That'd be great!" Night blurted out.

He felt like he was back in high school, failing at cool again.

He hung up and thought, *I'm damaged.* He was seeing things, and himself, with extreme clarity. He was deflated. But even in his weakened state, Night knew one thing for certain: He wasn't going back to Disney. The last time he'd felt this way had been after Harvey gutted *Wide Awake.* Night had known then that even if Harvey Weinstein were the last producer on earth, he would not make *The Sixth Sense* for him. There are surprising pockets of strength when you're crazy-mad. Night remembered that from the last time.

Night asked his assistant if she had ever received Nina's copy of the script. She had. Paula had held the script in her hands, thumbed through it, seen that Nina had written notes all over it, and taken it to the shredder. She knew Night wouldn't want to see Nina's notes. Nina was no longer a believer. Paula still was.

Night was consumed with casting questions. It was crucial, make-or-break, that he find the right actor to play Cleveland Heep, the building super. Cleveland was in nearly every scene, and how that role was cast would determine the movie's fate. Night had been thinking about Tom Hanks, among other actors.

He had been reading the book *Blink,* by Malcolm Gladwell. The subtitle, *The Power of Thinking Without Thinking,* interested him. He did his thinking with thinking, but he recognized Gladwell's theme, about how we use intuition. While reading the book, Night came across a section on casting in which Tom Hanks was featured prominently. From what I could tell, coincidences like that seemed to happen to Night all the time.

Night was fascinated by the book's description of the Coke-Pepsi wars, about which cola wins the sip test on a supermarket sidewalk and which wins the take-home test, the soda you actually drink with your Sunday-night pizza. Night realized there was a corollary in movies. *Unbreakable* and *How the Grinch Stole Christmas,* a Universal movie, had opened the same day. *Grinch* had a better opening weekend. "*Grinch* is loved," Dick Cook had told Night at the time. The way Cook had said it made Night feel alone in the world.

Reading *Blink,* Night figured out that *Grinch* had won the sip test, but *Unbreakable* had won the test that mattered most to him, the take-home test. *Unbreakable* lived on in a Kanye West rap, in doctoral theses, in chat rooms, in highbrow film magazines. The modern Disney, Night realized, was too worried about the sip test. Under Walt Disney, the company had been all about the take-home test, movies that lingered in your mind forever.

Gladwell described how Tom Hanks was cast for his first big role. "He came in and read for the movie *Splash,* and right there, in the moment, I can tell you what I saw," Gladwell quoted the producer Brian Grazer as saying. "We read hundreds of people for that part, and other people were funnier than him. But they weren't as likable as him. I felt like I could live inside him. I felt like his problems were problems I could relate to." What Grazer saw in Hanks in 1983 was what Night was seeing in him over twenty years later, even though Hanks had become one of the world's best-known actors. Night was impressed that you still felt his innocence, after so many years and so much success. Tom Hanks would make a fine Cleveland Heep.

Splash, directed by Ron Howard, is about a wayward mermaid, played charmingly by Daryl Hannah. Now, two decades later, Night had hired Ron Howard's daughter to play the part of what Night called a "sea nymph." When I asked Night about the coincidences, he said that when he was writing *Lady,* he wasn't thinking of *Splash,* and when he cast Bryce Howard, he wasn't thinking about the Ron Howard–mermaid connection. But he liked how the pieces fit together.

"There are no coincidences," Night said, echoing Freud. Night was one to process connections all the time. Everything fit.

In terms of fame, Tom Hanks was near the top of the list Night had been keeping, candidates to play the role of Cleveland Heep, the stuttering building super. Night was the rare director who could hire anybody he wanted, provided the actor wanted the job. On the list with Hanks were Johnny Depp, Kevin Costner, Matt Damon, Tobey Maguire, Bill Murray, Adrien Brody,

Philip Seymour Hoffman, Paul Giamatti. Tom Cruise had been on it for a while but Night decided his star power would overwhelm the role. Hanks, a different sort of star, was the most obvious choice. Many people will go to a movie just because he's in it. On that basis, Night knew that Paul Giamatti was the least likely choice.

But while writing the role, Night's head kept returning to Giamatti. He had loved him in *American Splendor* and *Sideways*. He felt Giamatti had the same everyman quality as Hanks, but with Giamatti, the audience would have no preconceived notions. Night could tell Giamatti was smart but didn't want people to know it. Cleveland Heep was like that. Giamatti made unlikable characters likable, starting with Pig Vomit, Howard Stern's boss in *Private Parts*.

Paul Giamatti was the son of a star, in a manner of speaking. His late father was A. Bartlett Giamatti, the former Yale president and baseball commissioner. He was a towering figure in two important American institutions, a man with a commanding presence. Compared to his father, Paul Giamatti seemed so unactorly. He always looked like some guy sitting in a coffee shop, lifting the pickles off his tuna-fish sandwich.

In *American Splendor,* he played the cartoonist Harvey Pekar, and you couldn't help but feel for the guy. You knew Harvey had no power over his abrasiveness. In *Sideways,* Giamatti's character stole from his mother, was an insufferable wine snob, and was pretentious about his lousy writing. And you liked him anyhow. Paul Giamatti was funny. He was funny as the obnoxious producer in *Big Fat Liar,* he was funny as the straight-man detective in *Big Momma's House,* he was funny as Pig Vomit. Cleveland Heep had to be funny, at least sometimes.

Paul Giamatti didn't look anything like a leading man from central casting (he was round, balding, with his hands often shoved deep in his front pockets). Night liked that. He sensed

Giamatti had a deep honesty about himself. It's crazy: You make a living pretending to be other people, and the thing you need most is honesty. Not in the Boy Scout sense of the word. Night had known great actors who were great liars in their everyday life, and why wouldn't they be? Night meant honesty in the willingness to lay oneself bare. That's how he'd written Cleveland Heep, and that's how he saw Giamatti. Cleveland Heep had to get the residents of an apartment building to come together. They'd do that only if they believed him. Night thought Giamatti could pull it off.

Still, Night knew his casting idea was not for the faint of heart. Paul Giamatti's biggest acting gig (in terms of people reached) had been as the voice of Frank the Talking Headcover, a puppet on a golf club, in the Tiger Woods spots for Nike. *That* was the guy Night was thinking of hiring to play the lead in a movie that would open on seven thousand screens across the world. In a script that was like nothing Night had done before and like nothing that other directors were doing. Night would be asking Paul Giamatti, who had never had the lead in a big-time, big-budget mainstream movie, to carry his next movie. He decided he should do the conventional thing, for a change: meet him before hiring him.

They met for lunch on a winter day at the Mercer, a chic hotel in lower Manhattan. Night arrived first and positioned himself so he could see Giamatti as he was coming in. The main dining area of the restaurant was in the basement, one level below the lobby. Night saw Giamatti coming down the exposed steps. It was a cold, icy day, and Giamatti was wearing sensible shoes. That was the very first thing Night saw: Paul Giamatti's solid plain brown left shoe. Then he saw him take a step. There was something slightly awkward about it; the toe went a little low and the heel came a little high. The image of the shoe and the step got stuck in Night's head.

They shook hands. Night noticed there was a science-fiction book in Giamatti's coat pocket and fresh paint on the sleeve.

"What happened there?" Night asked playfully.

"Oh, yeah—wet paint," Giamatti said. He shrugged and made a face.

They had lunch. They talked some about movies but mostly about books, about science fiction, about Ian Fleming. They had dessert. Giamatti was funny, and Night laughed often.

Night had come to the lunch hoping to get some kind of confirmation. He suspected that the most critical casting question of the movie could be answered with the least likely of choices. Night made his decision about his lead actor the moment he saw Giamatti's brown shoe and halting step, descending the stairs to the Mercer Kitchen dining room. He made possibly the most important casting decision of his career on the basis of a shoe. The voices were there, turning instinct into analysis.

It's so human, that shoe.

Dude, it's a shoe.

Actually, it's not. Paul's the guy for the job.

When Night recounted that whole scene for me, with the voices showing up in the end, I still didn't get it. We all have conversations in our head, to sort things out. Or we replay a mental tape of conversations we've had, who said what, and what did it actually mean. But as Night explained it, this was different. Paul could have said, "Your movies suck, they bore me to no end"—and it wouldn't have mattered to Night. Why? Because Paul's shoe was talking to Night, telling Night what was really in Paul's heart, triggering an in-the-head conversation.

I know, I know; what bullshit, right?

———

Alan Horn sent a Warner Bros. jet to Philadelphia to fly Night to Los Angeles. The plane had low ceilings but was commodious in every other way. It had two pilots and one short, perky stewardess. The plane could have easily fit a dozen or more people, but the only passengers on board were Night; Jose, who had once been Night's assistant; Marc Glick, his New York lawyer; Paula; and me. The cabin was all polished wood and marble, and everywhere you looked, there were baskets piled high with fresh fruit. There were strawberries and melon slices and kumquats. There were newspapers and magazines to read, all crisp and new. It was exceedingly elegant.

Night, a voracious eater, had French toast with hot syrup and scrambled eggs with fresh avocado for breakfast. There was a library of movies to watch, and Night went straight to the *U* section, hoping to find *Unbreakable,* like a kid rifling through baseball cards in search of his favorite player. *Unbreakable* was his favorite of his pictures, the misunderstood child, the movie that haunted Night. But under *U,* the only thing he found was a Steven Seagal movie.

"*Under Siege 2?*" Night asked the flight attendant incredulously. "How can you not have the original?"

The stewardess laughed and said, "Nothing but Warner movies on this jet."

Night and I, with her cooperation, began a little competition to see who could guess more biographical facts about her on intuition alone. Night won: She was from the Midwest, unmarried but still looking, still hoping for children, the clock marching on. But there was something maternal about her. When she said her favorite movie was *The Notebook,* a love story based on the Nicholas Sparks novel, Night nodded knowingly. *Of course, of course.* It was like he was testing himself, seeing if he could still get inside somebody else's skin, wondering if the Disney breakup had robbed him of his most essential skill.

As we neared Los Angeles, Night went into the lavatory to change out of his jeans and T-shirt and into a white dress shirt and an elegant black suit, the suit he would wear to meet with Alan Horn. It had been made for him in Italy, for the Italian premiere of *The Village*. When he came out, there was a round of light applause. He looked so in control. I wondered if he was getting his game back or if he was acting.

"You know, if you and our stewardess were in a burning building and I could only save one of you, I'd save her," Night said quietly. He says things like that, provocative, odd, interesting things. Amused and startled, I asked why.

"You already believe in something. All she's got is hope. No faith, just hope. She's trying so hard. She's trying with her hair, trying with her makeup, trying with her smile. But life's beat her down. Her expectations are low. She's hanging on by a thread, but she's hanging on. Save her from the burning building, she'd have faith for the rest of her life."

To a mortgage officer examining financial statements, it would seem that the stewardess and the writer-director had nothing in common. But of course they did. The whole time, it seemed to me, Night had been talking about himself: *He* was hanging on by a thread. *He* was having his faith tested. Night needed to know there was someone who would pull *him* out of a burning building. In a manner of speaking, he was looking to be saved.

His movies were rich in faith. Devout Christians flocked to *The Sixth Sense*, which Night found intriguing. He was not Christian, but he had gone to a Catholic school through eighth grade and an Episcopalian school from ninth through twelfth, and images of Jesus of Nazareth had surrounded him all his life. "I find it much more poignant to think of Jesus as a man, doing what he did purely on faith," Night once said. "By making him a god, he can't be an example to me. If you have every piece of magic available to you, and then you walk on water, what's the big deal? I can't emulate that. But if he's a man—if he's Martin Luther King, if he's Gandhi—*that's* real. That's attainable. That's a model. If Jesus made a blind man see on faith alone, *that's* awesome. If he went to the cross as an ordinary man with just unbelievable faith, how inspiring is that? I'd be in awe of that man. I'd put his picture on my desk, even though I'm not Christian. But by making him a deity, by giving him magical powers, I think you reduce him."

As a child (but never as an adult), Night would pray for things: for a coach to put him in the game; for a girl to like him; for the voices to go away. (He didn't know how to use them then.) But in his boyhood prayers, he never thought of his God in any sort of human form, not even when he was eight. He was being raised by Hindu parents, and he thought differently from all the other second-graders at his Catholic school.

The stewardess could not have known Night's purpose in flying to Los Angeles, but she was rooting for him. She said, "This is the *funnest* flight I've ever had." There was a bonding thing happening on the plane, because of Night. He was emitting a spectacular energy, just as he had that evening at the Burch house. But this time it was different, twinged with nervousness and vulnerability. We all felt it.

When the plane was on the tarmac and heading for the Warner Bros. hangar, I saw that Night had two *Lady* scripts on his lap. I wondered when, if ever, I'd get to read it. And at that exact moment, Night said to me, "When you get to the hotel, Paula's going to give you a copy of the script, if you want to read it. Cool?"

With everything he had going on, how did he have time to calculate when I should read the script? Could he have known that I was thinking of that subject right then? His timing was improbable. I had always thought there *were* coincidences. You're at the gas station, you're thinking of calling a friend for Ping-Pong, and there he is. You say, "What a coincidence!"

In any event, I had never been so well managed—and I don't mean that crassly—in all my life.

There were two gleaming black SUVs and several muscular, we-mean-business security men waiting in the gleaming Warner Bros. hangar. ("Their specialty is the cavity search," one of the SUV drivers later said.) Night, in his black suit and his white cuff-linked shirt, went directly from the plane to the Warner Bros. lot to see Alan Horn and Jeff Robinov, the president of production at the studio. The rest of us went to the Hotel Bel-Air, an oasis amid the mansions, low and rambling, with bougainvillea and lilac and roses growing everywhere. Paula instructed me to bring the script back to her as soon as I was done reading it.

When Night had told me he asked his basketball buddies and his housekeeper and his nanny to read the script, it struck me as unrealistic. It's far more difficult to read a screenplay than a book or even a play. If you're reading the screenplay of a movie you know, that's different. *Annie Hall, The Sound of Music, Goodfellas,* I thought those scripts all made for excellent reading, but I had already seen and loved those movies. Doing it the other way, script first, is tough. It's hard to be moved by a screenplay. You know what you're missing: music, colors, movie stars, the company of strangers. I read the script for *Jerry Maguire* before it was made. (It was given to me by an NFL agent I was writing about, the impossible Drew Rosenhaus; he claimed that Tom Cruise's part was based on him, but it had to be another character in the movie, Bob Sugar, the agent played by Jay Mohr who steals Cruise's clients.) I thought the *Jerry Maguire* script was obvious and unrealistic and trite. *You had me at hello.* Please. Who talks like that? Couldn't stand it. But when I was sitting in the movie house with Christine, and

Renee Zellweger delivered that line, I bought the whole thing.

I brought some history to my reading of *Lady in the Water*. I knew the outline of the story but not its details. I knew the Disney people didn't get it, and that as I was reading it, Night was delivering it to the bosses at Warner Bros. I knew Night wanted Paul Giamatti to play the lead and that he had already asked Bryce Howard to play the female lead. I had their faces in my head. I had heard about the dedication page. Now, shortly after flying cross-country in a private jet for the first time in my life, as a temporary member of Team Night, I was seeing the script for the first time. It was striking to turn the cover page and see the dedication.

> *To my daughters,*
> *I'll tell you this story one more time*
> *But then go to bed.*

It was stranger than I had imagined. Really, *very* strange. I struggled with Lin Lao Choi, the gigantic Korean party girl/ university student who had tripped up Nina and Zimmer. The vocabulary—*narf, tartutic, scrunt*—I found daunting. My tastes are simple, and this whole thing was in the category of mythic bedtime story. (My bedtime stories to my kids were about falling through the ice while skating and other real-life horror stories with semi-happy endings.) The scary parts of the script—the scrunt, for example, with its long wet teeth— weren't scary on the page. There was bathroom humor I found coarse. It was not conventional in any way. There was something crazy about it. Almost nothing happened.

And yet . . .

It was funny, moving, odd in a good way, deeply beautiful. I liked the feeling of claustrophobia implied by the script, of getting inside an apartment complex and never leaving it, and all the while you're dying to get out and see the rest of the world. It reminded me of *Rosemary's Baby* that way and in other ways. There, the residents of the apartment building come together for satanic reasons. People also come together in *Lady in the Water,* but in Night's script, they're defending an angel. It reminded me of no other single movie. It was *The Englishman Who Went Up a Hill But Came Down a Mountain* meets *Harold and Maude,* if that means anything, and it probably doesn't. It was talky, like *Mountain,* and humorously morose, like *Harold.* Nobody saw those two movies, not compared to *Signs.* But they're both excellent and memorable. To my taste, *Lady in the Water* worked in the same way. There was something odd, fun, and moving about it. It was inspiring.

Cleveland Heep, the building superintendent, was sad, humorous, realistic, overqualified and overeducated for his job, desperate to connect with another person. (Night *had* to get the perfect person to play him. Any misstep there would just kill it.) I didn't think of Story, Bryce Howard's character, as a pool creature—or a "sea nymph," as Night described her—but simply as a magnificent young woman with red hair, and I didn't imagine she and Cleveland were ever going to get together because that seemed too easy. It was unrequited love, but not like anything you've seen before. The apartment filled with the fivesome of smokers I found funny. Early on, I was making one note after another, but at about the halfway mark, I stopped. There was a race-against-time quality to the script, and I got caught up in it. It read vividly, much more so than any other screenplay I had ever read. It felt like the kind of movie Christine and I would see with pleasure on a Saturday night, or on a drizzly weekday with the kids at school.

But not at a suburban multiplex loaded with kids eating gummy bears. To me, it read like the kind of movie we'd see at the Ritz Five, our favorite art-house theater in downtown

Philadelphia. There was something magical about the script, but also rare. How it could open on seven thousand screens across the world, how it could be a movie for the masses, I had no idea. Then again, I had thought the script for *Jerry Maguire* was banal.

When Night asked for my reaction to the script, I gave him the whole thing.

"Oh, I like that," he said. He was laughing. "Keep telling me that: 'How can this be anything other than an art-house movie?' That's good."

There were so many qualities of the athlete in him. The more you challenged him, the deeper he reached.

"Don't let me forget that."

When Night went to Warner Bros. that day—Warners, the Hollywooders call it, as if Jack Warner and his brothers still ran the place—he was experiencing sensory overload. He couldn't shut it off. As he was waiting to be ushered into Horn's office, he looked out a window and saw a hedge. Most people would have said it was perfect, straight out of the barbershop. It was not to Night.

There's something wrong with that hedge. What is it?

He kept staring at it. The hedge was like Paul's shoe. The hedge was yapping away at him.

That hedge shouldn't be next to a trash compactor. That's so demeaning to the hedge. Somebody robbed that hedge of all its art.

Night knew he was fixated on what any teacher would call the "wrong" thing, but he couldn't help himself. That's how he was. He'd look at a page he had written and his eye would go straight to the problem. He'd look in the viewfinder of a camera and Bruce Willis would be in the middle of it, in costume and makeup, ready to work, but Night's eye would go to a tree behind the movie star, a tree that was too green, too vibrant, somehow wrong.

Night was carrying the two scripts from the plane, one for Horn and one for Robinov. An assistant suddenly said, "Do you want me to take them for you?"

The voice startled Night. She couldn't possibly know how Night guarded his scripts. But Night managed to say the socially appropriate thing. He usually did, no matter what he was thinking.

"No, that's okay, I'll hold them. Thanks, though."

A door opened, and Night heard another assistant from another direction say, "Mr. Shyamalan, Mr. Horn will see you now." But his name got twisted into *shy-mo-LION*. It made him nervous. It made him wonder if he would be able to inspire Mr. Horn.

Night set the two copies of the script on a coffee table dominated by a potted plant. Everybody was anxious. Horn's office was spotless and austere. He was a tall, fit man with wire-framed glasses, still and intense, like Harrison Ford in *The Mosquito Coast*. Robinov was shorter, quirkier, less exacting. They were both asking Night questions, picking his brain. Night was pleased. That hadn't happened at the Lacroix dinner.

Warner Bros. has a reputation for marketing its movies astutely overseas, and Robinov asked Night for his theories on why Hollywood had traditionally struggled when marketing black stars as leading men in many parts of the world.

"Well, you have two groups. You've got guys like Eddie Murphy and Martin Lawrence and Bernie Mac, great comic actors. And you've got guys like Denzel Washington and Sam Jackson and Morgan Freeman, some of the best dramatic actors working today," Night said. "Foreign audiences are happy to be entertained by black comic actors. Chase movie, guy jumping out of a plane, whatever. They'll go there. But if you've got a black guy walking down the sidewalk and he falls in love with the girl in front of him—the kind of thing where the audience has to be in the guy's shoes—foreign audiences are less willing to do that than we are. The thing that gives you hope is that the chasm has been getting smaller and smaller here, so it should happen there." Night felt Robinov was connecting to what he was saying.

After a while, not even a half hour, Horn glanced at the coffee table, at the scripts. Everybody knew that everything now rested on what Horn and Robinov thought of the script. It was 11:15 A.M. They would be reading it as soon as Night left. It's not easy to get two top executives to read a script on your timetable, but Night had managed it.

Horn asked, "Would it suit you if I picked you up at your hotel at four-forty-five?"

"Of course," Night said. One of the rules of sales is always be agreeable.

Night checked in to the Bel-Air, in the hotel's presidential suite, a $3,500-per-night mini-house with fresh flowers and fresh fruit and a fireplace stacked with seasoned wood. Normally, he found staying in expensive hotel rooms—particularly when he was paying for them himself, as he was here—empowering. He felt he had earned the right to be in them. This time, he felt nothing but frayed nerves. He was one thing in public, and another by himself. He got out of his salesman's suit. He knew he could do nothing about Alan Horn and Jeff Robinov by force of personality now. Night's need to lead, his need to connect with other people, his gifts for talking and coaxing, none of that mattered right now. The only thing that mattered was the script and how people responded to it. And at that exact moment, Night's faith in the script was weak. Once he had thought there was something great about it, but now he was not sure.

Thank you, Nina Jacobson.

He imagined 4:45. Night would get into Horn's car, and they would drive silently somewhere. There would be attempts to start conversations about some inconsequential thing, but they would go nowhere. Horn and Night would arrive at some fancy restaurant at an absurdly early hour, when the waiters were still putting out silverware. They would sit in an empty cocktail lounge—drafty, bad music—and Horn would finally say, "We want to be in business with you, but not on this script. What else you got?"

Paula had organized a full afternoon for Night, meetings with different special-effects companies and puppeteers, the people who would make his scrunt, his scary creature with long wet teeth and thick, spiky matted grass for fur. Night wasn't ready to head out. He sat on the edge of his bed, dazed, his cell phone in his hand. He couldn't understand why he had not heard from Paul Giamatti.

He kept looking at his watch, which he still had set on Philadelphia time. He kept looking at his phone. He kept twisting his rings. His head was spinning.

He wondered what he should do with Giamatti if the news from Horn was bad. Should he still call him? He decided he should. He wanted to take Giamatti with him wherever he went next. Night wanted to make him an insider. He sat on the bed and tried to sort through all his problems like that, systematically, one at a time, but he couldn't. The room was giving him no comfort.

He put on his boots, mud from the farm still on their soles, and headed out for his afternoon meetings ready to once again be the public Night.

Alan Horn picked up Night at the Hotel Bel-Air. They did not drive to an empty restaurant. They went straight to Horn's house. On the short, winding drive there, Night's heart was racing, but Horn exuded calm. The house was filled with art and books. Nobody was home. Night saw his script sitting on a bare kitchen counter. He liked how it looked there.

Robinov arrived, carrying his own script. Night was waiting to hear the judgment.

We love it.

It's weird but we like it.

We don't get it but we know you'll make it work.

We don't get it but we know your fans will.

It's weird. Can you help us understand it?

We want to be in business with you but not on this script. What else you got?

He was waiting to hear some overarching thing.

Instead, they jumped right into it, offering specific notes, asking questions, going through the script page by page. "Anything we say here, it is only in the area of suggestion," Horn said. "Things you might want to think about."

Night was in a daze. At one point Horn said that the "humor in the walkie-talkie scene plays a little young." Night was normally a good note-taker, but all he wrote down was something like *young walkie-talkie no laugh*, and when he looked at it later, he had only a vague idea of what it meant.

At one point Horn left the house for a half hour or so, picked up his daughter from her after-school sport, and returned home. Night liked the whole casual manner. But all the while he was distracted. He thought he could tell, by the way Horn and Robinov were talking and the things they were saying, that they wanted to turn the script into a movie.

But maybe that's not the case, because if they liked it and wanted it, wouldn't they just come out and say so?

Maybe they don't want to be so direct.

Maybe they don't want to play their hand early.

75

Maybe they disagree.

Maybe they don't know what to say.

He needed something from somebody.

When Horn returned, Night said, "Can I ask something here? Maybe I'm missing something, but I'm not clear: Are you guys in on this thing?"

He felt all the blood in his body abruptly pooling in his forehead. A pinprick would have created a geyser.

Horn nearly laughed but didn't. "Oh. Oh, yes, of course, of course. Absolutely. We're in. We're totally in. We want you to make this movie for us."

Night wanted to feel relief, but he didn't. He didn't know if they were responding to *Lady in the Water* or to the $2 billion his other movies had grossed. Night *did* feel like he had a clean slate, a place where he could start over. But the most important questions to Night were still unanswered. Could he inspire them? Could he turn to them when he needed help? He knew he didn't know. He was just starting out, and he was already exhausted.

The meeting ended quickly after that. Robinov had his copy of the script, Horn had his. Night had his scrawled notes.

"This might seem a little strange, but I don't like to have my scripts floating around, I've had problems with—"

"Here, we have two. Take mine," Horn said. "I've written some notes in the margins, and if they're useful to you, use them."

Notes from an executive that are appropriate for the director to see. Wow.

Horn asked, "Is it okay if we hold on to the one?"

"Of course."

Night knew he had to say that. They were going to give him at least a $60 million budget to make a movie, and they would spend substantially more than that to market it. For them to be able to hold on to one copy of the script, the way Nina used to, that seemed reasonable to Night. He could do that.

He flew to Los Angeles, Night said more than once and with admirable candor, "to try to sell the script to Warner Brothers," and after he did, he seemed different. After his meeting with Horn and Robinov, he was more assertive, slightly edgier than I had seen him at home. Somewhere on that trip, he slipped out of his middle-of-the-night writing robe and into his director's outfit, his shirt unbuttoned to mid-chest. He said he was tired of writing, that he was ready to direct again. Directing was like a break. It's not that hard to get people to do things for you when you're paying them. But try to get exactly the right 25,000 words down on a 135-page script, leaving just the right white space—it's hell.

One night, after Warner Bros. had bought the script, Night and his cousin Ashwin Rajan, and Jose and Paula and I, went out for dinner at Mr Chow. It's a Beverly Hills institution, a classic see-and-be-seen place, but a half-week behind the news, I'm guessing. It was loud and crowded, with some people, Ash among them, wearing funky woven woolen hats. The old rule, no hats inside, was meaningless at Mr Chow. Ash was a fledgling agent at United Talent, the agency Jeremy Zimmer and Peter Benedek owned. He and Night were like brothers. A few tables away from us, Burt Reynolds and Sylvester Stallone were having dinner with two well-coiffed ladies and a young, quiet, smooth-skinned Hispanic man who looked like he was ready to contend for the welterweight title tomorrow. Both Stallone and Reynolds had skin that was weirdly tight. They looked a little spooky.

Night asked his cousin Ash if he had a UTA business card and whether he knew how to flash it. Night went off on a long bit on the sleight-of-hand methods that old-school Hollywood agents would use to produce their business cards: out of the breast pocket, from behind the ear, out of the sleeve. Night must have picked up these moves from old movies. He was too young, and his visits to Hollywood were too infrequent, for him to know the routine firsthand. He has fast hands and deft fingers, and the bit was funny for a while, but he played it for the whole night. This was not the contemplative person I had talked to sometimes for hours at a stretch in his office at the farm in the heart of Wyeth country. When we were leaving the restaurant, he sent Jose out first to make sure the car—the enormous, gleaming black Warner Bros. SUV—was idling and ready to go, and then he rushed us into the waiting car as one group, saying, urgently and low, "C'mon, c'mon, c'mon!" There were three or four photographers he was trying to get past. I could call them paparazzi, but I don't want to get sued by some paparazzi union for defamation. One looked to be a middle-aged housewife with a pharmacy Instamatic. One girl waved and politely tapped on Night's window, autograph book and pen in hand. Night lowered the window and signed for her, then hit the up button and said to the driver, "Let's go!" The driver turned on his left blinker, checked his mirrors, and slipped carefully into the mellow late-night Camden Drive traffic.

The next night we went out to eat at a restaurant called Koi, which had delicious food and a sprinkling of models and actors hovering at the bar. Ash, no surprise, had made the reservation. He knew the spots, as fledgling agents should. As we went through the lounge area on our way out, a young woman in a bulky sweatshirt—a tourist from the Midwest traveling with her family—slipped past all the models and actors, approached Night, and, with no particular urgency, said that her younger sister, sitting twenty feet away on a sofa, was an enormous fan but too shy to approach Night.

"We were just saying if we could only see one famous person during our trip here, who would it be, and she says you, and then here you are," the tourist said. "How strange is that?"

There was no reason to doubt anything she was saying. Night went over and said hello to the kid sister, who spent two minutes describing to Night each of his movies as if he had never seen them, and what she took from each one. She was sweet and articulate, not breathless.

"Cool, cool," Night kept saying. "Thank you."

There was no hysteria. She didn't ask for an autograph, and my guess is had Night offered one, she would have declined it. All she wanted was to connect, brain-to-brain, with the person who made the movies that had a life deep within her, and that's what she did.

When we got to the sidewalk, Night was nothing like he had been the previous night, on the way out of Mr Chow. "They were so nice," Night said, speaking of the midwesterners. He sounded vulnerable and needy. It was endearing.

A lot of "industry" people stay at the Hotel Bel-Air, so in addition to the crisp free copies of *The New York Times* and the *Los Angeles Times* and *The Wall Street Journal,* there are copies of *Variety* and *The Hollywood Reporter* available, too. On the morning we left, Night's move from Disney (or "the Mouse House," as *Variety* calls it) to Warner Bros. was front-page news in both trade papers. They had only the main points of the deal worked out, but enough to go public.

There was no evidence of the move's true drama and emotion in the stories. In an era of press releases and prepared statements, news stories often become sterile and neat, the way the participants want them to be. What's lost is how messy life is. Still, for what they were, they were accurate.

There was one quote in the stories from an unnamed Disney employee: "We have a terrific relationship with Night, and although we didn't agree creatively on this particular project, we look forward to working with him in the future."

A more truthful statement would have been: *At times we have had a terrific relationship with Night, and although we didn't "get" his new script, we offered him a $60 million budget to make it for us anyhow. But he walked. We hope he'll make another movie for us again someday, although when he said goodbye to us, it sounded like he really meant it. You know his whole thing with Harvey!*

You don't expect deep truths in those kinds of stories. You expect sanitized bullshit, and that's mostly what you get.

Paula, Jose, and I were in the second row of the gleaming black SUV, with our luggage in the back. Marc Glick was staying in Los Angeles to work out the details of Night's contract with Warner Bros. The contract would be worth around $20 million, to buy the script and secure Night as the director, plus a percentage of the gross. In other words, the kind of deal a movie star gets, a big-time, top-tier, A-list movie star who can pretty much guarantee a $50 million opening weekend and a movie that will gross at least $200 million. If you had 5 percent of the gross, that's another $10 million. Plus a cut of DVD sales and all the rest. You can't even use the word *payday* to describe such sums.

Night had dropped his idea to finance half the movie's budget. He didn't think it was the right time or place to go so far out on a limb. Nina Jacobson and Dick Cook and Oren Aviv had been so sure of themselves when they said they didn't get it. Night was wondering then—and would be for a long while to come—if they were right.

Night had been eager to make a big bet on himself. He was in the process of buying an enormous Main Line estate not far from his farm and office. It was maybe the grandest of all the horse-country estates, with a house where you could shoot a remake of *Howard's End,* once Night was done rehabilitating it. The project would take years and would cost tens of millions of dollars. If he had a half-interest in one movie that became a phenomenon, the whole project would be paid for. But Night didn't feel ready to make that bet. Doubt had been deposited in his head.

Night got in the car last but right on time at seven-thirty. (He took punctuality seriously.) He was furious. I'd never seen him like this. He tossed copies of the trades on the dashboard and said to Jose, "Did you see this shit?"

Jose nodded.

"Get Zimmer on the phone."

Despite the early hour, Jose tried to get Zimmer on the phone. Night continued to rail about Disney. "What the *fuck* is that all about? We had an agreement. We all agreed about what we would say. We agreed that we would all be gentlemen about this and not turn it into something. Then they say this shit about creative differences? What kind of shit is that?"

There was a literal truth in Disney's statement that "we didn't agree creatively on this particular project." Had they agreed creatively, Night would have been making the movie for Disney. But Night, in full Johnnie Cochran mode, plowed right through the narrowness of that claim: "What happened to 'Here's sixty million dollars. Go make the movie for us'?"

He was staring straight through the windshield, and his words were bouncing off it and reverberating to the three of us behind him.

"Where is that? If I had known they were going to go talk about creative differences, then I would have said, 'I left Disney even after they offered me sixty million and final cut.' But I took the high road."

He was steaming.

"You got Jeremy?"

Zimmer was not picking up his cell phone or his office phone. Jose didn't call him at home.

Night was shaking his head.

I asked, "Can you do like the athletes do? Can you take your anger and turn it into performance?"

Tiger Woods has that move. He'll miss a short putt or a camera will go off on his backswing, and he'll get, as the old-school ballplayers say, "the red ass." He turns his rage into effort and wallops a 330-yard drive; he turns his rage into concentration and delicately plays a half-swing pitch shot. Even in a rage, Woods has different speeds. More than that: He becomes keenly aware of everything in his arsenal. It raises his game.

The time between the end of my question and the beginning of Night's response was 0.0 of a second.

"The only way this movie's gonna be good is if I can find peace. All my unhappiness with Disney, the whole 'we don't get it' thing, I've got to bury all of that or this movie will suffer. You can't inspire people when you're angry."

The words spilled out of him without a moment of reflection. It was not the answer an athlete would give, not an ordinary one, not even Tiger, who never tells you what he's thinking anyhow. It was an answer from a Zen master, except that Night was not a Zen master. He made movies. He lived in the world where art, commerce, and lies collide.

For a while Night had been telling me that he thought of himself as an idiot savant, to use an expired phrase. Like Dustin Hoffman in *Rain Man*, but Night's gift was not for counting toothpicks when they tumbled out of a box and onto the floor, or knowing when Fernando Valenzuela would pitch. Night's gift was for knowing feelings instantaneously. Not all the time, but sometimes. His gift was an ESP for frame of mind, his own and others'. "The voices," they popped in and popped out, sometimes useful, sometimes not. That business about Paul Giamatti's shoe and step and how it had revealed Giamatti to Night: Interesting stuff, but what did it actually mean? Then on the plane: I had been thinking about when I could read the script, and out of the blue, Night had invited me to do so. You could call it a coincidence, if you like.

But this instant search-for-peace response, that was something else. When Night evaded Harvey in selling *The Sixth Sense,* he'd made the move to survive. Now Night was dealing with rejection, pride, anger, insecurity, invincibility, betrayal, *fatherhood*—and doing it all at once. But even in the thick of it, he had it all sorted out. He had identified the problem, stripped it naked, and figured out the solution like a grown-up doing first-grade arithmetic. *That* was the savant in action.

Sitting there in the SUV, I felt as if I had a spyscope that let me see into the place where the oval head shots of Nina and Dick Cook and Oren Aviv were floating around, where the picture of the trash compactor was filed, where Lin Lao's mother was invented while sitting in a hotel lobby after the breakup dinner at Lacroix. In a moment when he was riddled with conflict, the voices were telling Night to go placidly, etc. We've all been there, so angry and red-faced and mad that all you want to do is kick down a door. Night was in that exact spot, and all he was thinking about was his need to find peace only because the voices were screaming a single message to him: *Find peace, find peace, find peace.*

4.
_____

I t's not easy to make a living as an actor. Cindy Cheung was born in 1970, and by the spring of 2005 she had a full-time office job; her acting work could barely pay her cell-phone bill, the only phone she had. As a tall Asian woman, she didn't have much to audition for. When the studios were casting Asian women, they usually wanted someone short to stand behind a counter at a dry cleaner or something. Still, Cindy Cheung kept at it. There had to be thousands of other thirty-five-year-old actresses doing the same thing, clinging to the hope of discovery. In that way, she was no different from the stewardess on the Warner Bros. jet to Los Angeles, the woman Night had imagined pulling out of a burning building.

Cindy didn't come to acting until she was a senior in college, majoring in applied math. After graduating from UCLA, she could have taken a job at Northrop Grumman, the aviation defense contractor, as a software programmer. Instead, she got a gig performing at Los Angeles elementary schools, reciting poetry while wearing a bowling shirt and bouncing around as if on a pogo stick. She made the rounds in Hollywood, but it was slow going. She got a day of work on *Seinfeld* as Woman No. 1, but when her episode aired, Cindy's role was cut.

She moved to San Francisco to study at the American Conservatory Theater. In her classes, she was urged to "get in touch" with herself, and the self she touched, she quickly discovered, was depressed. Her parents had divorced and a guy had broken her heart and she was living on the top floor of a musty old Victorian house in Chinatown, with the dark wigs of the previous tenant, now dead, shoved in old drawers. A therapist advised her to go for a bike ride. The fresh air helped. Prescription medications helped more. After a year or so, she was off the meds and feeling good about herself and her acting. She had won the female lead in a Horton Foote play that did not call for a tall Asian-American woman. A triumph. She felt the lure of New York, and in 1998 she moved there. She was twenty-eight and single and looking to lead the acting life.

Whenever she did audition—for Broadway, off-Broadway, TV shows, commercials, studio movies, independent movies— the casting directors could see she had talent. She was tall and slim and attractive, with a beautiful singing voice, a knack for imitating people, and an excellent sense of humor. But in the end, it was nearly always the same. If the casting people were looking for an actress, no ethnicity or race specified, they looked at Cindy Cheung and saw a Chinese actress, even though she was a native Californian with the mid-country voice of a Des Moines weather lady. To the casting directors, she was tall and Asian—a freak show. There wasn't much out there for her.

Night's casting director, Douglas Aibel, needed help. He knew he wasn't going to be able to cast Lin Lao Choi by normal means. The over-the-phone notes Doug had gotten from Night added up to a character nobody had ever seen—except Night, in his head: *She's in her early or mid-twenties. A gigantic Korean-American. Dresses like Britney Spears. Six feet tall. Rolls of fat. Confident. Comfortable in a bikini. Sweet, funny, mystical. Fights with her mother but respects her. Movie pivots on her.*

Aibel asked Night if he could hire a scout to work Korean

neighborhoods, turn over rocks in Hawaii, in Korea, on bas-ketball rosters, in women's professional wrestling, anywhere. ("Hire anybody you need," Night said. He could say that; he was one of the movie's two producers.) Out of habit and a sense of fairness, Aibel made plans for open calls and for no-tices in *Back Stage* and on various websites. He wrote a charac-ter breakdown, to be sent out to agents and managers, trying to honor Night's vision but broad enough to find *somebody*. *Rolls of fat,* Doug could not use that.

He expected conventional searches to yield nothing. "The people who respond to those things are people who want to be actors," he said. "The person who's going to get this role doesn't even *know* she wants to act yet." He wanted to honor Night's vi-sion, but this one would be tough. Night was looking for a freak.

After the meeting at Alan Horn's house, Night was desperate to reach Paul Giamatti, but he could not find him. Not in his apart-ment in Brooklyn, not on his cell phone. When he finally did reach him, all Paul said was that he hadn't read the script yet.

Night's heart sank. Reading the script wasn't a major time commitment. You could do it in ninety minutes, less if you liked it a lot or not at all. But he buried his disappointment and summoned his inner salesman.

"Listen, dude, I wrote this role for you, man," Night said. "I really want you to do it, and so does everybody at Warner Brothers. I gave them all *sorts* of opportunities to tell me they didn't want you, and they said, 'No, we think he's great. We want him.'" Paul said some noncommittal thing and the con-versation was over.

A week passed. Night had still not heard back. He didn't know if Giamatti had read the script or not, if he liked it or not, if he wanted the job or not. No news was bad news.

One day in that period, I was at the farm for lunch. I mentioned to Night that Christine and I had seen *The Upside of Anger,* with Joan Allen and Kevin Costner. It had been our Saturday-night movie date.

"How was it?" Night asked.

"Excellent."

"How was Costner?"

Costner plays a retired baseball player, often drunk, who has a sports-talk radio show, except he won't talk about his baseball days. He's slovenly and cranky.

"Outstanding."

"Is he funny?"

"Extremely."

"How's he look?"

"You know, he's got a little paunch. He's losing his hair. He looks kind of beat up. He looks good."

"I've always liked him," Night said. "I met him once. He punched me in the arm and said, 'I know you.' I liked that. Very endearing. Was he likable in the movie?"

"Very much so."

"Life's caught up with him. He doesn't have that invincibility anymore. *Damn!* Jose, don't tell them anything's up, but call Costner's guy and see what his availability is."

Twenty minutes later, Jose had an answer for Night. "He's got an independent movie that has him tied up for the first two weeks in August, and then he's available after that." *Available* is a loose word in these kinds of discussions. Shoots run longer than scheduled, and agents have multiple irons in the fire in the "available" periods. Most things don't come through.

The voices were going off.

Maybe it's not Paul. Maybe it's Costner. Costner has warmth. Costner grabbed my elbow. Cleveland Heep has to have warmth.

Paul hasn't even read the script. Does that mean anything? My God—is there someone I can talk to besides myself?

"It's not ideal, but we could shoot other things first," Night told Jose.

He asked Paula to get Sam Mercer, Night's producing partner, on the phone.

Night's first words to him were, "I'm starting to have second thoughts about Paul."

It was startling. What about *Listen, dude, I wrote this role for you, man?* What about Night's moment with Paul Giamatti's shoe? That day his decisiveness had been overwhelming. The voices were loud and clear. They were telling him that he didn't need Tom Cruise or even Tom Hanks. Night wanted the guy with the meager beard who played the flunky writer in *Sideways.* And now that actor didn't seem to want Night. The traffic wasn't moving two ways, like it was supposed to. As Night was flooring it toward Giamatti, Giamatti should have been coming straight at him. And he wasn't. He was . . . *nowhere.*

Night couldn't see the reality, that Paul Giamatti was an actor in demand with a lot going on. Night wasn't accustomed to dealing with real-world intrusions. You were supposed to get sucked up into Night's world and to hell with everything else. But that wasn't happening.

"What do you think about Costner?" Night asked Sam Mercer.

It wasn't common for Night to ask Sam creative questions. But he needed someone to turn to, and Sam was there. "Is Costner too graceful for this role? You believe Paul as a building super. But this is a super who is not a super, you know? Waiting like this for an answer from Paul, it makes me wonder. Maybe he just doesn't want to do it."

Night went outside, collar up against the wind, alone with about the biggest casting question of his career.

One of the things Sam did for Night was have the conversations Night didn't want to have or didn't know how to have. He protected Night from some of the harsher realities of moviemaking: negotiating with union bosses, landlords, agents, managers. Sam was a fixer. He could say, to anyone, "Are you in or are you out?" He didn't brag to Night about his methods. He did the opposite. He protected Night from them.

Several days after Night had asked Sam about Kevin Costner, Night got a call from Paul Giamatti.

"Dude, I am so *Lady*," Giamatti said. This was in March, five months before shooting was supposed to begin, an eon in moviemaking.

"Stop it," Night said playfully.

"I'm telling ya—I am."

Night didn't need to ask Paul what had taken him so long. The thing was, he was in. And for a moment Night was healed.

Every time Night said Paul Giamatti's name, my heart raced. I had first met Paul over twenty years earlier, when he was a skinny, curly-haired impish high school student wearing red high-top Chuck Taylor Converse basketball shoes, which even then was a retro look. We were briefly neighbors when I had my first job after college, working as a year-round reporter on Martha's Vineyard. I knew Paul only enough to say hi in the summer of 1983 and the summer of '84. But for those summers I knew his parents well. And there was Night talking about Paul with such fervor all those years later.

The Giamattis—Bart and Toni and their three children—had a summer home on the Vineyard, on a little hill in the woods. Their modest rancher was separated by ten yards of crabgrass from the one I lived in. Our other neighbor, John Farrar, was the EMT who had pulled Mary Jo Kopechne's body out of Ted Kennedy's 1967 Oldsmobile. Bart and Toni and I were all fascinated by a peculiar book, for which Farrar was a source, called *Teddy Bare,* a diatribe by Zad Rust, who called bullshit on every claim Ted Kennedy made about the death of Mary Jo Kopechne. Bart and Toni loved the peculiar. The kids I didn't know about.

Bart was the baseball commissioner when he died of a heart attack in 1989 in his house on Martha's Vineyard, eight days after kicking Pete Rose out of baseball. He was fifty-one. Paul Giamatti, newly graduated from Yale, was in the house at the time. So was Toni. The timing of his death was not a coincidence. There were other serious underlying health issues, but the matter of Mr. Rose, as Bart politely referred to the tsuris wrought by Rose's gambling problems, killed him.

In *Sideways,* when Paul's character goes to his mother's house and steals money from her bureau, there are a dozen or so family pictures on top of it. They're movie props. But one of the photos shows Paul standing with his father. It's a graduation snap, happy and real, on the screen for maybe a second. When the picture came into view, Christine says, I gasped. Bart was a seminal figure to me as a kid out of college. In a different way, Toni was, too. Some years after Bart died, I wrote a play about him. It had a brief run in a small theater. And nine years later, there was his son telling my new subject, "Dude, I am so *Lady.*"

My minor link to Paul, I mentioned it only in passing to Night, and I mention it here in the interest of disclosure and for another reason. Early one day in preproduction, when Paul met Night in New York City for a wig fitting, I was surprised that Paul recognized me immediately. He knew nothing about my being around, and we hadn't seen each other in twenty-one years. ("My memory for faces is scary," he said later.) Paul was bearded and schlumpy and endearing. I saw him and thought of my struggling twentysomething self; Paul's theater-loving parents; the unlikely path of Paul's career; the circular nature of life. I was beginning to understand what Night meant when he said there are no coincidences.

As soon as she moved to New York, Cindy Cheung realized it was where she was meant to be. She felt that when she was first living in Queens and more so when she moved to Manhattan.

For two years, she worked side jobs that let her continue to act. She worked as a cocktail waitress, although she knew nothing about liquor. (People would ask for a Glenfiddich, and she would say, "Glen who?") She worked as a hostess at an Italian restaurant where the manager instructed her to seat the old people in the back. She worked at a travel agency that catered to old people, and once she called somebody to follow up on a recently mailed brochure only to be told the intended recipient had died. She had a back-office job at Prada where she was the one person who didn't speak Italian, resulting in the misfiling of many order slips.

But all the while, she continued to act. She needed people to hear her. She went to workshops, she performed for free, she attended readings for new plays.

Cindy and a group of Asian-American actor friends founded a group called Mr. Miyagi's Theatre Company. On rented stages, they did a revue of scenes from the collected works of John Hughes: snippets from *The Breakfast Club* and *Pretty in Pink* and *Sixteen Candles*. People found their way to it, even after the group started charging five dollars a head.

Then Cindy performed in an off-off-Broadway play called *Masha No Home*, in which she played a Korean-American wife. D.J.R. Bruckner from *The New York Times* found *his* way to it and wrote: "Samantha Quan as Masha and Cindy Cheung as Annabell have the big roles, and they do them proud." He said Cindy was "incendiary" and "explosively funny." Somebody was hearing her.

In their next outing, Cindy and her Mr. Miyagi's Theatre Company accomplices wrote and performed a sketch comedy piece called *Sides: The Fear Is Real,* about the auditioning process. People found their way to that one, too, including a reviewer for *The Wall Street Journal,* Terry Teachout. He wrote: "Collectively written by the six terrific Asian-American performers who make up Mr. Miyagi's Theatre Company, *Sides* is a zany catalogue of everything that can possibly go wrong at an audition . . . Catch it now and in five years you can tell your friends how you first saw Sekiya Billman, Cindy Cheung, Paul Juhn, Peter Kim, Hoon Lee and Rodney To back when they were still struggling actors."

Two people had noticed her. It helped her keep going.

When Night returned from Los Angeles with a deal for *Lady* in place, he started hiring people quickly. His first hire was a famous cinematographer, Chris Doyle, who had shot one of Night's favorite movies, *In the Mood for Love.* Actually, to say Chris Doyle shot it doesn't do him justice. He *shrouded* it in lusty carnal darkness. Night wanted that look for *Lady.* Night didn't want a director of photography who would just execute the shots Night already had in his head. He wanted Doyle to bring him options. That was what Night told him when he hired him. It was a risky move. Night knew Doyle could make or break him.

While Night was making his preproduction hires, Paula was preparing for her June wedding, after which she would be leaving Night to open her own gift shop, something she had wanted to do for years. Night was worried about her departure. Paula wasn't a student of film, but she knew exactly how her lactose-intolerant boss liked his hot chocolate. Paula was training her successor, a Bryn Mawr College senior named Maddie, who was something close to an authority on Japanese black-and-white horror movies, among other genres. Night was amazed by what she knew.

Night was starting anew. He was bringing in many new people for *Lady*, more than he normally did. Betsy Heimann, who so expertly chose the leather-and-polyester wardrobes for Quentin Tarantino in *Pulp Fiction*, was hired as the costume designer. Martin Childs, an Englishman who had designed the sets for *Shakespeare in Love*, was hired as the production manager. Night hired Mary Cybulski, David Mamet's longtime script supervisor, a sort of accountant of words. Night liked that they all worked often on non-studio movies. They could think for themselves.

Night brought in a bunch of old hands, too. Brick Mason as his storyboard artist, the person who turns the screenplay into an elaborate comic strip before it becomes a movie. Barbara Tulliver as his editor, the director's bullshit detector. Jimmy Mazzola, formerly Woody Allen's prop man, as property master, in charge of the things the actors handle. Bill O'Leary, a veteran New York gaffer, as the lighting chief. Night the working writer was in hibernation. Now he was the bossman, always decisive in public. He was running a company that was growing bigger daily.

"I have a need to lead," Night said. Typically, writers are not leaders. The fringe is their home turf. But Night had no trouble being in the center of a swirl. Even when he was between movies, he had lots of people on his payroll: Franny the driver, Michael the cook, Dana the nanny, plus a farm manager, various gardeners and handymen, at least one assistant and often two. Then there was a steady stream of people hired on an as-needed basis, which meant close to full-time, including architects, landscape designers, sound engineers, pool people and

security people and horse people, a piano teacher, a projectionist. There was always somebody at the entrance gate at the
farm, waiting to be buzzed in. Night did not live by Thoreau's
maxim: *Simplify, simplify.*

His days had become much more scheduled and mecha-
nized, with lunches and job interviews and conference calls
and visits to possible shooting locations. He was still thinking
about the script constantly, tinkering with it when he could.
But there were no more afternoons whiled away in front of the
computer. He was in preproduction now. He had become an
evangelist for his movie, constantly defining it for people who
had not read the script. He'd say, "It's a fairy tale." Or "It's
about a dream." Or "It's an epic love story!" He was a one-man
marketing department. In preproduction, he spoke often of the
"tone of the movie" and how each person he hired would need
to influence the tone; he said that the movie would succeed
only if he got a hundred tonal decisions correct, or a thousand
or ten thousand.

His preproduction months were March through August 22,
the first day of shooting. All he needed was someone to play his
sister, someone to play Lin Lao Choi, a place to shoot the movie,
a way to make the mechanical scrunt move like the bastard child
of a wild boar and a hyena . . . His lists, which he kept on long
narrow cards left over from *The Village*, were endless. He had
good days, when the mental picture of Nina wouldn't visit him
once all day, and more bad ones, when he couldn't run her out.

Don't get it; don't get it; don't get it.

Night couldn't tell if it was his voices, spurring him on like
a mocking coach, or if Nina was saying something he would
someday find to be true, that *Lady* really did *not* make sense.

———

Cindy Cheung left nothing to chance. She spent twenty dollars a month, under the table, to get a daily e-mail intended for agents and talent scouts, which gave her a one-day jump on the major plays, movies, and TV shows being cast in New York. She scanned the report daily, looking for the word *Chinese*. Day after day there was nothing. Then one day in spring 2005 she saw a character breakdown, submitted by Doug Aibel, the likes of which she had never seen before. It was for a Warner Bros. movie to be directed by M. Night Shyamalan.

Lin Lao Choi—20s—a big, tall (6 feet or so, at least 5-9) young Korean woman, average looks. She's an endearing, intelligent young person, very traditional, yet very much of today. She's steeped in the history of her family, and yet dresses like Britney Spears. Not necessarily heavy, but she's a commanding physical presence. A memorable character. Has an accent. Lead.

Cindy was five-nine. She was one eighth Korean (although she didn't speak a word of it). She looked younger than thirty-five; she could pass for twenty-nine. *M. Night Shyamalan.* The word *lead* was not meant literally in these write-ups, but Cindy knew the role had to be significant. Cindy immediately called her agent, Paul Hilepo, namesake of a small boutique agency called Hartig-Hilepo, and asked, "Did you see that M. Night Shyamalan breakdown?"

She didn't know that Paul Hilepo had already received a call from Doug Aibel about the role. Doug's casting assistant, Stephanie Holbrook, knew Cindy's theater work. She was a fan. When she read Doug's character breakdown for Lin Lao, she got out a glossy picture of Cindy and pinned it to Doug's office wall. Doug had auditioned Cindy for other roles, and he liked her, too. But Hilepo didn't tell Cindy about the call. Too much information can backfire on an auditioning actor. He said, "Believe me, I saw that and started salivating." For once a big-name director was looking for a tall Asian actress for a studio movie. For once, Cindy had a chance.

Several days before her audition, Cindy was given her audition scene to read, three individual pages pulled out of the script. Sides, they're called in the business, like the name of Cindy's play. In her scene, Cleveland Heep asks her about the word *narf*. Cindy looked it up on the Internet and found nothing. (There was a Native American Rights Foundation and a Nike Animal Rescue Fund, but no *narf*.) One line seemed funny to her: "University gives many pages of homework. What they think? I have no social life?" She remembered that Joaquin Phoenix in *Signs* had been funny. She decided she'd go for funny. She knew that if she got the role, she'd be working with Paul Giamatti, one of her acting heroes. She tried not to think about Paul Giamatti. She tried not to think that the role would pay a living wage. She concentrated on the words on her sides and what they triggered in her head. In her apartment at night she'd rehearse, her novelist husband filling in for Giamatti. They'd read the lines in bed before falling asleep.

The day she read for Doug Aibel, she wore black pants and a lacy black-and-white tank top. She put on eye shadow and blush and mascara and plum lipstick. Her straight hair was curled and all done up. Doug looked at her and said, "Take off your earrings. You look too . . . pretty."

She could hear disappointment in his voice. She had made the wrong choice. A chance, a rare chance, was slipping away.

"It said in the breakdown that she dresses like Britney Spears," Cindy said, explaining.

"That's only when she goes out," Doug said.

She performed the scene for Doug and a video camera on a tripod. Doug read Cleveland's lines, softly and with almost no inflection. It took maybe two minutes. Night would see the videotape if Doug felt it was worth his time. After the first stab, Doug asked Cindy to try it again.

"Throw it away more this time," he said. He wanted her to play it more casually. Less funny. Slower.

She knew Doug had worked often with Night. She trusted him and did as he suggested. But it didn't even feel like acting to her, that second take.

She was the first person reading for the role. Plenty of others would come after her. It was a studio movie. Tall Asian English-speaking women would come out in droves. Cindy figured the odds were slim. They always were.

Night had a wish list for his various male supporting roles. The names William Hurt, Philip Seymour Hoffman, Sidney Poitier, Richard Dreyfuss, Chris Cooper, Gene Wilder, Terrence Howard, Alec Baldwin, Vince Vaughn, Bill Irwin, Don Cheadle, Tom Wilkinson, Danny Glover, Forest Whitaker, Bob Balaban, James Cromwell, Steve Buscemi, Peter Sarsgaard, Jeffrey Wright, Vincent D'Onofrio, Wallace Shawn—and many other less familiar names, ones usually offered by Doug Aibel— kept coming up. Not counting the five smokers, Night had four remaining acting jobs for men to fill.

He looked at a list of names, running his finger over them. The voices kicked in.

I need angels, I need angels, who are the angels?

One day Night was interviewing somebody for a job on *Lady in the Water* who had recently seen Alec Baldwin.

Alec's on the list. Maybe that's a sign. Maybe that means something.

"How'd he look?" Night asked.

"Chubby."

"Hmmmmm."

"But he'll lose weight if you tell him to."

"Is he heavy in the face?"

"He can lose it."

Night looked unconvinced. He'd been down that road with other actors.

"I want to see his eyes. He has those great eyes."

For Night, filling the male roles was an embarrassment of riches. He offered a role to Philip Seymour Hoffman, had a couple of conversations with him, in an unguarded moment allowed him to read the entire script. Hoffman let him down gently—*loved the script, liked the role, just too much going on now*—and the disappointment lingered in Night only briefly, maybe two days and part of a third. He knew there were other actors who could do it.

But filling the two main female roles, after Story, consumed Night with worry. Where on earth would he find his Korean heavyweight, Lin Lao Choi, with her comic manner and her rolls of fat? And who would play Anna Ran, sister of the stalled writer Vick Ran, the role Night had reserved for himself?

It would be by far the biggest part of Night's acting career. He wondered what it would be like, the whole acting thing: finding his voice, playing off the actors, seeing himself in their eyes, applying for membership in their club, having the public respond to him in another way. He knew critics would be watching him, hawk-eyed, to see what he could do with the role and why he had cast himself. I had never heard anybody in Night's camp, or anybody at all, challenge Night on whether he was the best actor for the part. When I asked him about it, he said, "I wouldn't even want to *make* this movie if I couldn't play Vick." That's a statement that a director whose last four movies have grossed over $2 billion can say. He knew he wasn't hiring the most technically skilled actor he could find to play Vick Ran. But Night needed an actor he knew would believe in the role, and he had found him. There were other motivations. If the movie became some sort of phenomenon, the credit would come back to Night every which way: as writer, as co-producer, as director, and as an actor playing one of the leads.

Vick Ran's kid sister, Anna Ran, needed to be (or look) Indian, funny, and a few years younger than Night. She needed to be sardonic and confident, able to jab at Night's character, even though the real-life Night was directing the movie.

Doug Aibel had ideas for Anna, and Ash Rajan, Night's cousin, boy agent at the United Talent Agency, had a candidate, too, young, cute, and Indian. Night had had mixed feelings about helping Ash get a job at UT, his own agent's firm. Night despised any system that kept insiders in and outsiders out, where talent didn't carry the day. But he saw in Ash, newly out of college, his own intense ambition at that age, and he knew Ash would make it or not on his own. This was the first time Ash had suggested a client to him. All Night was willing to do was take a look.

In high school on Long Island, Doug Aibel was what Broadway people call a "second-acter," someone who went to the great midtown theaters and sneaked into plays at intermission, on stolen nights and Sunday afternoons. His day job, as the artistic director of a New York theater, the Vineyard Theatre, was consuming, and so was his second job as a casting agent for a small group of movie directors and producers, including Scott Rudin, Wes Anderson, Tim Robbins, Night, and a few others. His tiny windowless office at the Vineyard was crammed with head shots and tapes and scripts, and his phone rang constantly. Trying to get some work done for Night one day at lunchtime, he said to his assistant, "Absolutely hold all calls—unless it's Scott Rudin."

Doug had never known a director able to make such quick, intuitive decisions about actors as Night. Over the years Doug had picked up on something that Night did subconsciously: He chose actors with good mental health. Night chose actors he knew he could live with for the half-year of shooting and editing.

For the role of Anna Ran, Doug sent Night a dozen tapes of the auditions he liked best. When he sent them, he also included the tape of Cindy Cheung, the first Lin Lao candidate he had seen. Night gave Cindy a quick look. He thought she showed promise. She had no rolls of fat, but he figured he could be flexible about that. Still, he knew the search would be long and that many more would be coming. He moved on to Anna.

He quickly got it down to two candidates. There was, in Night's shorthand, "Ash's girl," Sheetal Sheth, young and cute and bouncy. She had recently finished work on a movie Albert Brooks was making for Warner Bros. called *Looking for Comedy in the Muslim World*. And there was Sarita Choudhury, a New Yorker who worked often in independent movies. Night didn't recognize most of the movies on her résumé, but he smiled when he saw *Law & Order*. To him, that was like an actor having a high school diploma; it showed a survival instinct, too. If you were living in New York and trying to make a living as a working actor, you got yourself on *Law & Order*. There was a built-in problem with Sarita—she was several years older than Night, and he had written Anna as his younger sister—but he wasn't going to allow that to void her chances for the job, not when Doug Aibel had such high regard for her. You could always find a negative, and there were negatives that could not be overcome. What Night was always looking for was a sign, some overwhelming positive, about why a candidate worked. Among those who worked, he tried to find the one who worked best.

That didn't mean he always hired the most technically skilled actor. He had, after all, cast himself. There were other factors.

"The famous example," Night told me once when he was going to New York for auditions, "is *Back to the Future*. Originally, Eric Stoltz was hired to play the role of Marty McFly. They shot scenes with him. It didn't work. He was too actorly, too serious, I don't know, but they fired him and brought in Michael J. Fox. He killed it in all three of those movies." The sitcom actor was the right one for the role.

Night saw his two Anna candidates, Sheetal and Sarita, on the same day, in a small windowless room on the top floor of an old building in lower Manhattan with a slow elevator, in an audition space called the Three of Us. Aibel was there with his assistant, Stephanie, who taped the auditions. There were acting classes and other auditions going on in other rooms, and actors sitting on benches in the hallway, reading from sides. The place was filled with dangling nerves. Many of the people, out of necessity, were wearing psychic blinders.

Night rode the elevator with a mother and her young actor son. The elevator stopped on every floor, and Night tried gently but repeatedly to engage the kid in conversation. (His need to connect and his curiosity were interchangeable.) The kid's answers were emotionally dead and monosyllabic, and the mother never bothered to make eye contact with Night.

"The sad thing to me," Night said after we got off the elevator, "was that had the mother figured out who I was, then she would have been all over me. You know, 'Can you put my son in one of your movies?' Like that. But rather than take a chance, she just decided that I was another kook in a New York elevator. She was too closed off from the world to let a stranger in, a stranger that could have changed their lives. She paid no attention to the moment." He felt deflated. He had failed to inspire them.

Sheetal auditioned first. With her plump lips and light skin and light eyes, she looked nothing like Night. Night looked beyond that. He felt you could believe her as Night's kid sister. She had grown up in Pennsylvania, she was a scholastic star in high school, she loved basketball, she had gone to Tisch at NYU. Her engineer father had responded to her choice of profession in pretty much the same way that Night's doctor father had with Night. Night was laughing, they were so similar.

If she was nervous, you could not tell. The only thing coming out of her was spunkiness and desire. She wore no makeup, or very little, and was dressed like a girl in a Gap ad—the American girl (of Indian descent). When she moved quickly, you could see her flat stomach and navel above her low-slung jeans. She had brought a prop not in the script: Fritos corn chips in a Ziploc sandwich bag. Doug read Night's lines. She seldom needed her sides. She had prepared. Night laughed and smiled frequently, moving from a metal folding chair to the floor, sitting cross-legged five or six feet away from her, looking at her as if she were the only actress in the world.

But the Fritos were distracting him. She was doing a whole *thing* with them, carefully placing each chip on the tip of her tongue with the tips of her fingers, then swallowing it whole, as if to avoid getting any yellowish crumbs stuck in her perfect white teeth.

Did she count those Fritos out before coming in here?

Night knew he was thinking about the wrong thing, just as he had with the hedge below Alan Horn's office. Night asked her to put the Fritos away, so he could focus on her acting. She didn't seem embarrassed at all. She exuded confidence.

Sheetal's Anna was funny, annoying, cute, believable. Night felt she could play the part. He was worried, though, that she could play the role only one way, and that if, on the day— shooting day—Bryce Howard wanted to try something different,

Sheetal wouldn't have another move. When Night asked her to try different things in the audition—"Let's go for more like 'I'm tired of making my brother dinner every night' "—the perky, cute, funny, slightly annoying Anna emerged all over again. But Night was okay with that, because her one note worked.

"You could see her as so annoying you'd want to kill her," Night told Doug when Sheetal left. "I like that. She's Anna as I wrote her." You couldn't ask for a better endorsement.

Doug Aibel was a study in discretion. He wouldn't bring anybody he didn't think could play the role, and he indicated his preferences with subtlety. He'd say, "Now, this is an actor you probably haven't heard of, but she's well regarded in theater." (You almost never heard Night or Doug use the word *actress*.) It was on this basis that Doug had pointed Night to Cherry Jones, a celebrated Broadway actress who had significant roles in *Signs* and *The Village*. Regarding Sarita, Doug said, "She works a lot in India and in indie film, and she's a real New Yorker, well known in the downtown scene." In other words, she was an artist hanging out with other artists. By Doug's standards, that was whacking Night in the head with a script.

Sarita came in. She was dark, voluptuous, obviously older than Night, with long dark hair and high cheekbones. There was something exotic and glamorous about her. She looked like a young mother. She also looked slightly bored, but that had to be acting—there were rings of perspiration under her arms. There aren't many big-budget movies calling for actresses of Indian descent, and the stakes were high for her. Her reading of Anna was totally different from Sheetal's, and different from how Night had written the role. Sheetal had screamed the line, "Mr. Heep's a playa!" She had made it funny and exuberant. Sarita dropped the exclamation mark and the pseudo-urban pronunciation and calmly whispered, "Mr. Heep's a player." She made it real, something said with inside knowledge.

Night asked her to read various lines in various ways, and when the session was done, Night said, "Wow." They were together only about fifteen minutes, but those fifteen minutes were so intimate they had felt like a day. When Night asked Sarita about her background, it illicited a brief, rich family history. Sarita had grown up in India, England, Italy, and Jamaica and had lived in New York for years. At the audition, she spoke English with an American accent.

Preparing to leave, she got on her toes to give Night a kiss on his right cheek. Night was a little surprised, and then there was a split second of awkwardness when she went to the other side to finish off one of those European double kisses. She briefly seemed undecided about whether to complete the double kiss.

The voices went crazy.

Got it. Okay. That's the real Sarita.

In that moment, Night saw her awkwardness, her vulnerability, her earnestness, her desire, her truthfulness. She had let down her guard, the years of rejection that are part of the acting life when nobody's knocking on your door, when you're closing in on forty and still running all over Manhattan, riding in rickety elevators and carrying a pillowy day bag that holds a swimsuit and a pack of cigarettes, your cell phone and your daughter's artwork, the *Times,* and a little black book crammed with the numbers of agents and friends who have spare beds in a half-dozen different countries. In that moment of hesitation, with Night so close to her he could smell her, she won the chance to get the role. Without it, the part was going to Sheetal. With it, Night was undecided.

Sarita left and Night said to Doug, "I don't think I'd have to rewrite the role for her, but I'd have to rethink it. She'd be the older sister who looks out for her kid brother."

He called his cousin. "I liked your girl. Sheetal, right? She's really, really good. I'm thinking about her, dude. She's in the running." He wanted to sound like a leader, like he was in control. And except for the Fritos, what was there not to like? Sarita was the more skilled and accomplished actress, but Sheetal *was* Anna. It was turning into Eric Stoltz versus Michael J. Fox—and Night had no idea what to do.

Chris Doyle had a big reputation. Everywhere Night went, he heard the same thing: Chris Doyle is a genius; Chris Doyle cannot be controlled. He was a native Australian who lived in various hotel rooms around the world when he wasn't in Hong Kong. His Chinese name—he regarded himself as Chinese in spirit—was Du Ke Fung, which translated as "like the wind." There was a quote from Doyle under his biography on IMDB, a movie website: "Du Ke Fung is an extremely poetic name, as opposed to this piece of shit sitting before you. This person called Du Ke Fung with no past or parents or ID card makes these films and at night he turns back into this drunkard called Chris Doyle." Doyle had worked extensively with the Chinese director Wong Kar-Wai, whose movie *In the Mood for Love* had made such an impression on Night. He had also been the director of photography on the Jet Li karate movie *Hero*, which Night found exhilarating, and Gus Van Sant's remake of *Psycho*, which Doyle had done without having seen the Hitchcock original. Doyle had only one experience working with a big-name director on a mainstream big-budget American movie, as Barry Levinson's director of photography on *Liberty Heights*.

Night saw Levinson at a Directors Guild dinner. "Did you really hire Doyle?" Levinson asked.

"Yeah." Doyle's fame had stayed within the cult of moviemaking. Most people who pay for movie tickets would not know his name.

Levinson was shaking his head, and Night knew what it meant. He was crazy.

The experience of writing *Lady,* the experience of leaving Disney and signing up with Warner Bros., it *had* left him a little crazy. At his core, he wasn't a changed person. He was still his disciplined, responsible self. But there were pockets of madness where there hadn't been before. Night was okay with that. A little inspired madness would improve *Lady.*

One day, in the midmorning tranquillity of a workday at the farm, Chris Doyle arrived.

"Good morning!" Paula said. She had that cheerful quality.

"What's good about it?" Doyle answered.

He immediately launched into a recitation about Betty Ford, something about her being so desperate she was drinking hair spray. He asked Paula to get him a cup of coffee with "this much" whiskey, holding his bony thumb and index finger about an inch apart.

Doyle was wearing a faded green short-sleeved turtleneck and thin tight cotton pants with no belt. (Who knew that turtlenecks came in short sleeves?) His arms were hairless and tanned. For shoes, he wore bizarre zippered contraptions, thick green rubber pads that might have served as loafers for moon dwellers, unzipped so they flapped around his heels when he walked. His black goggle-style glasses—chic in Soho and few other places—hung around his neck on a black cord. No jewelry. He was just a slip of a man, not much bigger than a jockey, with a weathered face. He looked like Keith Richards of the Rolling Stones, all weathered. He wore his hair in the Lyle Lovett manner, an abrupt updo shaved nearly to his scalp on the sides, then puffy and curly on the top.

At his request for a drink, Paula went nowhere. Standing at her tidy antique desk in Night's beautiful farmhouse, Doyle launched into an introductory discourse. This—not verbatim, but close—was how Night's hand-picked DP introduced himself to Night's assistant.

I am still on Hong Kong time, or maybe I'm on London time, I'm not certain, but I do know that I spent last night at the Rittenhouse Hotel in the city of Philadelphia, and did you realize, you beautiful thing—what did you say your name was? it really doesn't matter—did you realize that the bars in Philadelphia close at two A.M., *and there are no decent bookstores in the city, and the porn offerings both on the hotel TV and in other parts of the city are banal and middle-class and terribly dated, and could you kindly get me that coffee, ahem, as soon as you possibly can, my dear beautiful Paula, you vision of loveliness, of course I know your name—and by the way, how do you feel about three-ways, but we can undress that later, I mean address, address, ha, ha, ha!—but could you kindly contact the production people or whoever is responsible for my hotel accommodations and inform them, or she or him or it, that I cannot, under any circumstance, stay overnight in Philadelphia again for the duration of my work on this grotesquely overbudgeted, potentially extremely beautiful movie I will be making for the very honorable, the very reverend, His Majesty Dr. M. Night Shyamalan, and that for the duration—the six months or six years or whatever the fuck it turns out to be—to please arrange a room for me at the Soho Grand Hotel in New York, New York, and that the services of a car and driver will be needed daily, and, ahem, nightly, preferably a yellow driver, ideally female, fluent in Cantonese, who is very tall or, at the least, very, very leggy . . .*

The cinematographer had arrived. This was Night's man.

Night came in and Doyle said, "The Philadelphia traffic, it's as bad as the traffic in Bangkok. It takes longer to get from downtown Philadelphia to your farm than from lower Manhattan."

This was comically untrue. New York was over two hours from the farm by car, Philadelphia maybe a half hour. Night laughed easily and then Doyle started laughing, exposing his little teeth, yellow and dry. Before long he was saying, "I got this haircut at the Bangkok airport. Never get your hair cut at the Bangkok airport. Fifteen minutes later, I was still feeling horny, so I went to the other side of the airport and got a shave."

Doyle was able to change moods without notice or provocation. He went from cheap sex in the Bangkok airport to the beauty of the orange evening sky in downtown Bangkok, and how the evening sky in Venice is green "because of the canals," and he asked if Cleveland Heep's apartment building was meant to be in Philadelphia or in the suburbs so that he could start thinking about light, about evening skies, and about what Cleveland Heep's bungalow would look like at dusk. It was a theme a minute with him, and before long he was talking about an early scene where Story is in Cleveland's bungalow. "I see her with bare feet, wet, leaving water marks where she's been, the whole thing imbued with wetness." And before the loveliness of the image could settle in, he went on, "And we all know what wetness is a metaphor for." He put his hands on his hips and simulated a sex act. "All my references are from Japanese porn."

All the while, Night was laughing. He was face-to-face with a manic person, a person who had so obviously rejected societal conventions, a person who made such a blatant effort to stand up and scream, *I'm an artist!* Night was happy. Night, who kept careful track of how many pages of script he and Brick Mason waded through every day while storyboarding, who knew when his kids had dental appointments, was not at all scared or worried about Doyle's lunacy. He found it inspiring. Night was purging the things that made him comfortable, purging himself of Disney.

An insight came to Night immediately about why Doyle was so blatantly vulgar: It enhanced the beauty of his art. It made it even more unexpected.

Night and Doyle and Brick went into a converted barn on the property where there was a small screening room and a big, airy meeting room above, to start going through the script. In the meeting room, there was a model of a scrunt at the table where they were about to work, and Doyle said, "May we move that?" His chair had a cushioned pad on the seat, attached by little strings. He removed it entirely. His script was already dog-eared and marked up, many pages crammed with notes, drawings, and doodlings. He may or may not have been ready to work. He sipped occasionally from a bottle of Heineken (Paula kept him away from the whiskey) and described his annual mourning every January 3, the anniversary of Freddy Heineken's death. He also made references to John Milton and Salvador Dalí and Philip K. Dick, the writer. At one point, when Night was talking about how a scene could be shot, Doyle popped out of his chair, made a lens out of his thumbs and index fingers, and stalked the creaking floor as if carrying a handheld camera. Once an hour or so, he'd say cryptic, semi-poetic things, like "the basement is the underground of life." Night liked that one in particular. Stephen King had once advised Night to write in his basement, to make himself uncomfortable, and Night had taken him up on the suggestion. It wasn't one of those creepy cellars, with puddles and bugs, but it was underground, and it was there that much of *Lady in the Water* had been written.

The poetic moments were only occasional. When Night asked Doyle if he wanted some hummus—Doyle ate almost nothing—his retort was "Hummusexual?" When Night reminded Doyle that he and Brick were on page 69, he sang, "Everything's fine when you're doing sixty-nine!" When Night talked about the movie's "broken rhythm," Doyle said, "The rhythm method!" When Night said to him, "Don't ever give me an Americanized Chris Doyle—I want the *Asian* Chris Doyle," Doyle grunted back, "Yellow."

In the weeks after that first visit, Doyle came to the farm from New York day after day, but only because he had to. He was unaccustomed to Night's regimented workday, and to the formality of storyboarding. In Hong Kong, working with Wong Kar-Wai, he had taken years to make movies. Not only was there no storyboarding, there was no script. Night was Kar-Wai's opposite. He had to plan out everything. There were few directors who did such thorough storyboarding. Doyle was forcing himself to adjust to life on a clock.

One day Night announced to Brick and Doyle, "You have me until three-forty-five." (He'd remind his collaborators periodically that he was the boss.) The time came and Night departed, leaving Doyle and Brick in the room. Brick, despite his best efforts, could get no work out of Doyle for the rest of the day. He theorized about this and that, pontificated about the state of film, went into long monologues about his sex life and his drinking, and waited for six o'clock, when one of the production assistants—a young man with a Polish surname from Philadelphia and not a leggy Asian woman—was authorized to take him back to the Soho Grand in New York.

When they started working together, I was eager to hear how Brick and Night and Doyle would approach the first scene of the movie. It's a comic scene, of no particular consequence that I could tell. There are a bunch of screaming Spanish-speaking sisters, terrified by a hairy bug of some sort, and Cleveland comes in and squashes the thing. I was interested because Night had once told me that the most significant thing he had done as a filmmaker was in the first scene of *The Sixth Sense*. The scene shows a woman in a cellar illuminated by a bare lightbulb. Night said he'd had a creative breakthrough that related to that opening scene. It came in waves: first while he was writing it, then while he was storyboarding it with Brick, and finally, while he was shooting it. There's not a spoken word in the scene. The first sentence in the script is an instruction: "A naked lightbulb sparks to life." The woman runs her fingertips over some wine bottles in the basement. She wears a narrow smile. She sees her breath. She suddenly leaves. There are no spoken words. The whole scene is described in the script in twenty-two short sentences. The last two are: "The lightbulb dies. Dripping black devours the room."

"Everything I did in *The Sixth Sense,* and everything I've done since then, is because of what I learned in writing that opening scene," Night said. "It shows up in everything I write. It influences everything I read."

"What is it?"

"I can't tell you." He said this playfully. He said almost everything playfully. It made you take notice when he used another tone.

"Does Brick know?"

"Yes."

"Will he tell me?"

"No."

"Will you tell me?"

"I'll confirm it for you if you figure it out."

So when Brick and Night and Doyle were discussing the first scene of *Lady in the Water,* I paid close attention. I thought maybe the secret related to openings and I would get an insight through Night's handling of the shrieking Perez de la Torre sisters (named after Jose's mother). Night said things like "I want to set the tone early that this movie is fun." Brick talked about whether you'd have Cleveland in the same frame with the screaming sisters. Doyle asked whether the sisters would have wet hair. I tried to read something into it, and got nothing.

———

There was something ungoverned about the Friday in late May, the Friday of Memorial Day weekend, when Sheetal came to the farm. Night wasn't calling her "Ash's girl" anymore. She was the actress he might be playing opposite, the actress who would carry much of the movie's humor. It was a big day.

When Night introduced the young actress to his director of photography in the morning, Chris Doyle kissed her hand and did an elegant little waltz with her, carrying her away to another room, half singing, "Come away with me." He ran his fingers through her luscious hair and stared clinically at her translucent eyes. He pronounced her a gift to the camera. She went with it all very easily. You would have thought she was an old pro. Doyle said, "She will be a star."

Chris Doyle was filled with declarative statements that day, some of them decidedly uncharming. The long, structured workdays were taking a toll on him, his days made much longer by the commute of his own choosing. He was spending at least four hours each day on the road, being driven from lower Manhattan to Night's farm on the outer reaches of Philadelphia's Main Line each morning and then being driven back each night. A lot of time on the New Jersey Turnpike.

It was a gorgeous day, and Michael the chef served lunch outdoors. Afterward, Night and Sheetal went to the paved driveway to shoot baskets while discussing the part. When they were gone, Doyle said to me, "Everybody knows I drink too much and I fuck my brains out, but on the set I'm all business." He often made a case for himself, even if nobody was asking him to. "I made seven movies with a man who uses no script. Now I'm with a guy who storyboards *everything*." He was like that with Night, too, mocking him by establishing how foreign Night's methods were to him. He said scripts, in general, were "inconsequential," and he was including *Lady* in that as-sessment. But what he liked, he said, was Night's view of the world and, most significantly, the subject of the movie. I asked him what that was. He said, "The poetry of people." That was the best description of the movie I had heard yet.

We could hear Sheetal dribbling. When Night played bas-ketball on Tuesday nights, it wouldn't be uncommon to see him shoot five three-pointers in a row. But with Sheetal, he was let-ting her do most of the shooting. He was working the whole time, sizing her up as his kid sister.

She read for Night in the barn, with Jose reading Night's lines. As Night looked at her, he cocked his head at strange an-gles, as if that would change his perspective. He seldom looked at the script on his lap. He was tougher on her than he had been at her New York callback, when Doug Aibel had read the part of Vick Ran, but he had warned her that he would be. "I'm gonna be brutal, as if we were shooting today," Night said. He was sit-ting on a hard, austere wooden bench, something you'd see in a Quaker meetinghouse or on the set of *The Village*. Night asked her "to convey an idea that's not on the page." They were not re-hearsing a high school production of *Arsenic and Old Lace*. Night was treating Sheetal as a seasoned pro, despite her greenness.

She was leaning so far forward in her chair that only half her bottom was on it. She was scratching her palm with her fin-gers; she looked anxious but sounded confident. When she was confused about how to read one line, she asked, "Can you give me something here?" She talked about her frustration with di-rectors who won't tell you what they want. "You wanna say, 'Dude, just *say* it.'" She asked, "Do you rehearse a lot?"

Night thought that was a cheeky question but consistent with her character, both her real-life character and the charac-ter she would play. He was enjoying her work. Night's "brutal" was actually quite civilized. He said, "I'm not buying the way you said *banned* there, but I'm digging everything else." Later he said, "There was a lot of good stuff in there, but you got too sincere too early."

When she was about to leave, Night gave her a hug and said, "You did really, really well. I'm psyched." (With Night, there was a lot of hugging.) He thought she had the job, and she must have, too. Her trip to the farm had confirmed what he'd felt in New York: She was Anna, as written. He could live with her for five months. She could make the part come alive. Chris Doyle was even more effusive. He predicted she could be the next Nicole Kidman.

The next morning, the Saturday of the three-day weekend, Night woke up in a spare bedroom at a relative's house in Maryland. The bed was unfamiliar and the walls were bare and his first thought that morning was about Anna and who should play her: Sarita, the older downtown New York actress with the European kiss, and not Sheetal. In that guest room, stripped of his regular surroundings, Night realized it did not matter whether Anna was his kid sister or not. Night knew Sarita would play the role differently from how he had written it, how he had intended it. She would improve it. If Paul or Bryce—or Night—wanted to try something different on the day, Sarita would make the corresponding moves. For his movie, he needed Eric Stoltz, not Michael J. Fox. Maybe Chris Doyle was right; maybe Sheetal Sheth would someday become Nicole Kidman. But Night knew her potential as a future Nicole Kidman would not improve *Lady in the Water* now. Sarita would make Night a better actor. She would raise his game and improve the whole movie. Or she could.

After spending about two minutes watching Cindy Cheung's audition with Doug Aibel on videotape, in which she had so dutifully dressed in her Britney Spears getup, Night called his casting director and said, "Let's bring her in." He liked her enough to see her in person.

To prepare for her callback, Cindy was invited to Doug's office at the Vineyard Theatre to read the entire script. Cindy spent two hours with it, with earplugs in. Doug was solicitous. "Do you have enough light? Would you like some water? Do you have everything you need?" He had an abiding respect for actors and acting.

Cindy was impressed by the size of the part and the peculiar beauty of the script, in that order. Before she left, Doug had some more fashion advice for her. For the callback with Night, she should dress "as neutrally as possible, pretty much the way you are now." She was wearing mid-ankle khaki cargo pants, a loose gray T-shirt, her hair up in a high ponytail, and almost no makeup. "It makes you look younger." He knew Night was looking for someone who could pass for twenty-five or younger. Doug also told Cindy to allow one hour for the callback. She was surprised. Most of her auditions lasted between thirty seconds and ten minutes. She was given a date for the callback, a weekday afternoon in early June, at the Three of Us audition space.

Night, driven by Franny, left his home for New York early that June day. His first stop was in Tribeca, his adopted neighborhood in New York. He had recently bought a large two-story apartment there that he was rehabbing. It was on a sliver of a street, a holdover from old New York. Night believed in real estate as an investment, although he would never word it that way. He bought houses that he and Bhavna and the girls would use. They planned to spend four or five weeks a year in the Tribeca apartment, plus assorted overnight stays. When Night arrived at the apartment that June morning, there were thirty workers there, laying down floors and installing sound systems and hanging art, getting the apartment ready for a large family housewarming party that would celebrate Bhavna's earning her doctorate. The place was in a state of chaos, with sawdust on the floor and several languages being spoken at once and different heads of different construction departments vying for Night's attention. But through the clamor, Night could see what the apartment would look like in five days, on the night of Bhavna's party. That was one of Night's skills.

From the apartment, Franny drove Night to Nobu, a chic Tribeca restaurant, to meet Bob Balaban. The actor—a tiny, trim, nearly bald man wearing pressed pants and a pressed shirt on a hot day—was waiting for Night outside, by the front door. He looked stiff. The veteran actor (and author of the charming *Mc-Growl* book series) was up for the role of Mr. Farber, the film critic in *Lady*.

Bob Balaban had recently wrapped *Capote,* in which he played William Shawn, the editor of *The New Yorker;* he had also been in *Close Encounters of the Third Kind* and *Waiting for Guffman* and nearly sixty other movies. His work was known. Typically, a director doesn't ask an actor with Bob Balaban's history to audition for a smaller role. What a director could do is have a meeting with such an actor, to gauge interest and chemistry, and that was what Night was planning to do that day at Nobu. But before Night got out of his car, he saw Balaban on the sidewalk and said to himself, *Farber!* It was just like when he first saw Paul Giamatti. He knew he had his guy.

Balaban knew a limited amount about the role, and over lunch Night told him more. The actor told the director he'd take the role if it wouldn't give small children recurring nightmares. Right then and there, Night decided he'd let Bob Balaban read the script. Not just the Farber sides but the whole thing. Neither made an explicit commitment to the other over lunch, but that didn't really matter: They both knew it was a done deal.

Night moved on to his Lin Lao problem. Cindy was already

at the Three of Us audition space when Night arrived. Taking Doug's fashion suggestion literally, Cindy was wearing exactly what she'd worn when she went to Doug's office to read the script. The building was unusually quiet for a weekday at three o'clock. Night introduced himself to Cindy and said, "How *are* you?" as if he had known her all his life. He asked if she had any questions.

"Yes, one," she said. "Does she have any sort of crush on Cleveland?" Cindy thought maybe that would explain why Lin Lao was so willing to give Cleveland books and information.

"No," Night said. He could have given a five-minute response to that question, or any question about the script, but he limited himself to a single word. She was on a need-to-know basis. She wasn't in the circle of trust. And with that answer, Cindy, on the spot, had to rethink her approach to the character.

Doug Aibel started reading Cleveland in his neutral way, and Cindy played Lin Lao Choi almost as Annabell from *Masha No Home*—over the top and heavily accented. She wasn't throwing it away. Just the opposite. She was extremely loud. If she was an actor who needed to be heard, she was getting heard, likely in the adjoining rooms.

And Night was cracking up from the very first word. He was giggling, he was cackling, he was in hysterics. He sneaked a peak at Doug that said, *Is this really as good as I think this is?* Something magical was happening.

He had specific requests of Cindy, as if he were shooting the movie that day. "When he says to you, 'Can you look up the word *narf* for me?' you're surprised that he doesn't know the word. It's as if he's asking you if you know who Little Red Riding Hood is. You're like *How can you not know?*"

It didn't completely compute for Cindy, but she accepted what Night said—after all, he had written it—and she immediately worked in his Red Riding Hood idea.

Later in the script, Lin Lao makes a reference to her mother, saying, "She doesn't trust Americans. She says they watch too many game shows." Cindy read it the first time with dripping sarcasm. Night had another suggestion for Cindy there: "Say it like this is a really big problem, watching too many game shows, and that you agree with it." The second time Cindy recited the line, showing respect for the mother's considered opinion: Americans really do watch too many game shows. In that tone, Lin Lao hardly seemed American herself. It was completely different.

When they were done with all the funny scenes, Night said to Cindy, "All right, I hate to make you do this, but we've got to switch gears here and do the big climactic scene at the end. This is life and death here."

Cindy immediately became slow and still. She took a deep breath. She took her time. Night no longer was laughing. Like Cindy, he was quiet and still. She could feel that he was letting her affect him. His arms were not crossed, literally or otherwise. She had read once that Night liked to feel the weight of the shaving cream in his hand before shaving, to be really aware of the moment. She felt that during the audition, and it inspired her.

They finished the scene and Night said, "That was beautiful."

He looked like he wanted to hug her, but he didn't.

"Would you mind waiting outside for a moment so I can talk to Doug?"

The door closed. "I think she's really, *really* good," Night said.

"I agree," Doug said.

"I don't think we're going to find anybody better."

He brought Cindy back into the audition room and talked to her.

From the moment he said "How *are* you?," Cindy never felt she was in the presence of a celebrity. She imagined that auditioning for Steven Spielberg or Clint Eastwood would be a different experience, that their fame would be overwhelming, that you'd be too nervous about taking up too much of their time to do your best. She felt the opposite from Night. She sensed that he was completely absorbed by the moment and had no expectations about what would happen next.

"Tell me about yourself," Night said casually. "Tell me about you and acting."

Cindy told Night a brief version of her odyssey in acting. Her discovery of it as a senior at UCLA, her bouts of depression, her San Francisco years, the near-death of her acting dream, her return to acting through writing her own material.

Night was overwhelmed. Everyone was so certain Lin Lao would be impossible to cast, and yet here was Cindy Cheung, right in front of him, so, *so* good, sending him a powerful message, that the movie *could* work, that his faith in it would be rewarded. He could see that Cindy was a kindred spirit.

Night said, "You got the part."

Cindy Cheung didn't shriek or cry or do much of anything. She was ecstatic and surprised, but she barely showed it. She hugged Night and Doug.

Night was impressed by her response to the news. It told him that she understood what was happening, that the audition was merely a start. She had gotten the role on merit and faith and work and timing. Not because she had a dream. Not because she prayed. Her role in *Masha No Home,* at forty dollars a night, had everything to do with what happened in the Three of Us audition room on that afternoon in early June. So did the dead lady's wigs left in the dark San Francisco apartment and the early-morning poetry gigs at the Los Angeles elementary schools and the turning down of the job at the defense contractor and everything else. It had been a long haul already. All it was doing now was continuing. Magic was no substitute for work.

Night told Cindy he had seldom done that, offered a role

right on the spot. He had wanted to do it with Haley Joel Osment, who played the young boy in *The Sixth Sense,* but he couldn't because he "didn't have any clout with Disney then."

He had said the Disney name, and nothing happened. His day had been going so well—touring the apartment in a construction zone, casting Bob Balaban as Mr. Farber, finding his Lin Lao in the first box he opened—that there were no cracks for Nina to invade. The oval headshots of the troika, the voices helped keep them at bay, this time. It was a constant battle.

Night said to Cindy, "This is good timing. If you had been working in Hollywood all these years, you'd have the same exact seven moves that all the working Hollywood actors have. But you still have your whole range available to you. I think you're in a perfect place in your life for this to be happening to you."

Night had wanted to shoot *Lady* in one cloistered location, a sanctuary of moviemaking, his Eden, where he could block out the intrusions of real-world show business and do his priestly thing. Cindy was a stand-in for the stewardess on the Warner Bros. jet, the one who loved *The Notebook* so, looking for real life to give her a reason to believe. Night was pulling Cindy out of the fire, that's how he felt. She was so deserving and so talented. She had done the work and would do the work. She got that it was a long road. Offering her the job, right there on the spot, he hadn't felt so sure of anything else he had done in a long time.

The money people came in. They always do. Paul Hilepo represented Cindy Cheung, and Sam Mercer represented Blinding Edge Pictures and Warner Bros.

Sam offered $65,000 for the ten-week shoot, the SAG minimum. Bryce Howard had received the SAG minumum for *The Village,* her first studio lead. Night was paying himself the SAG minimum to play Vick.

It was not close to what Hilepo was looking for. Taking the role would be a big move for Cindy. She would have to quit her stable job, and who knew when she would get acting work again? Nothing much had changed: There still was little work for tall Asian-American actresses. He told Cindy he thought she should get $250,000. Trying to get there, the agent—without revealing his negotiating strategy to Cindy—asked for $1 million.

Sam Mercer was amused and a bit appalled, but he negotiated with Hilepo as if the agent had said something realistic. Mercer went up $10,000 to $75,000. He added a two-room suite in the Ritz-Carlton in Philadelphia for the entire nine-week shoot. And seventy-five dollars a day in meal money.

Hilepo said it wasn't enough. He knew the bankroll behind Mercer was immense. He knew how much Night wanted Cindy. Night had said it, right there in the Three of Us audition room. In that moment of revelation, Night had given away a lot of bargaining power.

Weeks went by. Cindy asked her agent, "Is Night aware of what's going on?"

"Don't worry about that. This is what you pay me for," Hilepo said. He would get 10 percent of Cindy's deal. He was doing his job, getting the best payday he could for an actor who had been paying her dues for years. "He's not going to hold you responsible for any of this. It's all on the agent."

Night knew how it worked. Marc Glick and Jeremy Zimmer had just done the same thing for Night with Warner Bros., gotten him the best deal they could with his new studio.

"Oh, no," Cindy said. "I *want* him to know. Based on what he said that day at the audition, I would think if he knew what was going on, he'd say, 'Get it done.'" She wasn't worried. That day in the audition room, something *had* changed. Night had guessed that, and he was correct. She knew that if she didn't work in Night's movie, something else would soon come through.

Cindy was mistaken about Night: He did know what was going on. And he felt the SAG minimum was a fair rate for an actor with no experience making her first studio movie. Money complicates everything. That day in the audition room, he was certain he had found exactly the right person to play the role. But at $250,000, she was not. There was a number, a dollar figure, at which Night's belief in Cindy was compromised by the limit of what he was willing to spend, and what he thought was fair. Sam Mercer and Jose would sometimes say to Night, "It's show *business*." They didn't need to. He understood that. He was an intuitive businessman.

One day in late June, Night said to Sam, "Make them a final offer, and if she doesn't accept it, we'll start auditioning again."

In the audition room, Night had been certain he knew where Cindy was in her life, that there was a reason their lives had intersected when they did. He felt so good about what he had done. But now he realized he had been wrong. The person he thought she was, that person would have jumped right on just to see where the train would go, even at the SAG minimum. Reading people, that's what Night did. That's what allowed him to write, to cast, to direct, to lead. But he had misread Cindy, misread the room, that day. He had offered Cindy the chance to be on his team, but it was not enough. Night's faith in her would not pay Cindy's bills.

For Night, where there had been assuredness, now there was doubt. Nina was back in his head again. He was all fucked up.

5.

Things were moving fast. A building, the Cove apartment complex, was going up from scratch. The blueprints called for five stories with fifty-seven apartments, plus a pool and a bungalow for the super. It was being built on a derelict lot in Bristol, Pennsylvania, a working-class suburb of Philadelphia. A year earlier the building had existed only in the imagination of a father and his two daughters. Now it was a union bonanza.

Every day brought new people, new questions, new issues. Cindy Cheung was offered $100,000 to play Lin Lao Choi, take-it-or-leave-it, and she took it. Night decided to disassociate her agent's cheeky salary demands from the actress before him, "for the good of the movie." That had become a regular theme for him. He talked often of defending the movie, defending actors, defending characters, defending angels. It was exhausting, all this work in the name of defense.

As a decision-maker, Night was at times a willful procrastinator. He'd sometimes say, "Let me wait and see how I feel on the day." That is, the day the scene would be shot. More often, he was scary fast, a Vegas card-counter knowing when he wants a hit on 17. Once he had Cindy signed on—signified by her head shot going up on Sam Mercer's office wall—Night quickly settled on an actress to play Lin Lao Choi's mother. Night hired a tiny Korean-American woman named June Kyoko-Lu, who promptly informed Night that Lin Lao might be a legitimate Chinese or Vietnamese name, but was definitely not a Korean name. Night, just as promptly, came up with a new name for Cindy's character: Young-Soon Choi. Mary Cybulski, the script supervisor, made certain the next iteration of the script included the name change, with the hyphen.

Mary protected the *Lady* script, in its every detail. Betsy Heimann, with as many words for brown as Eskimos have for ice, did the same for the movie's wardrobe. There were zealots everywhere—a wig man who might have put a hairpiece on every last actor, given the chance. These were people immersed in craft and many of them were kings in their departments. Night had brought in all these people to serve his script, and along the way *Lady* became their movie, too. Only Night belonged to no department. He didn't have a little crew working under him, but everybody, hundreds of people, in competing departments. He talked all day, hugged often, laughed easily, gossiped occasionally, and at the end of the day, he looked exhausted and alone. The best sleep he got was in the car when Franny was driving him home.

Night made his movies near his home because he could and because he wanted to sleep in his own bed and see his wife and girls, and because he could claim Philadelphia for himself. No one else was making movies in and around Philadelphia on a regular basis.

Between the city and the suburbs and the farmland beyond it, greater Philadelphia had everything Night needed. All three had character, the city most particularly, with its peculiar evening light, yellowish and dark, with short midnight shadows in the old graveyards in the courtyards beyond Independence Hall. Night liked the way John Landis shot the city in *Trading Places* and how Peter Weir shot it in *Witness* and especially the way John Avildsen—or should the credit go to Mr. Sylvester Stallone?—had shot it in *Rocky,* one of Night's favorite movies. The city is gray and gorgeous in *Rocky.* The rotting fruit on the streets of the Italian Market. The blunt yellow rock of the Art Museum's outer walls, an impenetrable fortress of good taste, not built for anybody named Balboa or Shyamalan or Duwayne, unless they were cafeteria workers or guards or something. What a movie.

Night wanted to shoot *Lady* in the city, but there were logistical problems to every building he considered, namely live tenants. Still, he held on to the idea that he could shoot in the Philadelphia city limits.

Night had shot much of *The Sixth Sense* and *Unbreakable* in Philadelphia, and he and Bhavna had a charitable foundation that helped working families buy homes in the city, with the idea that home ownership could improve blocks, schools, and lives. Dealing with city bureaucrats, right up to and including the mayor, had triggered so much headache and heartache that Bhavna and Night often wondered if the program was worth it. But they saw tangible results, and were committed to the program.

Philadelphia had a look all its own: glass high-rises and sagging warehouses and row homes and brown-brick churches with spires that have stood since Benjamin Franklin's time, all practically abutting. But the best chance to shoot in the city was to build a building in the vast Philadelphia Navy Yard, even though it was near the Philadelphia airport, which meant problems with jet traffic. There was back-and-forth between suits from the mayor's office and Sam Mercer, even a discussion of rerouting jet traffic. But when Night heard the particulars he decided it was too risky, which was why he was led, reluctantly, to a thirty-five acre fenced-in industrial site called the Bristol Commerce Center, formerly a 3M plant, near the intersection of I-95 and the Pennsylvania Turnpike, on a street that only sounded quaint, Green Lane. Night had stipulated that the set be within forty-five minutes of his house, and Night carefully timed the length of the trip when Franny drove him there the first time: forty-three minutes.

Martin Childs, the production manager Night had imported from England, had already drawn a simple sketch of a modern five-story apartment complex shaped like a squared-off *U*, with an oblong heart-shaped pool in its center. Beyond the pool, surrounded by woods, he drew an old-looking bungalow, a vestige of another era, where Cleveland Heep would live. It was terribly drab. Night loved it.

Now Night was going to see if Martin's building could work on an industrial site in the suburbs.

It was dusty and hot the afternoon Night first saw the place where Martin's sketch might come to life. The cement parking lot was all cracked. The office space was musty and institutional. There were enormous dark warehouses the size of airplane hangars, and a huge flat field choking with weeds. Night was shown a large rectangular room with two doors and no windows and told that it could be his office. The whole place was uninspiring, with bad orange carpeting and mushy fake-brick wall coverings. There were signs everywhere, remnants of the industrial age: NO SMOKING BEYOND THIS POINT; HARD HAT AREA; WATCH FOR MOVING VEHICLES. There were calendars keeping track of consecutive days without an accident.

The place where Martin's oblong heart-shaped pool could go had been staked off with yellow caution tape. Down the street were a trucker motel and a biker bar. Across the street from the old plant was a small neighborhood, the residents all black, and a white-painted cinder-block church, the kind you see in the Deep South, in the little towns ignored by time.

The site had been a factory and still felt like a factory. It did nothing for Night. It was sequestered, soulless, dull.

"Let's take it," Night told Sam Mercer. A vision of what it could be was in Night's head. "Let's do it here."

On his way home, Night noticed black kids bouncing basketballs on the sidewalk, on the other side of Green Lane. The houses, many of them, had sagging porches and gated windows. Night wondered about the lives in those houses, the untold stories they held.

Affluent white America treated Night as if he were white. He was rich, educated, accomplished, fun to be with. But Night saw himself as a person of color, as an American minority, just as Cindy Cheung saw herself. Indian-Americans, Native Americans, Asian-Americans, African-Americans, Spanish-speaking Americans, these were his people. The residents of the Cove, they were the American mosaic.

Night took his own fashion cues from the city, from black Philadelphia, not the suburban country-club world that remained a mystery to his golf-addict father who played only public courses. There were no polo shirts in Night's wardrobe. When his father the internist, accompanied by a Jewish doctor friend and a black doctor friend, went apartment shopping in Philadelphia in the late 1960s, he came back with stories, told with more humor than indignation, about American segregation. ("Dr. Sham, let me show you a neighborhood I'm certain would better suit your needs.") Night had grown up with his father's sensitivity to and awareness of class, race, and ethnic prejudice. Outwardly, he had inherited his father's you-gotta-laugh-at-it sensibilities. But underneath, for Night, there was a checked anger at the injustices of the world.

Night liked black culture. He liked the ease and candor and

humor and anger of black speech in all its varieties. Night's neighbor in the suburbs, for a while, was Allen Iverson, the star guard of the Philadelphia 76ers, African-American and speckled with tattoos. He wasn't Night's favorite player; his defense was too erratic, and he shot too much. Still, Night had an NBA superstar for a neighbor. Iverson wasn't around much. Sometimes they'd see each other and wave, driveway to driveway. Once, when Night was shooting baskets with one of his little cousins on his driveway basketball court, Iverson was on his driveway court with one of *his* little cousins, talking trash and playing more defense than he usually did in televised games. Night liked that, how Iverson wasn't pampering the kid, wasn't constantly murmuring "good job" the way the suburban Little League dads do when a gifted child hits a weak infield grounder and trots down to first.

Night's office was now in Bristol, in the old 3M plant, which was being turned into a modern movie set. In the code language of the movie business, the set was now base camp. In the same vein, Night and the other lead actors had campers, not trailers. The ones for Night and Paul Giamatti and Bryce Howard were luxurious, with leather sofas and kitchenettes and queen-size beds and all the essential electronic gadgetry. Portable restrooms were brought into the base camp, marked DESI and LUCY. A catering trailer arrived, serving outstanding food, eaten under an elegant giant white tent, the kind you might see at a country-estate wedding. On the menu was grilled fish and beef, sushi, chicken alfredo, fajitas, all sorts of good stuff. At breakfast there was so much fresh colorful fruit, you'd have thought you were at a Marriott Sunday brunch. There was a young Hispanic man who made smoothies all morning long, *morning* being an inexact word in the movie business. Jimmy

Mazzola, the prop man, brought in the espresso machine Tom Hanks used in *You've Got Mail*.

There were days in July and August that were broiling, but Jimmy could always find a relatively cool spot. He'd go under a fire escape and have a cigarette and a double espresso and tell Martin Scorsese stories or Woody Allen stories or John Travolta stories to anybody who might be around. The roar of construction trucks accompanied his voice; the apartment building was going up at a pace that would have flabbergasted anyone who has ever tried to put in, say, a new patio. Every day at lunch, enormous union construction men, and some women, so wet with perspiration you thought their tattoos might drip right off, sat at the catering tables and engulfed huge lunches. Night talked with them, thanked them for the jobs they were doing, asked them how things were going, and treated them to afternoon Popsicles. You could see they liked working for him. They didn't blame him for the oppressive heat; that's part of the Philadelphia summer. Anyway, they were running up thousands of hours of double-pay overtime every day. They weren't complaining.

Actors were making sporadic visits for physicals and screen tests or just to check things out. When Night told Paul about Lin Lao's name change to Young-Soon, he said, "Flip-flop chop!" Cindy came to Bristol and she and Night went to wardrobe. Of everybody in the movie, only Young-Soon would have a modern look. Cindy slipped into a pair of jeans reserved for Young-Soon and transformed instantly from conservative math major to trampy pop diva. With her midriff exposed and orange extensions woven into her long black hair and wearing a tan cowboy hat, Cindy pranced around as if this were the real her. Her mother was snapping pictures with wild abandon. When Cindy apologized for the "momarazzi," Night saw again the real

Cindy—the one who needed to act, not just for the pay, but for others to hear her.

Bryce Dallas Howard showed up, and there was no commotion. There she was one morning, the daughter of an icon and the movie's leading lady, looking like an undergraduate on summer vacation. She was wearing a skimpy cotton T-shirt, thin cotton pants, flat sandals, and carrying her lunch in a thermos. She wore no makeup, and was warm and friendly. She hadn't turned twenty-five yet, and she looked younger than that.

Bryce was about five-eight, with pale, perfect skin and an exquisite face. In high school she had been an athlete; her father had a fantasy about her playing basketball at the University of Connecticut. (Sports ran in the family. Her younger brother was about to enroll at Pepperdine to play golf.) She had the muscular legs of a sprinter, not the matchstick legs you see on Victoria's Secret models. Viewed that way, that clinically, she represented another odd choice by Night. She wasn't a hot chick off the Paris Hilton assembly line, the kind seventeen-year-old boys would pay nine dollars to look at for two hours. Night had something else in mind. On *The Village*, Bryce had been Night's personal angel, and now he wanted her to play that role for the world.

She passed her physical, despite her liquid diet that had been giving her terrible headaches. As an eater, she wasn't sacrificing that much on the liquid diet. Even on her regular diet, she ate nothing but raw food. No meat, no fish, nothing that required the machine-tilling of soil. Her parents were recovering hippies, she said, who gave her a middle name in honor of the city where she was conceived. Every day was Earth Day with Bryce. Night didn't like the diet when he heard about it. He was afraid she was getting too thin, and told her so. "If you're too thin, moviegoers lose their connection to you," he said.

He also thought that the liquid diet was the act of someone

"trying on personalities, the way a lot of young actors do," he told me. It seemed antisocial to Night, to eat that way. It didn't seem like a real way to lead a life. But it was real to Bryce.

She explained the diet to Paul one morning, the benefits of "cleansing the system" with a liquid diet.

"I like that idea—cleansing the system—yes, that's appealing, *very* appealing, sounds really good," Paul said. His voice was so distinctive, an airy bass, like no other voice in the movies. He had a way of repeating information with different words and dropping his voice markedly at the end of a sentence. He could keep conversations going for as long as he liked, and almost never had to ask a question.

"I can tell you what's in it: mineral water, maple syrup, lemon juice, cayenne pepper," Bryce said.

"Cayenne pepper," Paul said.

"Yes. *So* good. I can write down the recipe for you."

"Sure."

"Really?"

"Yeah, I'm interested."

She started to write down the ingredients. One would not come to her. She pointed her elegant, interesting nose, with a bump in it courtesy of a high school basketball game, high in the air. She was worried about the spelling of *cayenne*. She liked to get things right. Her lines in her script were highlighted with a yellow marker. You could imagine her doing all the extra-credit homework problems as a seventh-grader.

"You know something—do you use e-mail? Can I e-mail it to you?"

"Fine, sure." Paul wrote down his e-mail address for his costar. "I might try it. I could lose a few pounds."

"Don't do that. If you get smaller, *I* have to get smaller."

Paul was meeting Bryce for the first time, knowing they would be working intimately together day after day for the next several months. He had made *Cinderella Man* for Bryce's father, but he went out of his way not to mention him to her. Paul figured it was tough enough being the daughter of Ron Howard, trying to make it on her own in her father's profession.

In the previous year, he had starred in *Sideways*, a sleeper hit; he'd been nominated for a Golden Globe for Best Actor; been a guest host on *Saturday Night Live*. But in manner, in appearance, in his small talk, he remained an all-world regular Joe. Choate, Yale, summers on the Vineyard, son of Bart Giamatti, there was no sign of any of that. It was all in the vault.

Night loved how Paul paid almost no attention to his clothes. The actor wore the same thing daily: Merrell sandals fastened with Velcro straps, original Levi's, and a T-shirt or a short-sleeved plaid shirt with the collar curled up by the humidity, like the madras shirt Richard Dreyfuss wore in *American Graffiti*. Paul was content out of the spotlight, off to the side, where he could listen to Jimmy Mazzola tell his "Marty" Scorsese stories and where he could be one of the boys. A compliment to him was to be mistaken as a member of the crew, a union painter or something like that.

One day during preproduction, Night called Paul, who was in his apartment in Brooklyn with window-unit air conditioners.

"I think you've put on a few pounds," Night said. Paul had recently returned from a vacation in Italy.

"I always look this way," Paul said. He normally played everything so lightly, but there was no joke in his tone now.

"I'm just saying, as the director, I wouldn't want to see you go any higher."

"I didn't know you wanted Brad Pitt," Paul said. He was

angry, and Night noted the tone, in case he needed it in the future. "If you were looking for buff, you should have hired somebody else."

"I don't want Brad Pitt. I'm just trying to say you're close to the line." He didn't want to antagonize his lead, but Night felt he was doing what he had to do. When he needed to, he'd take on Jose Rodriguez, Sam Mercer, Chris Doyle, the Disney people—anybody, really. "You can't be an everyman if you go too far in one direction." He was afraid Paul could turn into a John Candy, where size becomes a comic bit. That would not serve Cleveland Heep. Night wanted moviegoers to *see* Cleveland Heep, to see Paul.

There was silence and then Paul said, "I hate this shit."

It was a painful conversation, all the way around. Night knew how he must have sounded, like another Hollywood schmuck, judging Paul by the wrong thing. But in his mind, he was protecting the character he had invented. He was defending the movie. He had to do it. But it left him feeling all alone.

Night didn't really have a management style, he just believed things so deeply (most of the time) and acted accordingly. If Cindy's agent really thought Cindy was worth $1 million in her first studio acting job, he should have said, "We won't take less than a million." That's what Night did when he was selling *The Sixth Sense*.

No business school would teach that, Night's habit of laying all your cards on the table. On *Lady*, he had done it first with Paul Giamatti and then with Alan Horn and then with Cindy Cheung, kept saying, *You're the one.* And where was the reciprocity? He couldn't get Paul to read the script right away. He couldn't get Horn to open the meeting at his house with his verdict on the script. He couldn't get Cindy to climb aboard at the SAG minimum. Maybe they had seen that Night was crazy, off his game, riddled with doubt. He sounded like a man trying to re-create his first love. Any sane person knows it can't be done.

We're gonna do something magical together here, I can feel it. Are you feeling it?

Yeah. Listen, what time you gonna start on that Tuesday after Labor Day?

The rest of the world could not afford to be so unguarded. Not Cindy, not Horn, not Paul, not Sarita. Maybe Chris Doyle— maybe. He was crazy, too.

Shortly after Night's watch-the-weight talk, Paul was in Bristol for a day of rehearsals with Bryce. Paul came into Night's office, and Night rose from his big leather swivel chair. Night said, "Whaddup, bitch?" They hugged.

"What's going on?" Paul said through a laugh. "Look at all this!" he said with actorly wonder. He waved his hand at the walls of Night's office, which were covered with white copy paper, 231 carefully ordered sheets, each with three or four screen-shaped rectangular drawings. Paul didn't intend to give heightened meaning to everything he said. It just came out that way. Paul started to examine Brick Mason's storyboarding, his depiction of the movie's scenes in sketch form.

Night knew he *had* to have Paul with him for the movie to work. The voices were telling Night that Paul was losing faith in him, and Night had to turn that around.

When Paula had delivered the sale script to Disney that Sunday in February, and even when Night had brought Sale Script II to Warner Bros., he was never certain he had the ending correct. He played with it in his head at night. Paul was meandering among the storyboards like an art student at the Met. He was an illustrator himself. Paul looked at the final page of the storyboards, where Brick had drawn Cleveland Heep taping a handwritten note on his bungalow door for his tenants. Night said, "I'm thinking about a new ending," and told Paul about it. Paul was the first to know. Night needed Paul to know that he was his most important collaborator on the movie, more so than even Chris Doyle.

"A very bold stroke, my friend," Paul said with a heavy emphasis on the *k* in *stroke*. And in the response, Night heard Paul saying that he got it, not just the new ending, which was significant, but what Paul meant to him, and what Night was trying to do.

As Night and Paul talked about the new ending, people in other offices were working on the original one. One floor down, Jimmy Mazzola, the prop man, was preparing a portfolio for Night with different choices for the final scene: stationery in different sizes and different textures, handwriting samples written with different writing implements. Jimmy knew that someday Night would ask, "Would Cleveland use a pen or a marker?" Jimmy would be ready.

There were so many things like that, what Night called "tonal choices." What kind of cigarettes should the smokers smoke? Which of eighteen shades of beige was the right one for the apartment building's exterior? What books should be in the apartment belonging to Mr. Leeds, the character who did nothing but watch TV?

One day Night spent a full minute staring silently at his youngest actor, Noah Gray-Cabey, who was playing a boy genius named Joey. Night was wondering whether Joey would wear a plain short-sleeved T-shirt, a long-sleeved striped one, or something else. "Long is more complex," he finally told Betsy Heimann. The wardrobe queen nodded gravely.

Then there was Night going through his own wardrobe

questions for his role as Vick Ran. Betsy wasn't outfitting him with the frazzled-writer look. The movie was filled with writers: Vick, who can't get his pen in gear; old Mrs. Bell, animal lover and failed writer; Mr. Farber, the movie critic; Cleveland Heep, often writing in his journals.

"What are you, a thirty-one-inch waist?" Betsy asked. Chicago was all over her *R*'s.

"Yeah, but when we're shooting I'll probably lose an inch." It was impressive, with his massive meals. His nervous energy burned them right off.

She had a half-dozen different styles of designer jeans for Night to try on. Night put on a pair and looked at himself in a full-length mirror, dropping his chin, moving his shoulders forward, squinting, tousling his hair like Ben Stiller playing the airhead model in *Zoolander*. Betsy had Night in flimsy leather sandals and a T-shirt underneath a ripped T-shirt. Jesus as a fashion model.

"I gotta tell you, that's a very sexy look," Betsy said. *Vay-ree.*

Night shook his head. He knew better. He was playing a writer who could not finish. There was nothing "sexy" about it.

Then there was the question of whether Paul should wear a wig. Many hours on that one. Paul gamely tried on one wig after another. For preproduction, Night had brought in a famous hair-and-wig man from England, Peter King, a jolly chap, very funny and very white, wearing shiny white shoes and a white belt. His assistant was a young black man with a shaved head, also very shiny. Their examination of Paul was deeply clinical.

Night, you need to know this: If you cut off Paul's beard, it's not coming back. It's not really a beard. A beard grows. It's hair on a face.

Night asked, "If he wears glasses, what are the wig-and-beard implications?"

The wig man shot a look at Night that said the implications

were so far-reaching, it would take hours to answer the question properly.

"I'm only asking because I like the idea of the beard and glasses, that kind of look that Richard Dreyfuss had in *Jaws*," Night said. He saw movie analogies in everything. He had told a set designer he wanted the apartment where Joey lived with his father to have a *"Kramer vs. Kramer* quality to it."

Beard *and* glasses? Peter King did not approve. That gruesome combination would do nothing but diminish the greatness of his wig.

Paul thought the idea of him in a wig was ridiculous but said nothing to Night, not directly. With his regular beard and black heavy-framed glasses, and now with long locks taped on him by the wig men, Paul became a ringer for Bill Gaines, the founder of *MAD* magazine. "The transformation is *magical*," Paul whispered loudly, like an old theatergoer. The look was hilarious but not, in Paul's mind, Cleveland Heep. Paul felt Cleveland could handle his male-pattern baldness, but Night was close to putting Paul in a piece. The voices knew better. "I could have ruined the movie with that one decision," Night said later. *"Ruined* it." He wasn't necessarily overstating it. You could imagine people spending the entire movie asking, "You think Giamatti's wearing a rug?"

And then there was Bryce's wig: many, many hours on that. Bryce would definitely be wearing a wig. Night wanted her hair to be long, in the red family but leaning to orange, with bangs, kinky but not Laraine Newmanish. He was presented with dozens of options, all complicated by his requirement that her hair change color over the course of the movie, even though the action unfolds over several days. These were some of the biggest tonal decisions in the movie. When Night wasn't getting a good read on one red hue, Peter King said the culprit was Bryce's sweater, that the black was overamplifying the red.

Bryce jumped up and pulled off the black sweater. She was wearing a loose-fitting gray singlet underneath. Night looked at her in a mirror and said, "Okay, yes, now I see it. That improves it by seventy percent."

The question of the pool's drain weighed heavily on Night for a while. There was a scene in which Cleveland lifts the pool's drain and swims through it. If the drain was big enough to accommodate him, the movie would feel more realistic. Maybe a good thing, maybe not. If it was too small for that, it would feel more like a fantasy. Maybe a good thing, maybe not. So many choices. Night's days were filled with them. Most of the day, except when he was in rehearsals, somebody was nearby, waiting to ask him something about something. In the end, Night decided to use a duplicate of the drain used in the gutter scene from *Strangers on a Train,* a Hitchcock movie produced by Warner Bros. A subtle nod.

The 70 percent thing was common. Night was forever turning the results of his work into numbers and statistics suitable for *SportsCenter.* He said if he could get 90 percent of the tonal decisions correct in the movie, he'd be doing well. But he didn't want to make all the tonal choices himself. A movie had to be collaborative. If it wasn't, it didn't work. He took script notes from anybody. He hired people *because* they had strong tastes. He wanted them to make choices. He didn't want to dictate everything to them.

There were times Chris Doyle believed Night on all that— and times that he did not. One day the DP and Night were talking about a particular evening scene when Doyle said, "How many apartments will you want lit for it?" It was what Night would call a tonal question. The answer would tell you about the age of the building's residents, how compulsive they were, whether they were insomniacs or maybe working on side projects. The vibe of the building would be in the answer. But it was a question Night wanted Chris Doyle to figure out for himself.

In a calculated way, Night read him the riot act. "Don't give me that American Chris Doyle shit, okay? You can light every fucking apartment we have if you want. You decide." He said that even though he knew he wanted fourteen of the fifty-seven apartments lit. He was trying to free up his director of photography. He said, "I want the Asian Chris Doyle!"

"Yezboz," Doyle said, shuffling away. Doyle knew he was working in America. He could tell by the way a movie-set five-story apartment building went up just about overnight. On that day, Doyle would think of Night only as the bossman. Other days were different.

Most of the actors met Doyle for the first time when they came in for their screen test, a test not for acting ability but for how the actors looked in the lighting and the film stock and the various aperture settings Doyle was considering. On this day, the Asian Chris Doyle was out, the dangerous one. Upon seeing Cindy Cheung in her Britney Spears costume, Doyle said cheerfully, "You're looking very fuckable." Cindy did not take offense only because he said it so publicly and she detected no menace or sexuality in it. It was how he talked, how he paid compliments, how he called attention to himself. But Sam Mercer was worried. You never knew where a lawsuit might come from. The producer knew they'd have to watch Doyle closely. It didn't bother Night. If people were uncomfortable, that would be good for the movie. Night's own goal was to get out of his own comfort zone. He imagined what Nina would have said, had he tried to hire Doyle on her watch.

Night's worry was more immediate than Doyle's use of the word *fuckable*. Doyle's screen tests were outrageously muddy. "What's he doing?" Night asked one night after looking at them. "You don't do that leather-vest-with-no-shirt look on the first date. You gotta get the basics first and work your way up to the crazy shit." The screen tests didn't represent the American Chris Doyle (they would have been technically perfect) or the Asian Chris Doyle (they would have had art to them). They weren't inspired madness. They were just bad. Still, at least they were bad for a reason: Doyle was trying to do too much.

One day during preproduction, Alan Horn and Jeff Robinov came in for the day to see what their $68 million (the final budget) was buying. Night made certain to keep them away from Doyle, just in case the DP felt moved to pay them one of his patented compliments. Night, still getting to know the two executives, was being uncharacteristically cautious. There was one shot in the storyboards that was purely a Chris Doyle invention, involving the character Reggie, the guy who worked out only one half of his body, assuming an outrageous pose as he stares down a vicious scrunt. It was a comic moment in a scary scene. The possibility that Horn or Robinov would focus on that one shot among the hundreds in the movie seemed remote, but Night's worry was real, so he had the shot omitted from the storyboard wall on the day of their visit.

In their relationship, Robinov was typically the creative executive and Horn the analyst, the businessman. But during the visit, Night could tell for the first time what was happening internally at Warner Bros. Robinov was allowing Horn to have creative responsibility on Night's first movie for the studio. Night thought that took a lot of confidence, to allow your boss to do your job for you. He could not imagine Nina and Dick Cook having any similar kind of arrangement. It also underscored how Night had found his way to Warner Bros.—because Alan Horn called him that day in Paris after *The Village* had opened.

Night was more nervous than usual as he took Robinov and Horn and other Warner Bros. executives around the set, a construction site, really. When Night showed the group, about eight in all, the mechanical scrunt in action, he watched Alan Horn's eyes closely. Night saw fear. As Horn was leaving, he said to Night, "You wowed us." Night was relieved.

Yet he felt a certain emptiness. Originally, they were going to come for two days, with a visit to the farm on the first day. Night wanted them to see how he lived and worked. He felt that the better they knew him, the better the job they could do with his movie. But the two-day visit turned into a visit that lasted part of one day. They had other things going on in their lives. The tormenting picture of Nina Jacobson and Co. returned to his head, and Night wondered why Robinov had ceded (it seemed to Night) the creative onus to Horn. Was it because Horn and Night had a special bond? Or did Robinov, like Nina, have doubts about the script, too? Night knew these questions were only in his head, but that brought him no comfort.

Night was an odd sort of obsessive compulsive. He didn't expect every day to go well, or even close to well. He would have been perfectly fine with getting, say, 89 percent of the tonal decisions right, even if it was a full point shy of his stated goal. But certain things you had to get correct. The Horn-Robinov visit, that was an important one, and Night gave it a B-plus. You had to pick the right release date for your movie, and to do that, you had to know what the mood of the world would be like on that date. (Night was betting that on July 21, 2006, the world would be ready for a soulful movie with humor, for a world population weary of war.) You had to have the right trailer campaign and the right poster. You had to have certain key marketing executives, at least one or two levels below the ultimate bosses, who truly understood what you were trying to do in the movie. You could never get all of those people on your side, but you needed some of them. Certain hires you had to get right. You had to cast the right people in the right roles, on-screen and off. Same thing there: You would never get every casting decision right. Didn't happen even in *The Godfather* or in *The Sixth Sense* or in any movie. But there were about a dozen jobs—lead actor, lead actress, DP, casting director, caterer, maybe a half-dozen more—you had to nail. In other places, good was good enough.

For instance, the hiring of Mary Beth Hurt in a supporting role. She was so lovely as Laura in the 1979 movie *Chilly Scenes of Winter*. Once married to William Hurt, the most talented actor Night had ever worked with, she was now married to Paul Schrader, the director and screenwriter, most notably of *Taxi Driver*, the Martin Scorsese movie starring Robert De Niro. Night had hired Mary Beth to play Mrs. Bell, the animal lover who gave up writing because her one published book "sold like crap" and was a "terrible waste of time." At her audition, and again in rehearsals, with the script right in front of her, she would often trample the lines Night had written. There are many directors who are happy to have their actors improvise. Paul Giamatti, when shooting *Sideways* for Alexander Payne, had come up with the line "Write up my gay confession and I'll sign it." Payne used it. But Night didn't work like that, and every time Mary Beth Hurt inserted words of her own, Night wondered if there was some passive-aggressive thing going on between her and the script or her and Night or her and her own career. But Night wasn't too worried. She was a good actress, and she was in only a few scenes, and if you gave her enough takes, she'd get it right eventually.

And then there was Paul. He would ask if he could stutter on a different syllable than the one Night had indicated in the script. But he had opinions, too. He felt the stutter should be particularly emphatic when he was talking about children or near them. When Night heard Paul suggest that, he knew the actor really understood Cleveland Heep. Night knew that his single most important hire had been his best one.

Later on the *whaddup bitch* day, Bryce walked into Night's

office. Paul had been examining the teeth of a model scrunt and looked up.

"Did you hear about the new ending?" Paul asked her.

Night knew Paul wasn't going to give it away. Night liked seeing Paul like that, a little dangerous.

"No. What?"

"You *die.*"

Night cackled and Paul giggled and Bryce laughed, maybe a little excessively.

Bryce began distributing a food that looked suspiciously like haggis. A few days earlier, on August 1, there had been an afternoon break to celebrate Night's thirty-fifth birthday. (Jeff Robinov had sent Night a framed original poster of the 1939 film version of *Wuthering Heights.* He knew that Night had thought about the boy in it when he was writing *The Sixth Sense.* Night took that as a good sign—maybe Robinov *did* like the script.) Bryce was one of the few actors around that day. A couple dozen people—editors, tailors, set designers, accountants, prop masters, drivers, caterers, the on-set nurse, the wig people, the hair people, the makeup people, the security people—gathered around to sing "Happy Birthday" to Night and to eat cake, big slices distributed on thin paper plates. Bryce passed. "I don't eat anything that has animal fat in it," she explained to Night. Night was annoyed. He thought it was Bryce trying on a personality again, the vegetarian who must always announce she is an outsider.

Several days later, Bryce came in with a gruesome-looking vegan cake made with rice and honey and soy. You've never seen a grayer birthday cake or tasted one so gritty. In the name of kindness, Paul accepted a piece and pretended to like it. Night passed and said, "I won't eat anything that doesn't have animal fat in it." He was joking, but with a hint of hostility. Bryce ignored it.

She had changed. Night had first seen her on Broadway, in *Tartuffe,* where she was raw and emotionally bare. Based on that, he gave her a supporting role in *The Village*. Kirsten Dunst had been hired to play the lead. But Dunst dropped out in pre-production, to take the female lead in *Spider-Man*. Night gave the lead to Bryce. She was twenty-one, playing a blind woman in desperate love, and she had to carry the first real movie of her life. It didn't matter that she was the daughter of Ron Howard, that she had grown up in the business, that as an eleven-year-old she had handed out sandwiches to her father's crew as they watched the *Apollo 13* dailies. She was an apprentice, and she hung on every word Night said and played the role beautifully. Even critics who didn't like *The Village* praised her. She had saved the day, at the SAG minimum.

But since then she had worked with two artistic directors, Lars von Trier and Kenneth Branagh. She had become engaged to another young actor, Seth Gabel, and was making lists of names for her unborn children. She had lavish technical skills, and Night was eager to see her grow. But Night felt she was turning into an . . . *actress*. One of those people you see on late-night TV talk shows. He could smell neither her perfume nor her sweat. And she was one of the dozen key hires—she had to be on fire for the picture to work. From what Night was seeing in rehearsals, he was worried. Her torment felt manufactured. He wanted something more than her exceptionally cheerful and elongated "Hi, Night" whenever they saw each other. For the movie to stir people, he needed her acting soul. He needed the real Bryce Dallas Howard. She was Story, the lady in the water. She *was* the story. Just about every character in the movie would be trying to save her life. *Show me you're worth it, Bryce.*

One afternoon Night said to her, "Look into my eyes." They began a staring contest. "Tell me what I'm thinking." It went nowhere. She wasn't doing what Cindy did in her audition, what Night did in Cindy's audition: seize the moment, respond to what was happening right there.

The vegan cake was eaten, sort of, and Night and Bryce and Paul descended the back steps of the old 3M office building and went into a sealed-off room with a sofa, a few chairs, fluorescent lighting, industrial brown carpeting, and brown-paneled walls. The room hadn't been used in a long time and smelled of mildew. Night had turned it into a rehearsal room where he and his actors could go off into a drift.

Paul picked up a can of air freshener, a product called Oust, and started spraying it all around the room, as if putting out a fire. Bryce was talking about the documentary *March of the Penguins*. Night had his nose in the script. There were no windows that could open, and the only sound was a whirring fan. The room had once been a waiting area, but now the door was sealed with an accordion-style metal fence. Through the slats, you could see the frayed neighborhood across Green Lane.

Paul removed his sandals and took his wallet out of his back pocket and sprawled out on a sofa as if he had spent his childhood in that basement room, watching *Hollywood Squares* and eating Cap'n Crunch, except he was sipping black coffee from a Styrofoam cup and working on a movie that was paying him (Howard Stern got him to say in an interview) over $1 million. He was *not* trying on personalities.

They were working on an intimate scene between Story and Cleveland. Bryce sat right beside Paul. Night felt that the sexual tension should be one-way, from Cleveland to Story.

"Paul, you're like 'If this is a date, I'm throwing off the beeper.' "

Paul nodded cheerfully.

"Bryce, be careful not to become Lolita," Night said.

Bryce had her yellow highlighter resting across her lips and was staring with her translucent blue eyes up at Night, who was standing over her.

He pointed to her pouting mouth and said, "Be careful of *that*." She quickly moved the marker to her lap.

Night closed his eyes and put his fingers on his nose, mouthing words. He was lost in concentration. When Night was making *The Sixth Sense,* he had to figure out a set of rules for the living dead. One was that you wore for eternity the clothes you were wearing when you died. Now he was working on his rules for narfs, the under-the-pool species to which Story belonged, and he was talking to himself again.

Bryce was struggling with the line "I am scared." She asked, "Is she scared when she says that?"

"No," Night said. "She's rock-solid. She's strong."

Bryce considered that for a moment and said, "When I think of strength, I think of armor."

Story has no armor, verbal or otherwise. She talks very little and for parts of the movie, she wears nothing but one of Cleveland Heep's work shirts, or less. Her strength comes from her willingness to accept her fate and her wish to see Cleveland healed. At one point she admits she's a lousy narf.

"That's interesting. I think the opposite," Night said. "When I think of strength, I *don't* think of armor. I think of someone who is open about being vulnerable." He was defining himself. The rehearsal pressed on, three people trying to figure out the script, and one another.

Night's parents, both retired doctors, spent their days together, except when Night's father was on the golf course. They often ate lunch out, and got around in a big Mercedes. Their house was a tiny oasis of calm. There was something not quite American about it. There were almost no gadgets in it. It was filled with the music of their singsong voices.

Night's father was born in 1937 in southwestern India, in a

town of thirty-five thousand on the Arabian Sea called Mahe, under French rule for centuries. Shyamalan was his given name, not his father's surname. People called him Shyam.

Most of the people in Mahe were Hindu, and there was a small Catholic and Muslim population, too. Religious tolerance was the norm. Shyam's family were faithful Hindus. Shyam's father died when Shyam was six and his father was working as an estate manager in Malaysia. Shyam's mother put flowers on her husband's forehead and said goodbye. A holy man sprinkled water on the body. Young Shyam sat on a stone wall under a giant banyan tree and saw white smoke rise from the crematorium, fifty yards away. He thought his father had turned into a cloud. He could smell the sandalwood burning. The aroma was pleasant.

In Mahe, Shyam lived with his mother, four brothers, and one sister in a small house with clay-and-cement floors. They could not afford rugs. There were five temples within a short walk of their house. They went to temple almost nightly, and their mother would tell them to pray for sustenance. One temple had a large spring-fed pool next to it. Shyam and his family would bathe before prayers and eat rice dinners afterward. After Shyam's father died, the boy's mother sold her family jewelry to stay in the house. Even though the caste system was not as strong in Mahe as it was in most of India, there was no possibility of Shyam going to university; they were far too poor.

There was an oval rock wall around the pool, maybe fifteen feet high and three feet wide and smooth at the top. One day when he was twelve, Shyam was sitting on top of the wall, his legs dangling toward the pool, when a prankster started running at him as hard as he could. He was planning to jump over Shyam and into the pool. But the other boy jumped too late and caught Shyam square in the back with his foot. Shyam fell headfirst and should have smashed his head against the craggy, rocky wall—a likely death. But he fell outward before going down and landed on his hip in water deep enough to prevent any serious injury. From then on, his trips to temple stopped feeling like a duty.

Shyam aced his national achievement tests in high school, and scholarships were offered to him as Indian culture changed under Nehru. He went to college and then on to medical school, where he met his future wife. They came to the United States in the 1960s to get more schooling, and they stayed. They started in an apartment in Philadelphia and ended up in a house on the Main Line with an outdoor pool, an indoor pool, a tennis court, and a Japanese garden. They raised a daughter and a son, Indian kids in a land of white people, eating Sugar Pops in a kitchen that smelled of curry. Veena and Manoj learned about the gods, heard the stories, went to the festivals, ate the food. None of it held any meaning for the son, not that the father could tell. Except when it came to storytelling. From the time he was a boy, Manoj loved to hear the stories, the more ancient the better.

From time to time I'd see Night's parents at their house. Sometimes we'd have tea there or go to an Indian restaurant where the family had been eating for years, or to a local deli with Formica benches. Night and his father had the same giggle and the same habit of twisting their rings while talking. Night had his mother's warmth. He made regular visits to his parents. He was close to them.

Night's father's medical practice had been in North Philadelphia, in a rough part of the city. Most of his patients were indigent Hispanics and blacks on Medicaid and Russian émigrés paying cash. He often made house calls in unpredictable neighborhoods and worked many more hours to earn the same kind of money the Main Line doctors made, but he hadn't become a doctor just to make money. After *The Sixth Sense*, Night was in a position to encourage his father to retire, and his father did.

"In his movies, Manoj is explaining the supernatural, and doing that is part of the Hindu tradition of storytelling," Dr. Shyamalan said once over lunch. His English had the rich accent of his homeland. "I tell Manoj, 'There are things that are inexplicable.' I told him how I sometimes can still smell my mother helping me when I was a child, the feeling that she is right there. And I think maybe he took a little of that when he was writing *The Sixth Sense*."

He was proud of his son's career, but he remained convinced that Manoj could have been an outstanding doctor or lawyer. Either one.

Night's mother, Jaya, grew up near Madras, in southern India, in a house permeated by Hindu culture. Her father was a deputy police superintendent, and Jayalakshmi, her full name, was the oldest of eight. She was a renegade in her own unassuming way. Had she not gone off to college, she would have been married by arrangement. She evaded the caste system with a rare combination of determination and intelligence and became an obstetrician and gynecologist. Four of her siblings followed her into medicine. One became a hand doctor, another a kidney specialist, another a surgeon, another a psychiatrist. All of them moved to the United States, and all of them married doctors. There were years when family weddings had at least ten doctors present. Manoj used the children of those doctors as his actors in many of the forty backyard VCR movies he made (and starred in) in high school and before. Sometimes, they re-created hospital scenes.

One of the cousins, playing a female patient: "I'm pregnant."

Young Manoj, sounding like a soap opera MD: "Lie down, everything's going to be okay. I'm going to put you on a Pitocin drip." He had no idea that Pitocin was used to induce labor, but he'd heard his mother say it over the phone, and he'd seen *Pitocin* on the sides of the pens in the kitchen.

For years, Dr. Jaya Shyamalan held the record for the largest ovarian cyst any doctor had ever removed from a surviving patient at Mercy Fitzgerald Hospital, on the outskirts of Philadelphia: eighty pounds. (No wonder Night was such a stat man.) She had also delivered thousands of healthy babies, as well as some who were not. One pregnant woman, near term, did not believe that her unborn infant had died. Silently, Dr. Shyamalan handed the mother her stethoscope and held the grieving woman through her hysteria. Night's mother had debilitating arthritis and reluctantly retired in her early fifties, in the early 1990s, when her son was turning into Night at NYU.

When Brooke Shields wrote about her postpartum depression, Dr. Shyamalan read about it with interest. She knew it was a common problem in the United States, and uncommon in India, where the tradition was for mothers to spend several weeks at their own mother's home after delivery, one generation looking after the other. That was what Jaya had done with her own children.

Jaya and Shyam were still living in India when Veena was born, but they were living in the United States when Jaya became pregnant with their second child. Jaya spent the last five months of her pregnancy at her parents' house, which was then in the South India city of Pondicherry. Shyam stayed in Philadelphia, working and taking care of Veena. Manoj was born in a hospital in Pondicherry and spent his first six weeks at his maternal grandparents' house. He returned to India every two or three years until he was in his early twenties, when he started to go more irregularly.

When Night graduated from NYU, he told his mother he wanted to shoot a movie of his own in India. He had an idea—American college student of Indian descent returns to the motherland—but no script. His mother learned that scripts written by nonresidents had to be submitted to the Ministry of

Information and Broadcasting. Ten days later, Night had a script written. They submitted the script, raised money from family and friends, and went to India to make a movie. They rented cameras, hired an experienced cinematographer, rounded up a crew, and navigated India's bewildering permit requirements. Night hired the least inexperienced actors he could find by taking out ads in newspapers. In the tradition of Woody Allen and Spike Lee, Night played the lead.

Trying to leave the country with the exposed film, Night was required to put the film canisters through the X-ray security machines, and Night said, "There's a five percent chance that there will be no movie at all." But the film survived, and the movie he made from the film in those canisters, *Praying with Anger*, had a brief run in one theater in New York and a good review in *The New York Times*. And that was it. You cannot find a copy, and Night won't even talk about it. His mother told me she saw it once, cried all the way through, and never saw it again.

Night was close to his mother, but not in a sentimental way. One day, when finishing work on a scene with Brick, he said, "Well, as my mother would intone it, 'At least *that* scene will work.' "

Night loved being an actor. In the basement rehearsal room, particularly when he was working with Paul and Sarita, playing his movie sister, it was like a reprieve from the burdens of being the boss and a chance to hang out, as if he were just another actor, even though he was not. There was a sweetness to rehearsal days, amid the mustiness.

A few hundred yards away, the apartments in Night's mock five-story apartment building were being built, decorated, painted, and finished. A beehive of activity. On the other side of Green Lane, in the fraying black neighborhood, regular life was unfolding daily in a slow, summery way. Inside the rehearsal room, time seemed to stop altogether.

There was no construction noise in the rehearsal room, just the whirring fan and Night laughing at Paul's improv bits. The idea of a wig for Paul died at last, and in his relief he developed a gag in which he'd use four fingers to represent a toupee. He'd abruptly move his head a quarter-turn, like a spectator watching a tennis match, and a half-second later, the fingers would move. Maybe you had to be there, but it was funny.

Paul seemed to barely need the rehearsals. He had his lines memorized early, and whatever time he spent "finding" his character, he must have done on his own. But whenever Night would say something like "Paul, you up for trying one more time?" Paul's answer would be the same: "Yeah, sure—fine."

Paul and Night were about as different as two people could be. Night was a striver, like his immigrant parents, and he didn't pretend to be otherwise. Paul had the sensibilities of old Yale, in which admitting to ambition was a mark of crudeness. Still, a closeness was developing between them. The watch-your-weight phone conversation had been buried. Night could give Paul shit now.

"What happened with that remake of *Apes*?" Night asked lightly.

"Oh, I know," Paul said. In the 2001 version of *Planet of the Apes,* Paul had played Limbo, an ape with a sense of humor. "Hey—we tried."

"I saw it the night it opened," Night said. "I'm in this big theater, filled with *Ape* fans, and we're all walking out. Some guy kicks open those big exit doors and says, 'Da shee *suck*.' And we're all like 'Yeah, that shit sucked.' "

Paul laughed. He knew the truth, and Night did, too. You could never tell what a movie was going to be like, not until it came out.

Paul got the movie bug from his parents. He'd follow his mother, a high school English teacher, to pretty much whatever she was seeing. He was six when they saw *The Conversation*, the intense Francis Ford Coppola movie about paranoia. On Saturdays, Paul and his father would sometimes go to matinees. They'd see the Monty Python movies and anything with Peter Sellers in it, or apes, or horses. Bart loved Westerns. He talked often about writing the perfect Western. Bart was as dynamic in his family life as he was as the president of Yale or the commissioner of baseball. You can imagine the void brought by his death. Toni died fifteen years after Bart, in 2004. Toni's father, a legendary high school football coach in New Jersey, was buried on a Friday, at age ninety-seven, and Paul's mother died the next day. She was only sixty-seven. A month later, *Sideways* came out. It was a hit. After *Sideways*, there were fewer and fewer people saying of Paul, "Isn't he Bart Giamatti's son?" Now, on the *Lady* set, Paul was smack-dab in the middle of a studio movie, albeit a strange one. He was trying to keep the director sane, and trying to make an odd movie work. It was a tall task.

One day I left base camp and went into the neighborhood on the other side of Green Lane, which Night was curious about. The houses belonged to members of the working class, the working poor, and the just plain poor. It was a hot weekday in August. There were a lot of people outside. There was a man selling chicken wings from his front step, six in a Styrofoam container for $3.50 with a warm supermarket soda. You could smell the sweet aroma of grilling meat from another direction. There were two men fighting on the sidewalk, nothing too vicious, but there was a small crowd around. There were kids on low-slung bikes and toddlers in diapers in inflatable pools. They could see the Cove, Night's mock apartment building, going up through the trees across the street. Some mornings they saw the throngs of people gathered at the front gate—open calls for pool-party extras. There was enough going on in that little neighborhood to shoot a movie right there.

A woman named Tuesday Davis, with a tiny gold bar protruding through the flesh below her lower lip, was sitting on a stoop with two other women. She saw me with a notebook and asked if I was a talent scout for the movie. She continued as if I had said yes.

" 'Cause I'm ready for my close-up!"

Everybody laughed.

She was an attractive woman, but she looked painfully tired. She didn't have a job.

She said, "I heard they got a mermaid in a swimming pool."

"That's true."

"That's what I want to know: How'd they get that mermaid in that swimming pool?"

"Just, you know, movie magic."

"What kind of stars you all got over there?"

"Well, there's Paul Giamatti. He's the lead."

"I ain't never heard of him."

"Bryce Howard, she's the female lead."

"I heard of her. I'm pretty sure I heard of her."

"Maybe you've heard of the director, M. Night Shyamalan?"

"Yeah. He did *The Sixth Sense* and all."

"Did you see that?"

"Yeah. It was okay. I fell asleep. I fall asleep in the movies."

"Do you go to late shows?"

"I go at like six o'clock. But it's too dark in there."

We talked about this and that for a few minutes. When I left, she said, "You tell 'em all that Tuesday Davis is ready for her close-up!"

6.

Night was a dinosaur. He felt a script should be done before shooting begins, and he felt all the actors should be available for a read-through, held a couple weeks before the first day of shooting. In modern moviemaking, read-throughs are often conducted with fill-ins reading from scripts-in-progress. They could be listless affairs. To Night, read-throughs were holy. For *Lady in the Water*, the read-through would be the only time the whole cast would be together. Whether it went well or poorly, it would set the tone for the first days of shooting, and those two or three days, Chris Doyle had said, would set the tone for the rest of the shoot. Paul, Bryce, Cindy Cheung, Sarita, Bob Balaban, the five smokers, the five Perez de la Torre sisters, and two dozen other actors gathered in a hotel ballroom at the Rittenhouse in Center City Philadelphia. This was the agenda: a delicious buffet breakfast followed by an uninterrupted reading of the script, followed by a delicious buffet lunch. Food, work, food. Night knew from experience that the schedule worked. One of his management philosophies was never to skimp on food, in quality or in quantity. He knew it inspired loyalty and effort. Plus, he was such a big eater.

Some of the actors had their own scripts, and others, like the smokers and the Perez de la Torre sisters, were lent scripts for the day. (It takes a while to get in the circle of trust.) Alan Horn wasn't at the read-through, but Jeff Robinov was, looking more New Age bohemian than most of the actors, in a long-sleeved T-shirt, pants with many pockets, rubber sandals, and a sort of ski cap on his head, the kind the Santa Cruz surfers wear coming off the beach at dusk. During breakfast he showed Sam Mercer and Jose Rodriguez family snaps from deep inside his wallet, while nearby Mary Beth Hurt read *The New York Times*, and Cindy read *The Wall Street Journal*. Night worked the crowd, beaming and nervous, reaching into his pocket for TUMS when nobody was looking.

It was a gathering of movie people, and they talked about movie-people things. Mary Cybulski, the script supervisor, described a party in New York where Bill Murray had introduced her to a tall, bald black man named Michael. She had said, "Hello, Michael. Where do you live?" "In Chicago," Michael Jordan had said. Night's hero was just another man at a New York party to Night's script supervisor. Mary was better on the 1919 Black Sox. She had worked on *Eight Men Out*, the John Sayles baseball movie. Bill Irwin, the Broadway star hired by Night to play Mr. Leeds, had played Eddie Collins, the clean second baseman, in it. There was a lot of that going on, figuring out the degrees of separation. A lot of the people knew one another, or had an agent in common, or had some link, tangential or otherwise.

People were talking about other projects and other interests. Mary Cybulski had been trekking all over the world as the script supervisor for *Syriana*. Sam Mercer had just wrapped *Jarhead*. The last episode of *Six Feet Under*, featuring Freddy Rodriguez as a budding mortician, was about to air. Bryce had a theater group that was meeting in a barn on her parents' farm in Connecticut. She had dressed up for the read-through, wearing shimmering red lipstick and a shimmering green blouse. Her character was attracted to shiny things, and she was finding her character. On the set, Bryce said, she would be beading with shiny beads. Sarita wondered where she could find a lap pool in downtown Philadelphia, and Paul was looking for Vietnamese restaurants and secondhand bookstores. People were seeking him out, even though he did what he could to deflect attention. Everybody had something to tell him, a long series of unrelated non sequiturs, really. Paul didn't mind. For him, the weirder, the better.

"Hey, Paul, did you know Valerie Bertinelli was doing summer stock in Bucks County?"

"Really? No. No, I didn't. That's so strange. Valerie Bertinelli. Wow. No, I didn't know that."

Jeffrey Wright—who would be playing Mr. Drury, father of the boy genius, Joey—had been in *Syriana*; he and his wife had recently had a baby, and he called from the road to say he was running late. After he heard the news, Night's stress worsened measurably, for the read-through and beyond. Night's newest worry had nothing to do with Jeffrey Wright as an actor. Night thought he was brilliant and masculine in the best sense of the word. His portrayal of the artist in *Basquiat*, gay and black and addicted to drugs, was devastating, as was his work in *Angels in America*. What worried Night was that Wright was an actor who needed time to figure out a role, and his availability would be limited during the rehearsal period. But you never would have known anything about Night's anxiety if you'd seen him from a distance on the morning of the read-through. As he talked to one of the Perez de la Torre sisters, Marylin Torres, about her role in *Maid in Manhattan*, he was the picture of ease. His smile was not only pleasant, it was beatific.

Maddie, Night's new assistant, now a Bryn Mawr graduate and working her first big gig for her new boss, shepherded the actors to their assigned places at long catering tables that formed an enormous square. Bryce and Paul sat together. The smokers sat together. The Perez de la Torre sisters sat together.

June and Cindy, mother and daughter, sat together. Night was ready to start, but one seat remained open.

Stalling for time, Night said, "We're waiting for one actor. I don't want to say who it is—Jeffrey Wright—but in the meantime I'll do a little stand-up."

People laughed, and when they stopped, Night seized the chance to make an important *Lady* announcement, one he knew would sound even more dramatic in the dying laughter. (It's taxing, being so hyperaware.) "I have a new ending that will replace the old ending, so the last page you all have in your script, we won't be using that."

Upon hearing Night's announcement—it wasn't news to Paul, the director's designated insider—the movie's lead instantly ripped the last page from his script in one decisive stroke, crumpled it up, threw it at Night, and shouted, "Extraneous!" More laughter.

Night continued, "The idea for *Lady in the Water* came to me the same time as *The Village*." He was standing, and everybody was looking at him. Nobody was sipping anything or checking for text messages. "I had two stories I wanted to tell. One was about struggle. The other about loveliness. I had to write the one about struggle first. *The Village* is a movie about hiding. And *Lady in the Water* was hard to write after that. To write it, I had to feel vulnerable again. And it was tough, tough to get rid of the cynicism, tough to get rid of all the things we do to protect ourselves."

He was speaking quickly, with great emotion and energy, even more than usual. You could tell the ideas had been in his head for a while, waiting for the right moment to come out.

"I wanted to write a straight love story, but this script didn't want to be that. It wanted to be something else. It turned into a father-daughter story. It wanted to answer the question, What do we see when we see a narf? Who does each of you see when you think of an angel?"

A lean young actor named John Boyd, one of the smokers, immediately thought of the woman in the Bob Dylan song "Shelter from the Storm," the one in the song's enduring refrain: " 'Come in,' she said, 'I'll give you shelter from the storm.' "

Night was using *narf* like an everyday word, which for him it was. He might have used *angel* in the script, except the word came with such grand expectations of wings and harps. So he had invented a word with no expectations, and he had invented a nemesis for the narf, the scrunt. Paul had a bit about taming scrunts in a production called *The Scrunt Whisperer*. But if the movie worked, the scrunt would be terrifying.

The coexistence of good and evil—the theme of *Unbreakable*—Night could have made movies about that for the rest of his career. Night viewed *The Exorcist,* Satan taking up residence in an innocent girl, as more than a horror movie with a famous vomiting scene. He saw the film as a metaphor for life, his own or anyone else's. He fought the impulse to do or say or think some selfish thing, and tried to do something good or kind or inspiring. There were times when he failed. But it would have been easy for Night to lead a wholly narcissistic life. Instead, he kept regular office hours; worked hard but could also get away from work; set up treasure hunts for his girls on their birthdays; read Bhavna's doctoral thesis for content and typos; gave scholarships to the needy; treated his employees well; tipped generously at Christmastime. And he did it all with a distinct sense of fun. He wasn't going through the motions. It was exceptional, really. In my experience, watching elite athletes and others with off-the-chart drive, there's a certain obvious ruthlessness. To stay on top, you need it. Night's was beneath the surface.

The person talking to the actors on the morning of the read-through was the same person from that balmy evening at the Burches', when Night was so drunk with energy that he made everyone else there feel more alive. On the morning of the read-through, he was even more of a force, for he had endured a psychic blow since that balmy evening and survived it. He thought parents seeking perfect childhoods for their kids were deluded. He felt that childhood bumps made for stronger adulthoods. His childhood as Manoj, the outsider trying to find a way in, allowed him to write and direct as he did. (It particularly helped in writing *Lady*.) While Night talked to the actors, Noah, the boy playing Joey, sat on his real mother's lap staring at Night.

Jeffrey Wright, Noah's movie father, slipped in, cool and handsome and whispering apologies, and the read-through began. A man with a booming theatrical voice started to read: "Interior. Apartment kitchen. Morning. A group of Hispanic women are screaming. One is holding a broom. One is holding a spray can. One is holding a stainless steel meat cleaver. The last two are just screaming."

The group of Hispanic women, the five Perez de la Torre sisters, were all staying at a second-tier Philadelphia hotel, a Residence Inn, getting in character by speaking in Spanish and eating together at Mexican restaurants. They were all such lovely people, they might have been real-life narfs. In the days before the read-through, with nothing to do except work on their screaming, they did their work in parks and bathrooms. When they started screaming in the first scene, everybody became hysterical with laughter. That is, almost everybody. Robinov, the Warner Bros. executive, sat impassively. His face revealed nothing.

A tiny man, George Bass, playing the father of the sisters, read the first line of the script: "My daughter says she is very sorry for their scream. They are scared."

All through the read-through, the actors stared at their scripts. They took it all in with their ears but not their eyes. Except for Paul Giamatti. He had by far the biggest role, but he was already off script. Paul looked at George, who was across the room from him, fifty feet away, and delivered his first line: "T-tttell her not to be scared."

The room was arctic. You had no sense that outside, in the real world, it was a hot August day. Two of the Perez de la Torre sisters wore sensible cardigan sweaters. Jeff Robinov went into a steady, rhythmic shake, as if he were davening, or maybe he was just trying to keep warm. Everybody was focused. No cell phones went off. In rehearsals, Paul had joked about how the seat bottoms in multiplexes everywhere would start flapping the moment people heard Cleveland's stutter, but his *t-tttell* was endearing, just as Night had hoped.

There were no hovering hotel staff members or photographers or real-world intrusions of any sort. Night's eyes were darting constantly, working the room, going from the script to the actors to Robinov. He watched as Robinov made a hundred-foot walk to get something hot to drink. Night was mouthing every word being said. Often he was grinning maniacally. Sometimes he looked shocked, even though he knew every word and every stutter of the script.

Something fantastic was happening. For much of it, people were laughing, more than Night had thought they would. And then, near the end, there was a sudden, dramatic shift in mood, as there had been in the audition room with Cindy Cheung, when Night apologized for taking her from the comedy to the life-and-death part of the script.

Night read his own lines, the Vick part, very simply, as himself. Paul did not. With his body trembling and his lips quivering and his left hand on his broad forehead and his sandals off and his feet shaking, he delivered his lines with such power and conviction, you would have thought cameras were rolling. (There were no cameras at the read-through, and no Chris Doyle, either.) Paul's understanding of the script was profound.

The read-through came to an end after two and a half intense hours. There was applause and some whooping. Paul was about to make an abrupt exit.

"Wait, wait, wait, before you go pee," Night said.

"I've had to go since, like, page eighty-seven," Paul said.

"Just one thing."

Paul sat back down.

"The greatest thing about having made the movies I've made, with the success they've had, it's not . . ." Night didn't complete the thought, but you knew where it was going: It's not the private planes, the dinners out, the public adulation. He went on, "It's not any of the things you might think it is. The greatest thing is having the chance to write a movie like this and have it made by people who will let me cast whoever I want, and to get actors like all of you to play these parts and make it come alive. So, thank you. Now, Paul—go to the bathroom."

There was a magnificent spread for lunch, heaping bowls of delicious food, grilled vegetables and sliced fresh fruit and chicken with perfect grill lines. Night barely ate. He moved from table to table like a football coach at a pregame meal, listening and talking, giving pep talks and taking temperatures. One of the smokers said to him, "If the movie is half as good as this read-through thing, it's gonna kick ass." The Perez de la Torre sisters all hugged Night one by one. The room was filled with jazz and classical pieces played by young Noah on a grand piano with his mother looking on. One person after another congratulated Night. He had been fighting a headache and an upset stomach all morning, but now he was content. Not all the actors had found their voices, but that was to be expected. It was still early. The main thing was that the script worked.

Night could feel it. Jeff Robinov said some brief thing to Night, and Night smiled and patted him on the back.

After lunch, the workday was over for most of the actors, but Night had hours to go. He understood on the most primitive level that from that morning forward, there was a finite number of hours available to him to get the movie—this most personal of all his movies—as good as it could possibly be. He operated on the idea that the more time you spent on something, the harder you worked at it, the better it would be. Straight out of the Jordan playbook. He went to a suite in the hotel, and for the next five hours he directed rehearsals. His editor, Barbara Tulliver, was with him the whole time. So was Paul, now Night's trusted collaborator.

Other actors came and went at appointed times. Mary Beth Hurt came in, raised her script, and said, "I usually dog-ear these things. For this one I felt reverence." Maybe things were changing with her. At the read-through, she had read her lines as Night had written them. But Night had unfortunate news for Mary Beth: The script was too long, and he would be cutting some of her lines. She rubbed her bare summertime ankle in the vicinity of a tiny tattoo and said nothing. Paul started whistling as if he were hearing none of it. June and Cindy came in and worked on one of their Korean scenes. Sarita came in, flirty and confident, nothing like she had been on her audition day. Night called it her "awakening." He had notes for every actor in the cast, some more than others, a few of them written, all of them in his head. He had a perfect acoustic memory of how the line had been delivered in the read-through and what worked about it and what did not. He sat on the floor, looking up at his actors like a kindergartener staring at the teacher. His stamina was astounding.

Night gave Paul two notes. He had more, but he kept them to himself. He didn't want to overwhelm his lead. He was already worried about over-rehearsing him. Night said, "Sometimes I don't mind the word you decide to stutter on, but *narf* is a loaded word."

"Okay, fine," Paul said.

"So now this *narf* has come into your life, this angel they've sent down, and, just your luck, it's the worst one they've got."

Paul looked worn out. His eyes had spidery red lines across them. But he had taken it upon himself to keep Night laughing. He understood the immense pressure Night was under, and Paul was going to do what he could to keep him sane. He had worked for insane directors, and it was not pleasant.

Paul put on his professional voice-over voice and said: "Tonight on CBS: *Touched by a Crappy Angel!*"

At last there were no more actors around for Night to rehearse, and only the director and his editor remained. Night tried out something on Barbara, an idea for the closing credits, pictures of pools from all over the world, pools with nobody in them: Japanese pools, suburban American backyard pools, hotel pools, Olympic pools. Barbara, reserved by nature, did not start jumping up and down. She had edited *Signs* but hadn't been asked to edit *The Village*. She never knew why, and she had never asked. She was taking small steps back in.

Night's days were crowded, and everybody was trying to catch his eye. It wasn't easy to get his undivided attention. At the end of the read-through day, with the first day of shooting still two weeks away, Barbara saw a chance to say something about the script that was bothering her. A flaw in the script's logic, she felt. She knew from her work on *Signs* that you had to pick your spots carefully when you wanted to challenge Night. But she didn't want to have regrets later. If Night agreed with her, he could still do something about it. Her issue involved the scrunt's penchant for violence, when it pulled back and when it went all out.

Night was immediately defensive. "Are you giving me script notes? Because the writer's gone." He sounded like he had in Los Angeles, when he first shed his writer's skin and slipped into his aggressive director's outfit.

Barbara tried to persist, but she got nowhere.

Night said, "After twelve drafts, it should be air-fucking-tight."

He suddenly felt lonely and weary. The day had gone well, and he was looking forward to a cast dinner that evening, a chance to relax, hang out with the actors. There was nothing wrong with Barbara's question, but it made him feel like he had no one to turn to. All through the read-through, and all through the rehearsals afterward, he had been in a reverie. And now he was not. It made him feel that his script was failing, and that he was failing. The proof was right there: Barbara had found a hole when the script was supposed to be air-tight. It would never be right.

He said some appropriate conciliatory thing to Barbara—he'd think about it—and they started to head out. Script problems were back in his head. Then, as if he were in a movie, he got off the hotel elevator on the wrong floor and made a wrong turn and was heading to the hotel restaurant, Lacroix, scene of the Disney breakup dinner, as if on autopilot. He was almost at the maitre d's stand when he realized his error. Night hadn't thought of Disney all day, and suddenly the head shots—Nina and Co.—were taunting him again.

On the drive back to his house I asked Night what Robinov had said to him.

"Two words," Night said. There was frustration in his tone. " 'Good job.' That's it. Just 'Good job.' I thought there was magic in that room, I thought we had just done something brilliant.

When somebody gets up to get coffee right in the middle of a read-through, that's not a good sign. I didn't reach him. 'Good job.' What does that mean?" He felt just as he had with Barbara—*he* had failed.

His daughters were eating dessert when he got home, and he sat down with them. He could shift gears that way, even if it was a performance. Then he and Bhavna drove back into Philadelphia for dinner with the cast at a Cuban restaurant. Breakfast, lunch, and now dinner with the little United Nations of an acting troupe he had assembled, on the only day they would all be together.

At the end of a crowded day, Night went to bed thinking about Robinov's *Good job*. The voices were fighting.

Maybe he really doesn't like it—maybe that's why he kicked up the project to Alan Horn.

Maybe this, maybe that. Stop being a girly man, would you? He's just telling you that it's too early to get too confident.

Maybe there wasn't magic in the room—the one guy not hired by me says, "Good job."

Listen: Sometimes "good job" is just "good job."

Maybe Nina was right.

If she was, you'll find out soon enough. Just make your damn movie. Do the work and shut up.

Night and Paul had different ideas about fame. To Night, fame was a way to sell his movies. Paul didn't want people to know *him*, only the characters he played. He knew about the costs of fame.

In the New Haven of his boyhood, Paul's father was famous. A. Bartlett Giamatti was named the president of Yale when Paul was ten. Bart looked like an Italian movie star, a big man with dark skin and thick hair and sunglasses. In the 1980s,

Bart took on the Rev. Jerry Falwell and the educational policies of Ronald Reagan. He became a hero in a J. Press suit, at least to certain PBS viewers. Bart's term as baseball commissioner was only six months, from the start of the 1989 season, and the whole time he was burdened with the question of whether Pete Rose had bet on his team, the Cincinnati Reds. Fifteen years after Bart's death, it bothered Paul that his father was remembered mostly for Rose. To Paul, that was only a chapter.

The investigation of Rose, overseen by Bart, had been methodical and cautious (and proved to be correct). But all through it, Bart felt that *he* was on trial. On the August day in 1989 when Bart banished Rose from baseball, he was hanged in effigy in Cincinnati. Even though he had been a national figure for over twenty years, during the Rose matter, Bart endured a different level of scrutiny and fame.

"The actor Tony Curtis once told me that fame is an occupation in itself, that it is a separate thing," Bob Dylan wrote in *Chronicles,* a book that was popular on the Bristol set. "And Tony couldn't be more right." Some people are built for fame. Night was. People tried to sue him for this and that, usually claiming that Night had stolen material. Night knew what it was, grifters looking for pain-and-suffering handouts. Expensive lawyers sent them packing. There were crazy rumors about him on weird websites. Annoying, sometimes very annoying, but nothing Night couldn't handle. Bart had been built differently. He liked being a public figure when it was on his terms. But there's another kind of fame, fame as a beast you can't control, and Bart got that treatment only because the great Peter Edward Rose had a gambling problem. Paul watched it unfold from Seattle, where he was starting his acting career.

He didn't want to be a movie star, not in the conventional sense. Michael Caine wasn't really a movie star, he was a working actor, and Paul was filled with admiration for him. "The whiff of the hack," Paul said of him, *whiff* being the key word. It was praise. It meant this: You took a job, you worked it hard and well, you had a good time doing it, you deposited your check, you moved on. It takes a certain genius to make things that simple.

When Bart was a professor he was a rabble-rouser, shooting spitballs at the pompous and the stodgy, in touch with his inner wise guy. He was all mirth. Even as president of Yale, you could see Bart's wink: the raised right eyebrow, the twisted lips above the goatee. He was having a good time. And then he took another step up the ladder. Paul saw it all—the burden of ambition, the joys of mirth—and learned from it all. For Paul, mirth won. *Touched by a crappy angel!*

When you saw all the actors sitting together in the ballroom at the Rittenhouse, or when you saw Sarita or Bryce or Cindy or Paul hanging out in the production office in Bristol, eating bagels and throwing darts and playing Ping-Pong and waiting for rehearsals to begin, it became obvious how the movie was cast. All the actors were underworked, in different ways. Bryce was finicky about the directors she would work for. Paul had never been asked to carry a high-profile studio movie. Cindy had never been in a studio movie at all, and Sarita often went to India for work, daughter in tow. On and on it went. They were all character actors, really.

None of the actors was jaded. All of them wanted to be there. Nobody was there just for the paycheck. They all had a work ethic. There was not a true star among them. To the degree that Paul was, he was a reluctant star. He had no entourage. Nobody to spruce up his hair or select his shirt or entertain him at dinner. On weekends he commuted home to his wife and son in Brooklyn. He would have taken the train home, or driven himself, except the teamsters required him to have his own car and driver. He resisted the treatment where he could. When producers offered him an assistant, he passed. He didn't need somebody to make dinner reservations for him. His thing was to walk right in. He needed to travel light. If he let people treat him like a star, he'd lose the thing that made him good.

Night didn't have that problem. *Lady* would be marketed as *The Village* had been, as a movie written and directed by M. Night Shyamalan. He was the movie's star. Ever since *Unbreakable,* the selling of Night's movies had been shrewdly efficient. Whenever he was selling his current movie, he was selling the next one, too. If you sell one movie on Bruce Willis's name and the next on Mel Gibson's, you're starting over each time. When the *Lady* marketing campaign was being planned at Warner Bros., before the first frame of the movie was shot, Night was always in mind.

The actors treated the script like a text. They parsed it for work and for sport. In Cindy's audition, and during the read-through and at rehearsals, there was one consistently perplexing moment. It comes early in the script, when Paul asks Cindy, "Could you look up the w-word *narf* for me?"

In the early versions of the script, the response is what you might expect: "Why would I know this nonsensical word?" But in the sale script and the shooting script, Young-Soon's response is "It is a bedtime story, Mr. Heep."

At a rehearsal, Paul said to Cindy, "It's weird. Very strange. Here's this word, nobody's ever heard it before, and now the guy goes up to some chick sitting by a pool and says, 'Can you look up the word *narf* for me?' And she's like 'Of course. Yeah, sure. I was waiting for you to ask.' You know? It's amazing. Very strange. I mean it's cool. Very cool. But amazing." But Paul didn't ask Night to explain it. Night was the writer, and Paul knew how much thought the writer had put into each word. Night had chosen the name Cleveland because he felt people would underestimate somebody with that name. Paul figured Night must have had his reasons for Young-Soon's matter-of-fact response, and he was correct. Anyway, asking pointed questions, that wasn't how Paul worked. Cindy was comfortable asking direct questions, but Night had already told her how to play the line at her audition. (When you hear *narf*, think Little Red Riding Hood; how can you *not* know what it means?) If it worked for Night, she'd make it work for her. It was his script.

Night described that poolside exchange as "the most important scene in the movie." (It was an ever-shifting phrase for him.) When I asked him about the narf line, he gave me a five-minute answer. He could go for five minutes on any script question. He said that when Cleveland first says the word *narf*, the moviegoer is hearing a new word, but Young-Soon is not. In the casualness of her response, we're supposed to take a step into her world, popcorn bags on our laps. He had thought it all out. I'm sure there are astronauts who think like that, mapping out every possibility, but in my experience only Tiger Woods has that move. Tiger can play every shot in a tournament in his head, on a practice tee, before the event begins. He and Night both had not only intelligence, but discipline. If it was Eastern or not, for either of them, I did not know, but it was impressive. Sometimes, when Night was explaining the genesis of a line to the actors, they would take notes in the white spaces of their scripts, as if Night were a college professor and the material would be covered on the next test.

One morning at Bristol, Sarita and Paul and Bryce had all arrived early for rehearsal. Night was not there yet. Bryce said cheerfully, "Do you want to read lines?"

"Yes!" Sarita said.

"Yeah, sure," Paul said with limited enthusiasm. He was sipping a black coffee.

Bryce immediately suggested they turn to scene 53, page 67. It was a scene that had all three of them in it. She knew every page of the script.

Sarita turned to it. "But you don't have any lines here," she said. Bryce's work in the scene was all pantomime.

"Oh, let's not do it, then," Bryce said. She had her breakfast beside her, a murky-looking drink in a mason jar. "It's all about *me*!"

It was the kind of joke she never made around Night. She treated him as if he were a god, responsible for her birth as an actress, and she was often nervous in his presence, like Moses before the burning bush. Bryce once said to me, "When I'm around Night, I feel like I'm my inauthentic self."

But this morning, there was no Night. The three actors, with no parental supervision, before nine A.M., were working all on their own. The hardest-working people in show business.

In the scene, Cleveland is trying to learn more from Story about the rules of the narf world. Story speaks only in hand gestures, as if playing charades, and these are interpreted by Anna.

"I find this scene to be the hardest thing in the whole movie," Paul said. It was a long scene, six pages in the script, all exposition. (Nina had said to Night, "There are so many rules!" Night answered, "I know. I was thinking of putting in more.") Everybody else worked off a fastened script, but Paul carried a short stack of individual sheets, though he seldom needed them. Sometimes he'd curl the sheets into a tube and shove it into his back right pocket.

They were doing their work when Night arrived. Bryce said, "This scene is *so* hard."

Night nodded sympathetically and said, "This is a scene that can fall apart very quickly."

He made a few quick adjustments. He put Sarita on her

knees, her lower legs underneath her, as if she were praying. "Story's talking to you in sign language, and you're getting more and more fluent in her language," Night said. They did it again, and it was better. Bryce suggested another try, but Night said it was time to move on. Professor Shyamalan was in. Another day was under way.

During the rehearsals, particularly after the read-through, in the period leading up to the first day of shooting, an intimacy was developing between the actors and Night. He was being accepted as an actor himself. There was storytelling, much chitchat, revelations here and there. Bill Irwin did not own a TV. One of the smokers, Joe Reitman, was dating Annie Duke, the star poker player. The head smoker, Jared Harris, was the son of the actor Richard Harris. On it went.

Night had assembled a group of actors with no bombast. They were a study in self-deprecation.

Bryce said to Paul one afternoon, "Have you noticed rehearsals move much more quickly when I don't have any lines?"

"There's a reason for that," Paul answered. "*I* have all the lines in the movie. 'Vick, how long have you been writing your book? Wait, wait. Don't tell me. Six months!'"

One day they were blocking a scene—who stands where and when—and Bryce said to Paul, "Did you know my right side is my better side?"

"Really. How can you know such a thing?"

"I noticed something going on with my face, and I asked my father about it, and he said, 'Oh, yeah. I've known that for years. Your right side is more chiseled. Your left side is sort of rounded.'"

"Wow," Paul said. His constant state of astonishment made people comfortable around him. "I wish my father would have told me I have a better side. A chiseled side. Man. My face is a balloon."

Night, falling in with his actors, sometimes assumed that self-mocking tone, even though it wasn't his natural voice. He told about his first day of shooting *The Sixth Sense*, a kid director working with a big star, Bruce Willis. "I'm setting up a shot, and Bruce is in his trailer. Somebody comes up to me and says, 'Bruce wants to know what's taking so long.' Somebody else comes up and says, 'Harvey Weinstein's on the phone. He says he has to speak to you *now*.' And I'm like 'Oh shit—what do I do?' "

In preproduction, the hair and makeup people would try out different looks on the actors and take pictures, so they would have records. Sometimes Night would sit with them and thumb through magazines. In high school, it had always been work for Night to be social, trying to fit in, but now he was at the center of it all. He was reading a story in *Glamour* about Tom Cruise's girlfriend, Katie Holmes. "It says here that she's an ordinary girl from Ohio who has become Hollywood's hottest actress. Is that actually true? Because I'm a Hollywood director, and I've never thought about her for anything." Then he said, not with disbelief but because he wanted to know, "Who reads *Glamour*?"

The conversation went from Katie Holmes to Reese Witherspoon to Kirsten Dunst to Charlize Theron to Angelina Jolie. A hair lady was showing Night a picture of how he might wear his hair as Vick, but Night shook his head and said, "Too Bay City Rollers." She knew exactly what that meant: too 1975. Somebody said, "How 'bout that Angelina Jolie? She rode right through that incest rumor thing. Looked like it might slow her down, but she went straight damn through it." Something having to do with the actress kissing her brother at a long-ago Oscars. Night went back to Katie Holmes and Tom Cruise. He was fascinated by the hold Scientology had on the actor. He asked, "Who *is* L. Ron Hubbard?"

He was often funny that way, appealingly snide. In his office one day, Night was looking at a draft of a Warner Bros. press release that would announce the first day of shooting. Night read it out loud to a little group: " 'A journey into the heart of the human condition, exploring the epic beauty that can be found in the everyday and the extraordinary things we can achieve when we strive to find our purpose in life.' Why don't they just write 'Don't come see this movie'?"

But Night knew you had to think about marketing from the beginning. One day in his office before shooting began, a small group gathered, and Night showed a mock *Lady* trailer he had made, one that would go to Alan Horn and Jeff Robinov and some of the Warner Bros. marketing people. Technically, it was a mock teaser. About six months before a big movie goes out, movie audiences start seeing teasers, vague shorts designed to plant the idea of the movie in your head. Much closer to the release date, the trailer goes out, meant to give you a glimpse of the movie and make you want to see it.

Before showing the mock teaser, Night said, "If I could do *The Village* again, I'd market it as a romance. I'd lead with the romance in the trailer, then give them the scare at the end. I told the Warner Brothers guys they could bill *Lady in the Water* as a romance, and they were like *What?* But *Titanic* is the number one movie of all time. And it's a romance."

He turned off the light, Jose hit a button, and Brick's drawings from the storyboards filled a large-screen TV. A moody piercing violin solo came up. The pictures depicted Cleveland at the pool with a flashlight in hand. Cleveland carrying Story. Cleveland writing in his journal. There was no voice-over, only a tenor singing a snippet of a modern opera in Italian. Then, near the end, in a simple typeface, were the words: *Cleveland Heep's life is about to change. Forever.* Followed by: *M. Night Shyamalan's* Lady in the Water. *A Bedtime Story.*

You wouldn't think a one-minute movie made with still drawings could be so beautiful. Where the script was cryptic at times, the teaser was only simple and poetic and gorgeous. Bryce said, "People are going to go to the movies to watch *Dukes of Hazzard II* or whatever, and that teaser's going to be the most memorable thing they see." It seemed like a true statement. The teaser captured the particular kind of love at the heart of the story.

"I think it's great," said Sam Mercer, the producer. "It shows the true tone of the piece." By that he meant romance, of an odd sort, over creepy suspense.

You wondered how the real teaser, with the actual actors and the Chris Doyle cinematography, could be any better, to say nothing of the movie. If the movie turned out to be as good as that teaser, Night would have made something special. Everybody in the room felt that. Night was feeling exceptionally good.

Everyone in the room cleared out except Jose. Something was bothering him.

Night and Jose had known each other a long time, since before *The Sixth Sense*. They had met in a karate class and had become good friends before Night hired him. Originally, he had been Night's assistant. On *Lady*, Jose was the associate producer. It can be hard when friends work together and there's an imbalance in power, more so when the boss is seven years younger. In style and temperament, Night and Jose were totally different. Jose's feet were firmly on the ground, and Night lived for the esoteric. But there were things that only Jose could tell Night, because he'd been there when nobody else was. He had credibility that way. He used his influence judiciously.

"*The Village*, that idea about selling it as a romance?" Jose said.

"Yeah?" Night said quickly.

"I know a lot of people who said if they had known it was a romance, they never would've gone."

He had wanted to remind Night that *Titanic* was first sold as a disaster movie and that the teaser for *Lady* needed hints of scariness and suspense to keep Night's core fans coming back. But Night's impatience was palpable, and Jose stopped short.

Night was overcome with anger and loneliness and despair. He was on a high after showing his mock teaser, and now it was gone. It was the same sentiment he had felt with Barbara after the read-through: *I have failed; I am alone.* In his anger and frustration, Night pounced on Jose's "they never would've gone" and said, "Don't make decisions based on those people, or you'll be working at Burger King."

Jose did a lot of things Night never knew about. Sarita had mentioned that she liked a certain dish at the read-through dinner and Jose arranged to have a quart of it sent to her. He created goodwill. Burger King? Jose, hurt and angry, walked out of the office without saying another word; Night was left sitting in his big swivel chair behind his big director's desk, and now he was truly all alone.

Night wanted to edit the movie on film. Nobody was doing that anymore except Steven Spielberg. Studio movies were still shot on film. (Every so often a movie shot on videotape, like *The Blair Witch Project*, slipped through the cracks and into multiplexes.) But they were all edited digitally, on a computer, which allowed a director to look at dozens of different takes in rapid succession, with clicks of a button. Nobody was splicing anymore. The term *cutting room*, in a literal sense, had become an anachronism. But Night wondered why the movies that made the deepest impression on him—*The Birds, E.T., Lolita, Raiders of the Lost Ark, The*

Godfather, Jaws, The Exorcist, Being There—were all edited on film, as all films were until the early 1990s. Night wondered if writers wrote better on a typewriter or by longhand than they did on a computer. If writing is rewriting, as E. B. White said, it was certainly easier to rewrite on a computer. But Night thought "easier" was an unworthy goal. He imagined writers (screenwriters included) thought better and longer before committing something to paper in the days when rewriting was clumsy and time-consuming and expensive. He argued that writing was not actually rewriting but thinking. Editing on film was like writing on a typewriter. Editing on film forced a director to think more about the essence of the scene and how the scenes—141 of them in *Lady in the Water*—add up to a movie.

Sam Mercer and Barbara Tulliver were both wary of editing on film. There were reasons the whole movie industry—except Spielberg—had gone to the computer. Everybody else was saying that editing on a computer was faster, cheaper, better. Night would acknowledge only the first two, faster and cheaper.

"David Mamet," Night said to Barbara. She had edited eight of his movies. Mamet had switched to editing on a computer to save money. Compared to Night's budgets, Mamet's budgets were loose change. "He writes on a typewriter, right?" Like a good lawyer, Night knew the answers to his questions. "You keep talking about downtime for me. I'm not worried about it. I'll use that time to get a cup of coffee and think." Night was not actually a coffee drinker—he was wired enough without it—but he was making a point.

Sam said, "If you want to edit on film, it's going to be expensive." To edit on film, Spielberg needed a team of seven editors. To edit on a computer, typically on a system called Avid, you could do it with four. More editors meant a bigger payroll and the need for more space. After a movie is shot, editing typically takes place at an editing studio, but *Lady* would be edited in Night's converted barn at the farm. Night said he could make the space for the extra editors. He was ready to move the Ping-Pong table if that was necessary.

"You're talking to me like I've never edited on film before," Night said to him. He felt with Sam then as he had felt with Jose after watching the teaser. Sam wasn't honoring what Night wanted to be: an old-school director who really believed the old ways were better. "I learned how to edit on film at NYU. I edited my first movie on film. What I'm telling you is that I'm willing to sacrifice convenience for meaning. I'm telling you I'd rather walk to the restaurant than drive, because you remember things along the way when you're walking. You keep talking about how frustrated I'll be, waiting. Last couple times, I never left the editing room. I *want* to get out of the room. I want to see the scene in my head first."

Every time he had to fight for himself—with Barbara, with Jose, now with Sam—he was left feeling all alone. Maybe it sounds like Night needed a yes-man, but Night would tell you that wasn't it. He needed somebody who could give him what Nina took away that night at Lacroix. He needed someone who could help him drive out the doubt.

In preproduction, there were weekly meetings with all the department heads. The meetings always grew bigger and longer as the first day of shooting got closer. There would be reports from the stunt coordinator and the transportation chief and the editor and the prop master, all of the many departments in the surprisingly regimented business of making a movie. Surprising because, at its core, it's a creative business. The impetus for the whole enterprise comes from a writer. As business models go, that's pretty damn shaky. And in this case, the writer was the boss, and the boss was in a frail place.

There was always some tense area, somebody behind on something, often construction-related, usually because of permit requirements or the intense summer heat or a delivery failure or equipment malfunction, the stuff of everyday life. Rather than make unrealistic promises, people would lower expectations, and Night would get frustrated. As a boss, his standards were high, sometimes unrealistically so. If you had taken the gig expecting just another job, it was the wrong place to be.

There's a show-business axiom, attributed to W. C. Fields, that says you should never work with kids or animals, and Night had both in *Lady*. He was struggling to find the right child actors partly because he wanted to hire local kids, which meant fewer experienced actors to choose from. For his animals, Night wasn't sure what to do. After his bad experience with the computer-made alien at the end of *Signs*, he was determined not to go down that road again for his scrunt in *Lady*. He was thinking about putting a dog in a scrunt outfit but was convinced that a mechanical creature not only would be more practical, it would work better visually, too. Then there was an animal scene with monarch butterflies. Butterflies are hard to work with, as they don't readily take direction. The script required a butterfly to land on white-haired Mrs. Bell, played by Mary Beth Hurt.

At a production meeting, Night was going around the room when he got to Jimmy Mazzola, his prop man. Because an actor was going to touch a butterfly, it was by definition a prop, so the butterflies fell to Jimmy. Night knew that Jimmy had developed, for other movies, a mechanical butterfly operated by remote control, but Night was worried about how a mechanical butterfly would look on Mrs. Bell's arm in close-up. Night used few close-ups, so the shot would come under particular scrutiny. Jimmy was called upon to give his report on the state of *Lady* props. You had to be manic about detail to be a good property master. Jimmy was working on a flashlight for Cleveland Heep that would work underwater; a crossword puzzle with boxes big enough for the camera to pick up; an authentic Philadelphia public-transportation bus that would appear in the background. Scores of other things. This morning Jimmy didn't bother with any of that. When called upon for his state-of-the-props report, he uncupped his beefy hands, and out came a real monarch butterfly, flying up toward the fluorescent lights. "I got hundreds more—and a guy who can harness them and get 'em to go wherever you want!"

Night watched the butterfly with astonished glee. Jimmy was bringing honor to himself and joy to Night and reminding everybody in the room of the power of surprise and the magic of moviemaking. Night had failed to inspire Jeff Robinov at the read-through, Barbara Tulliver after it, Jose Rodriguez with the teaser, Sam Mercer with the idea of editing on film. But Jimmy he was reaching. He was inspiring Jimmy, and Jimmy was inspiring him.

Night organized and played in a weekly basketball game, often four-on-four, full-court, in a sweltering school gym. The group would play for close to three hours, with few breaks, and Night was seldom winded. He was the commissioner of these evenings, and he made up the teams in a reasonably evenhanded way, although his team won more often than not. The other players worked with computers or sold things, they had regular jobs, and they did not treat Night as an artiste. They hacked at him and got in his face. Nobody ever talked about work. They played three or four games—sometimes five—to eleven, one point for a regular basket, two points for anything from the normal three-point range. Night ran all night long.

Of any player, Night took winning and losing by far the

most seriously. He was like that in all games. He was a good Ping-Pong player, and if he could hold a fledgling player to seven points, it pleased him. But basketball was his main sport. At age thirty-five, he played like a starting guard on a decent suburban high school team. He dribbled well, ran well, played aggressively on defense, could get off a shot in traffic. His passing game was not a strength.

One evening Night's team lost the first two games, won the third, and was leading the fourth game 9–2. The game got tied, and Night made an urgent plea to his teammates: "Let's see if there's *any* manhood left in us—*c'mon!*" It was the same voice he had used with his cousins years earlier, trying to get them to will the cup into moving. But Night himself missed a fastbreak layup that would have been a game winner. Awful. The shot was one he'd make ten times out of ten if he was just horsing around. It looked like performance anxiety.

After the game, Night was analyzing what had happened, as if it mattered. "I get so agenda-driven," he said. "I start thinking about how much I want to win the game instead of just getting into the flow of the game." For him, it *did* matter. Why else do it?

A couple of nights before the first day of shooting, Night had invited everybody working on the movie—the actors, the teamsters, the caterers, Chris Doyle, everybody—to a screening of one of his favorite movies, *The Wizard of Oz*. He had rented a theater at a big mall multiplex with sixteen screens and sent out paper invitations. Paul had asked Night, "Can I bring a friend?"

Night wanted a crowd. Kids were welcome, spouses were welcome, Paul's friend was welcome. Bryce came with her fiancé. Night sat with Bhavna and the girls and several of his cousins. But attendance was poor, and Night was devastated. He wanted the cast and crew to think of *Lady* as the world thought of *Oz*, as something magical, but the message wasn't getting out. Chris Doyle didn't come, Paul didn't come. Only about twenty people showed up. Night blamed the turnout on the fact that he hadn't been involved enough in getting the invitations out. He hadn't put his stamp on it. Looking at the nearly empty auditorium, Night felt like a preacher with nobody to preach to.

Night hadn't seen the movie in a long time. Its lessons, this time, seemed odd to him. That the most important thing in life is not how much love you give but how much you get? The Scarecrow has no brain but becomes a genius because a wizard grants him a phony degree? But Night still found the movie to be powerful.

A trio of misfits comes together and helps a little girl get home—it's a win-win. Night hoped to do about the same in *Lady*. The residents of the Cove come to the aid of a creature called Story who's trying to get back home. They help her and she helps them. The whole thing may be a dream, or not. There's not a single profane word in *Oz* (which would surely get a PG rating today: *scary themes; melting witch; homosexual innuendo*). Neither was there any cursing in *Lady*, not even from the smokers. Most significantly, the movie was about faith, about what you can achieve if you believe. Dorothy is going to get herself home, one way or another. *Lady* dealt with the same thing. But that the opportunity to see a pristine print of *The Wizard of Oz*, on a big screen, as the guest of your director, that *that* did not draw a crowd worried Night to his core. He wondered if Nina was right, if nobody cared about the old magic anymore. After the screening he said to me, "I thought being old-school was a good thing for me. After the *Oz* screening, I wondered if I was even relevant."

Night and his little group were watching *The Wizard of Oz*

in Theater 1 on an ordinary Thursday night in August. Up and down the hallway, there were fifteen other screens in action. Across the corridor from *Oz* was *Hustle & Flow*, with Terrence Howard playing a budding rapper and reciting the lyrics to a composition in progress that would have sounded out of place in the Land of Oz:

> *You ain't know you fuckin' with a street nigga*
> *From the gutta pimp tight slash drug dealer . . .*

In the next theater was a small group watching one of the acclaimed chase scenes in *The Dukes of Hazzard*, the tension of the hunt heightened by the threat of motion sickness from a good-looking girl in the backseat. Nearby was a snack stand selling small sodas for four dollars (the real profit centers for the theater owners) and next to that another theater, virtually empty, showing *Deuce Bigalow: European Gigolo*. The theaters were all nearly empty, at the height of the summer blockbuster season.

The following morning, a Friday in mid-August, there was a final production meeting. Monday would be the first day of shooting. The group had grown so large that the meeting was held in the Bristol Moose Lodge, a mile or two from the set. Chris Doyle, normally so voluble, said almost nothing and wore dark oversize sunglasses, Elton-style. Betsy Heimann gave a terse report on the state of wardrobe and even Night, with his ESP, could not figure out what was bothering them. He asked Jose to find out the specifics, because he knew only the general category. On Monday, shooting would begin on a strange and complicated movie. If you wanted to believe in Night and what he was trying to do, you had to be nervous.

That afternoon, Night read a story in *The Hollywood Reporter*, comments from the new Disney CEO, Bob Iger, about the future of the movie in the movie house. The new Disney boss said the time had come for studios to consider releasing movies in movie theaters and on DVD at the same time. "The rules, in terms of consumption, have changed so dramatically," Iger said.

That subject infuriated Night. It wasn't just Iger. Whole sections of the industry were starting to say the same thing. Night was appalled. He wrote scripts and exposed film and edited it with only one thing in mind, ultimately: what the picture would look like to the moviegoer in a movie house. That's how movies were meant to be seen. That's where the magic happened.

His first great movie experience had come in early summer 1981, when Night was still Manoj and not yet eleven. He and a friend had gone to see *Raiders of the Lost Ark*. Manoj didn't want to see it—his interest in movies was only ordinary then—and when they arrived, the theater was practically sold out. Manoj and his friend couldn't get two seats together, and Manoj ended up sitting by himself next to an elderly couple. The old man said something to his wife and left. When he returned, he had a Coke and a popcorn for the skinny little Indian boy sitting next to him. Manoj was awed by the stranger's generosity. How it affected what happened next, Night never figured out, but the lights went down, the movie came on, and the boy went into a dream state. Three people had a major impact that day on young Manoj Shyamalan: the old man sitting next to him; Harrison Ford, playing Indiana Jones; and the director, Steven Spielberg. From that day on, his life had a path.

Night couldn't see straight, reading the news story. *Does Bob Iger understand anything about the magic of movies? Now Disney wants to ditch the theater experience in the name of greater profits?*

Night called Jeremy Zimmer. "Can you believe this Iger shit? Get me a reporter I can talk to, I've got to respond to this."

It was unusual; Night seldom wanted press, unless he was selling one of his movies.

"If Disney wants to go down this road, I'll fight them every step of the way. I'm in on this, and I'm in strong."

Before he left for the day, Night read a note Chris Doyle had slipped onto his desk. Doyle and Night had talked about how the whole movie should be shot in a gloaming, how the movie's days would never have any brightness to them, and how its nights would never be pitch-black. Doyle had been conducting experiments to achieve that look. It was dangerous, what Doyle was trying to pull off. It thrilled Night. He felt he had started to reach Doyle, and vice-versa. Doyle's note was a kind of haiku.

> *M'nght*
> *it works!*
> *our "night" is*
> *so romantic, ethereal*
> *and "true" to all*
> *I hoped to bring to you . . .*
> *(Thanks for your trust)*

Night smiled wanly. He stepped out of the old 3M building and into the late muggy dusk of an August evening. It had been another twelve-hour day, but Night wasn't counting hours, he was trying to use them. Franny was waiting in the car with the engine running and the air-conditioning on. Night got into the passenger seat and pushed it back as far as it would go. On the drive home, he fell into a deep sleep. Preproduction was over. Monday was the day.

7.

The night before the first day of shooting, I asked Night about the state of his head. "I've done six other movies, and I've never felt this level of anxiety. My hope for this shoot is to be ruthless, electric, and dangerous," he said.

He didn't sound like a man who'd found peace.

When Night arrived on the set at 6:25 A.M. on opening day, his director of photography was already lit. Night was wearing an embroidered button-down shirt, a departure from his everyday rock-band T-shirts, all done up, the way kids used to be for their first day of school. Chris Doyle was wearing a mustard-colored silk boxer's robe. There was alcohol on his breath and in every manic movement he made. He grabbed Jimmy Mazzola's genitalia (through his shorts), and he lifted the shirt of the head stuntman, Jeff Habberstad, to kiss him on the stomach. Jimmy was a character and a Brooklynite, a guy from the neighborhood, he often said, and he'd seen a lot in his years. He laughed it off. But Jeff was a lean runner from Washington State, with pictures of his wife and three kids on his travel coffee mug. His thing was to calculate and prepare for risk—he once jumped out of a truck that had been dropped from a plane—not to cater to the eccentric. There was pain in the stuntman's face. But it was the first of forty-five days, and he made no fuss. Then Doyle gave Paul Giamatti the same treatment as Jimmy Mazzola, and Paul did just like Jimmy, he rode it out. Doyle greeted Cindy Cheung with a sort of tackle, a kiss on her stomach, and immediately asked makeup to "make her elbows more beautiful." Who knew what was wrong with them, but Chris Doyle saw things that only he and the camera did. More than once Night said, "His eye is unbelievable. I can't imagine making this movie without him." That's how he felt, even with the muddy screen tests, the stomach kissing, and everything else. Doyle was helping Night feel dangerous. Doyle had come up with a new name for himself, this time an American one: Super Chris. As if he were indestructible.

On the back of his director's chair, Night's long surname was misspelled; the buzzing chorus of the August cicadas was overwhelming the sensitive boom mikes; and a boy actor, required only to lick his palm and slap his kid sister across the cheek in one fell swoop, could not get it done. It was the first scene Night was shooting. Movies are almost never shot in the sequence of the script, and Night was not scheduled to film the screaming Perez de la Torre sisters until much later in the nine-week shoot. Lick-Slap Kenny was supposed to steal the second scene, but Night had no reason to think he'd do well. The kid—hired through a Philadelphia casting agency—had been consistently, comically terrible in rehearsals, where his lick-slap was stuck in first gear, so slow it looked like he was lapping up the side of a delicate triple-scoop ice-cream cone. Night had said, "Here, let me show you how I used to do it with my cousins." Quick lick, quick slap. Slam-bam. But the boy had his own metabolism. In rehearsal, Paul was so amused by the slo-mo lick-slap that he hid his face behind his script.

There were four characters in the scene: Kenny and his sister, Alice; Mr. Farber, the film critic; and Cleveland. Paul had his game face on, muttering to himself between takes, walking around in circles. With his beard and his glasses and Cleveland Heep's drab green work shirt, Paul looked something like a young Fidel Castro. It was cool at dawn, but by late morning it was humid and hot, and by Take 7 there was perspiration coming through the back of Paul's shirt. Not what Night was looking for.

"Can we get wardrobe in here?" Night asked.

"I am a human being, do human beings not sweat?" Paul said, using the voice and cadence of Shylock. (*If you prick us, do we not bleed?*)

Paul was working. Upon seeing Kenny and Alice in the company of children, Paul went for his first big stutter, his own personal child protection act. The way he played the stutter, it was almost an epileptic convulsion. Cleveland was trying to warn Kenny and Alice to stay away from the pool after hours.

"It's not a"—suck air, suck air, suck air, suck air, suck air, suck air—"child-friendly environment."

Kenny had one line. One lick-slap and one line: "She's not supposed to talk about the boogers!" That's it. But the boy kept delivering it in a monotone he could not shake. It was as if the exclamation point meant nothing to him. Night ran through thirteen takes, ate up the long morning on it. In between takes, the boy nervously shifted his weight from one foot to the other, the international symbol for a child in distress.

Night wrapped the scene. He had been good-natured the whole time. You never would have known he was frustrated. The two kids walked over to a production assistant. She would escort them back to their mothers.

The boy playing Kenny said to her, "At the end of the movie, like after the credits, are they gonna show all my mess-ups?"

"Oh, no. They wouldn't do that," the PA said.

The boy was a true local. He lived near Bristol. He had his fingers curled underneath the bottom of his shirt, a mini–football jersey with a lineman's number on it, 92. It fit, all the way around.

"But you know, on the DVDs, they have those blooper sections? They put the mess-ups in those blooper sections."

Only Night knew that would never happen. For one thing, his DVDs didn't have blooper sections. For another, he'd be shooting the scene again. But the next time he wouldn't be casting locally. He'd be going to Doug Aibel and getting two new kids from New York, kids who had done plenty of commercials or Broadway or summer stock, little seasoned pros who could take direction. It was only the first day, and things were not going well.

In a casual way, Paul had been making a study of Lick-Slap Kenny. He was always watching. If something interested him, if it was peculiar enough, he could remember it for a long time. His range was impressive. He knew the names of various deposed warlords; select Spiro Agnew quotes; the books of the surfing novelist Kem Nunn; the music of the bluesman Skip James. He had a working knowledge of superconductivity and also prizefighting. He and Night were often citing bizarre, hilarious lines from the most obscure movies. From famous movies, he had impressive recall for little-known actors who dominated inconsequential scenes. From *American Graffiti*, for instance, when the actor Bo Hopkins, playing a gang leader, offers to make Richard Dreyfuss a Pharaoh, a gang member.

Paul had filed several Bob Balaban roles in his head, especially from the sequel to *2001*, called *2010*, a movie that had an audience of about eighteen people, by Balaban's estimate. Balaban was one of Paul's favorite actors ("I love that guy"), and on the first day of shooting, they had a scene together. Balaban didn't have a word in it, just a series of quizzical looks. After one of his many silent takes, Balaban looked at Night and said, "Was that too much?" Paul admired that kind of acting in general—raising an eyebrow, cocking the head—and Balaban's mute work in that scene specifically. But he didn't tell Balaban that, just as he didn't bring up *2010*. He wasn't being churlish (although he could be). In between takes, he and Balaban talked and joked about the acting life. But Paul wasn't comfortable talking about another actor's work in his presence, particularly an older and well-established actor. In Paul's mind, why would Bob Balaban, twenty-two years older than Paul, with appearances in *Midnight Cowboy* and *Close Encounters* and *Waiting for Guffman* and scores of others, possibly care what a tot like Paul would have to say about his work? There was a modesty there, the reason Night was so eager for him to play Cleveland Heep. Part of Paul's code was never to put pressure on another person to say some complimentary thing back to him. He never praised Night for that reason. He found fishing for compliments repulsive. About the only thing worse (in this category) was fulsome praise from an agent (his own knew better) or a producer, somebody like that.

"There was only one time I got upset during that whole Oscar thing," Paul said. He wasn't talking about the '06 awards, when he was nominated for *Cinderella Man*, but from the year before, when he wasn't nominated for a Best Actor award as Miles, the wine snob/crappy writer in *Sideways,* though many people felt he should have been. "That was when somebody said, 'I wish that guy would stop whining about it already.' That was complete bullshit, because I *never* whined about it." That had to be true. You couldn't imagine Paul calling attention to himself that way. Paul took the job on *Lady* not because Night had directed two monster hits (*The Sixth Sense* and *Signs*) but because he liked *Unbreakable*. Night had worked with huge, flamboyant, outgoing stars: Bruce Willis, who came with an entourage; Mel Gibson, who commuted from Philadelphia to Los Angeles every weekend in his private jet, inviting anybody who needed a lift to come along. Now Night had *this* guy.

During the rehearsal period, Bill Irwin was just completing a Broadway run of Edward Albee's *Who's Afraid of Virginia Woolf?* He had won a Tony for his role as George, the alcoholic history professor, a role made famous by Richard Burton. But when Irwin met Paul on the *Lady* set, one of the first things he said was "I heard you did a pretty mean George." Paul was astonished. He had done *Virginia Woolf* at Yale, in front of nobody, fifteen years earlier. He was curious to know how Bill Irwin even knew about it. But he didn't ask. Paul never wanted to seem like he was fishing.

It was a sort of situational coldness, what Paul had. I asked him if that quality might have been a taciturn New England trait left over from another generation. (Bart's mother was as Old Yankee as you could get.) "I don't think so," Paul said. "I think it's more a macho Italian thing."

There's a lot of downtime on a movie set, hours on end of it. You'd see Paul nod enthusiastically while somebody told a pinot noir story or some other wine story rekindled by *Sideways*. You'd see him grip a balcony railing with ten fingers and watch the dolly grip get ready for the next shot. You'd see him eat in twelve minutes before retreating to a book and classical music in his trailer, or sit around forever and talk about Werner Herzog documentaries. In time, it became apparent that the whole Michael Caine thing—take job, do job—was only an ideal for Paul. It wasn't his natural move, to make things that easy.

You could not imagine a less pretentious person, but in *Sideways*, Paul had owned Miles's writerly preciousness. (Could they have come up with a better name than Miles? Perfect.) You could hear affectation early on, when Miles goes to an arty coffeehouse and orders a *"spinach* croissant." That must take skill, to get so much out of one word. Paul shrugged it off. "Yeah, well, I've known a lot of pretentious people. So I just stole from those people."

Night saw in Paul not only exceptional humility but exceptional honesty. Paul knew himself. If you went down a road where your need for adulation or money or both was your highest priority, you'd become like a drug addict looking for a fix, selling your body to get stoned again. The need for applause and gaudy paydays could kill your art. Bob Dylan had avoided that road, and Paul was doing the same. He knew when his work was good. If, in your head, you allowed a worshipful public to build you up, then you had empowered those people to take you down, too. It didn't have to be a big group. If you measured yourself by the collective opinion of a clique of powerful executives, that could make you crazy. (Night had found that out.) Paul did a lot of smart things to protect himself.

For Night, the fame-and-money road always beckoned. After the success of *Signs,* he could have made easy money and mono-name fame his highest priorities. Instead, he made *The Village,* offbeat and brown. He stuck to storytelling just as Paul stuck to acting, taking over whatever character he had signed on to play next.

That opening Monday was a field day for Paul, with Super Chris bopping around in his boxer's robe, kissing people in odd places while union clocks ate up Warner Bros.' money at the rate of roughly $15,000 an hour. There were all sorts of spectacles for Paul to watch.

After the final lick-slap, Paul and Cindy Cheung and Bob Balaban assembled to shoot a scene. In it, Young-Soon is wearing distressed low-rider jeans as Cleveland introduces her to Mr. Farber. In rehearsals, Paul would say, "This is Young-Soon. She works in a brothel in Thailand." With film rolling (Kodak for the inside scenes, Fuji outside), he did it as scripted: "This is Young-Soon. She lives with her mother in 8A." Above Cindy's waistband, you could see a glimpse of two fluorescent yellow bikini strings.

If it was carnal, Chris Doyle would find it. While Night was doing something else, Doyle went over to Cindy and hiked the strings way up high, so they'd be completely in view.

The director of photography is not supposed to touch the costumes, and Betsy Heimann, from wardrobe, was livid. She went to Cindy and restored the strings to their original modest position. They were making a PG movie. (Nobody had told Doyle that; not that he would have cared.)

When Doyle saw what Betsy had done, he went over to Cindy and hiked them back up.

When Betsy saw that, she approached Doyle.

Cindy backed away and found herself standing next to Paul.

Betsy said to Doyle in a civil tone, "I think they want the bikini strings lower."

"I don't give a fuck what they want," Super Chris said.

The gloves were off.

"Well, that's *my* job, to decide how the costumes should look," Betsy said.

"Oh my God, I can't watch this," Cindy said to Paul.

"Really?" Paul said. "I've got to look. I'm fascinated. I see everything. That's my problem."

There was a guy who saw everything making a movie for a guy who heard everything—a perfect match.

Fourteen hours after the start of that first day, Night was in his trailer, drinking a Mike's Hard Lemonade. He had only a few personal touches in his camper. Two basketballs (there was a portable hoop outside his door). Spare clothes and a rain suit and a parka. Various hats. Several books with markers in different places: a biography of Arthur Miller; Dylan's *Chronicles; A Confederacy of Dunces*, by John Kennedy Toole. On the wall, two Dylan album covers, *Another Side of Bob Dylan* and

The Freewheelin' Bob Dylan, and a couple of drawings by his daughters. Various CDs on a low coffee table: Kanye West and Johnny Cash and the African singer Youssou N'Dour, plus a stack of CDs representing a hundred or so bands Night was sifting through, looking for a group to play a party scene late in the movie. But that Monday night, the only thing he had on his mind was Doyle.

"He's messy," Night said. Brick and I were in the trailer, and Night was unloading. He compared Doyle to Roger Deakins, who had been the cinematographer on *The Village.* Deakins was a severe Englishman, nominated often for Oscars (*Fargo* and *The Shawshank Redemption,* among others), who worked with a toothpick in his mouth, who was always in control, and who made Night look like a goofball. He could outwork Night. Night found him intimidating, but Deakins was a regimented pro. Doyle, in personality and style, was his complete opposite. (But Doyle and Deakins were close friends.) "I don't know how many times I had to say today, 'Chris—stay with the human beings.' He suddenly gets interested in Farber's key or something, but we don't *need* Farber's key, we haven't storyboarded Farber's key, Farber's key has *nothing* to do with the movie. Farber's face has *everything* to do with the movie. I'm like, 'Here's the storyboard. Let's see if you can beat it. You're not gonna beat it every time, but if you can beat it nine times out of ten, we're going to have an amazing movie.' Then he starts giving me these crazy hugs every time we get a good take. I'm like, 'Dude, we haven't done *anything* yet. Just keep the camera pointed at the actors, okay?' So then we're rolling, and I'm looking at Paul's face, and he's doing this amazing thing he might never do again. Ever. And I look in the monitor, and I'm looking at the stomach of the guy holding the boom mike!"

He was being just slightly hyperbolic, to make his point. Doyle's drinking, the stomach kissing, moving Cindy's bikini strings, none of that worried Night. (He distinguished between kissing stomachs and grabbing testicles.) The robe and all that, Night liked. Somebody on the crew said, "It's pretty arrogant, you hire a guy with a drinking problem and think he's suddenly going to work straight for you." That might have been a true statement about another director, but not for Night. He was a boy in these matters, devoid of cynicism. Doyle had said to Night before they started that his drinking wouldn't interfere with his work; Night had believed him then and still did.

Night was attributing the first-day lunacy not to alcohol but to Doyle's crazed and brilliant eye, the eye that had helped make *In the Mood for Love* so beautiful. The actors loved that movie, and they were comfortable with Doyle. All except maybe Lick-Slap Kenny. Doyle kept high-fiving the kid and jumping around in front of him, flapping the arms of his robe like bat wings. Poor kid. He didn't know what to make of it. There was nobody like that in the suburbs.

There was a knock on the trailer door. It was Maddie with a hoagie, a staple of the Philadelphia diet, various meats and cheeses with shredded lettuce lubed up by some congealed dressing on a long soft white roll. All the major food groups. Night's chef wouldn't make hoagies. Night unwrapped his second dinner, talking all the while.

"The most important thing is that he has an amazing way of seeing things. Of course, it's also entirely possible we don't have anything that's usable from this whole day. We'll find out tomorrow at dailies"—the daily review of the film shot the previous day.

Night took a bite of his hoagie. He had asked for mayonnaise. He always ate his hoagies with mayo. No mayo. It was a conspiracy. A plot. Had to be. The first day was over.

———

Call—starting time for work on the set—was widely variable. It could be six A.M. or six P.M. or any other time, all according to what Night wanted to shoot that day and what time the previous day had wrapped. There were September afternoons when the heat was smothering and some of the crew worked with towels around their necks to keep the sweat off their hands as they lugged cameras and light stands and an assortment of director's chairs. There were October nights when everything was drenched with artificial rain and the wind would blow right through you and the veterans wore parkas and rain pants. Most big movies change locations over the course of a shoot, but in *Lady*, it was back to the Cove day after day, for workdays that were typically twelve to fourteen hours long. At least eighty people, from various parts of the United States and other places in the world, gathered daily around a real pool surrounded by a fake apartment complex. After a while, you knew the entire wardrobe of the head gaffer's assistant's assistant.

The day's first meal was called breakfast, no matter what time it was served, and the second meal was called lunch. If call was for four-thirty P.M., breakfast was served first thing and lunch around twelve-thirty A.M. Sometime around three in the morning, the two craft services people might put out trays of steaming Chinese food. Shooting nights, there were many workdays that concluded at sunrise. They were tough, the all-nighters. The union crew members were all getting paid by the hour. But at some point they didn't care if the producers had mismanaged the day and were in an overtime union penalty period and guys with paintbrushes were now making eighty-eight dollars an hour. They just wanted to be in bed, and they were waiting to hear Night say, "That's a wrap." A half dozen or so assistants would then echo those words throughout the set: *That's a wrap, that's a wrap, that's a wrap.* In the parking lot, you'd hear people say to one another some variant of "Drive safe, now, hear?" And everybody would head back to their hotel rooms or their rented condos or, if they lived locally, their homes.

The great Pennsylvania Turnpike was the main street of this movie, the actors, crew, and Night using it as a gateway between the fantasy world of the Cove and the real world. One early morning, a tractor-trailer loaded with sheep and lambs turned over and the animals got loose and the turnpike was shut down and work started late at Bristol that day. Generally, though, there wasn't much overlap between the two worlds. The lead item on the AM news stations one morning was about three Pennsylvania Air National Guardsmen killed in Iraq. The flags at the rest stops along the turnpike were at half-mast. But once you got past the security guy and into base camp, the real world receded quickly. It was like being in a Las Vegas gaming room, where you can't tell day from night. In Vegas, they ply you with liquor. On the *Lady* set, they did it with food. You'd see the crew and Night and sometimes Paul eating oily pizza on cheap paper plates at three-thirty A.M., many of them—New Yorkers at some point in their lives—creasing the slices with the New York fold. The best bad pizza you've ever had.

The crew liked Night. There were tense moments, but many of the union workers on the movie said Night was the best director they had ever worked for. Part of it was his organization. Falling days and even weeks behind is an ordinary occurrence on many shoots, which can further complicate your home life and make planning for your next job impossible. Night was always close to schedule. He allowed for the Lick-Slap Kenny things to happen. Many of the crew had worked with Night on his previous movies and wore the faded crew T-shirts to honor their history with the boss. Part of it was his appreciation of good work. But more than anything, it was Night's accessibility that they found endearing. He'd talk to anybody about anything and seemed to be unaware of the severe pecking orders within the various guilds.

On Friday nights, a crew member's name would be picked out of a hat, and Night would award the winner an all-expenses-paid vacation for two to a European capital or Hawaii or some other lush place. Each week it got more elaborate, leading up to the biggest prize at the end: two weeks in the Far East. Night paid for the trips himself. It had nothing to do with Warner Bros., and it wasn't something other directors did. It was pure hucksterism, Night standing in the middle of the catering tent with a bullhorn in his hand, asking, with great fanfare, for an actor or a crew member to pick the name out of a hat. But it also showed a keen understanding of the people he was working with. They were like Night; they enjoyed a scene. It wasn't Night playing god, just Night having fun. Being a huckster was a part of his personality. He liked the trumped-up excitement of a lottery, even though it contradicted his earn-it ethic. He was no one thing.

Night worked at camaraderie. Jimbo Breen, the key greens-man (in charge of anything that grows), lived with his dog in a trailer on the set and had erected an elaborate after-work bar somewhere behind Cleveland Heep's bungalow, called Jimbo's. Jimbo had built these clubs on each of Night's studio movies, at the director's urging, and this one was his best yet. The theme was Polynesian, with a tiki-style roof and bamboo torches, and it had a pool table and a Ping-Pong table and bean-bag chairs. Jimbo tended bar. He was an amazing-looking man, with a stout belly, a big head, bronzed shoulders. He had a gravelly voice. Night had cast him in a small role in the movie, and Brick would sometimes refer to the "magnificence of Jimbo." He was a superb barman. By opening only occasionally, he made each evening at Jimbo's an event. Night always came, and he played Ping-Pong and shot pool and talked to everybody and stayed until Jimbo announced last call. Several veterans said they had never heard of anything similar working on other "shows," as they referred to shoots. Jimbo's, never part of the official tour of the set, brought the departments together. Many of the actors, the stand-ins and the stunt people, most of the hair and makeup people, plus the painters and the carpenters and the payroll people and the nurse and the caterers, would go to Jimbo's. If a day was going well, or if the Eagles were playing on *Monday Night Football*, Night would say to Jimbo, "You got to open tonight, don't you think?"

About the only person who didn't go to Jimbo's was Chris Doyle. (You seldom saw him in the catering tent, either. You didn't see Bryce there either, for that matter.) Doyle's first stop after work was a bar in Bristol where he had quickly established himself as the life of the party, after a near-brawl on his maiden visit. He'd be driven there by his young bilingual assistant, Elaine Liu, with whom Doyle spoke in Cantonese. From there, she would drive him another seventy miles to his room at the Soho Grand Hotel, unless he had one of his arty downtown parties to attend first, which he often did. Elaine lived in Manhattan but way uptown, in East Harlem, another half hour away. Her working conditions were terribly unsafe, brought on by Doyle's refusal to stay in Philadelphia and Sam Mercer's unwillingness to hire a driver for the movie's DP. Elaine knew Doyle had to be getting less sleep than she was, and she was getting about three hours per night. It often fell to her to rap hard on his hotel door at some ungodly hour to rouse him from bed and to start another day.

Sam watched Doyle carefully during his wild first week. Near the end of it, he sat down with Doyle and had a discussion with him about the facts of life as they related to sexual harassment lawsuits in the United States. It was a delicate conversation for Sam. If he said the wrong thing, or said something the wrong way, he risked losing Doyle altogether. Doyle could check out mentally or simply walk off. Night didn't want either of those things to happen, which meant that Sam didn't, either. But Sam knew he couldn't have the movie's DP continue to kiss people on their stomachs or grab their genitalia, because eventually, someone would see it not as an expression of manic energy but as harassment. Grab even one wrong testicle, and a $70 million movie could come to a grinding halt. Sam had to say that he understood it as a display of exuberance, but Doyle needed to behave.

The weekend after the first week of shooting, Doyle went to Amsterdam. (He said he got most of his sleep on planes.) When he came back, he was strangely subdued, with no hint of his regular self.

John Rusk, the assistant director, said to Elaine (THERAPIST TO CHRIS DOYLE, it said on her office door), "What's up with Chris?"

"I don't know," she said, "but enjoy it while you can."

But Night was terribly worried—he *needed* the manic Chris Doyle.

Nobody knew if the personality change was the result of Sam's talk with Doyle or if Super Chris was sick or going through some sort of detox or what. It was eerie, though. And then, slowly, the old Chris Doyle came back. One day he wore yellow caution tape as a headband. Another day, a surgeon's cap bearing the Viagra logo. One night he danced a lovely light-footed poolside waltz with an enormous African-American extra, playfully grabbing her bottom at the end. Some days he'd make visits to his secret stash of adult refreshments, hidden beside the tire of a production truck that was going nowhere; other days he ate solid food and didn't seem to be drinking at all. His personality was the movie's biggest variable. Paul Giamatti asked one morning, "Who's working the camera today, Dr. Jekyll—or Mr. Hyde?" One day Doyle wore a prison jumpsuit and a T-shirt underneath stenciled with the words NEW YORK STATE MENTAL INSTITUTION. It looked pretty authentic.

Dailies were shown after a quick dinner, in a trailer reconfigured as a long, narrow screening room, with a popcorn machine in the front and a projector in the back. Thirty or forty people would cram in, every seat taken and most of the steps, too. Night always sat with Barbara Tulliver, his editor. Doyle sat on the floor in front of the first row, his back sometimes resting against the legs of his lighting chief, Bill O'Leary. O'Leary was a pro, a veteran, blunt and able. He had known alcoholics in his life, and he found working with Doyle like a bad flashback. Doyle often slept during dailies, but somehow he knew what was going on. When Night said one day that his DP should feel particularly good about that day's work, Doyle rallied and said, "James Brown feels good. Super Chris feels *better* than good." He tried to kiss Night's foot, but Night wouldn't let him. Another time, when Night said he was "excited" by what they were doing, Doyle stood up, unzipped his fly, and said, "I'll show you excited." It was like he couldn't help himself. Night's comfort with it all was astounding.

Paul said there were two Chris Doyles, the working-class Aussie Chris Doyle obsessed with his own libido, and the cultivated Chris Doyle—you'd make him a Dubliner in a character breakdown—who would talk about his friends Gus Van Sant and the writer Simon Winchester or say clever things like "American football is not a sport—it's a promotion for supersizing."

There was both tension and affection between the director and the director of photography. Night once said, "We're actually very similar." When he told Paul about his ongoing saga with Doyle, Paul said, "You two need a marriage counselor."

When he hired him, Night had told Doyle that he wanted him as a filmmaking partner, but when he saw him focusing on, say, Farber's key, he'd get understandably nervous. Doyle had been hired for his eye, and about 28 percent of the time, it was brilliant. The rest of the time, Night was fending for himself.

There were parts of days and even whole days when Doyle was on his game, making a suggestion about lighting, about how an actor held a prop, about how a shot should be framed. But there were whole days and parts of days when Doyle was drunk or obstinate or both and the only thing Night could do was work around him. Among the crew, there was a running question as to whether Doyle would make it through the show, the way beat writers covering a ballclub place bets on when the manager will get fired. Would Super Chris quit? Would Night give him a moist towelette (his code language, with Jose, for firing somebody)? Would Doyle go to Europe for a weekend and forget to come back? Something had to give.

Bryce, Paul, and Night were the only actors who had stand-ins. Not stunt doubles but stand-ins. When Night and Bill O'Leary and Doyle (sometimes) were setting up shots, getting the lighting as they wanted it, having plants moved, creating shadows, lowering window shades, the stand-ins would stand where the actors would be later. The requirements for the job were a pleasant, easygoing personality—the job required hours of standing around, Doyle moving their body parts like a golf pro manipulating a student's limbs—and a basic physical similarity to his or her actor. Armando Batista, Night's stand-in, was a young Philadelphia theater actor, dark-skinned and athletic, who would read Samuel Beckett and Peter Brook while waiting to come off the bench. Jacqueline Sanders, an aspiring actress and screenwriter, had Bryce Howard's beautiful red hair and would bring a brown-bag lunch from home every day rather than eat the elaborate delicious free catered food she was welcome to. Paul's stand-in, Christopher Shookla, was an incessant talker who was six months older than Paul and nearly the same height and weight. Their faces and skin coloring and hair color bore no resemblance, but Chrismandu (his stage name) was growing a beard in an attempt to look more like Paul.

Chrismandu lived in a working-class neighborhood in Northeast Philadelphia with his wife and young son and got to Bristol each day by a combination of bus and train and, for the last mile, by foot. He had an extraordinary walk, with his feet splayed and his shoulders bopping from side to side, as if he were the designated goon in a street gang, even though he was always by himself. He often wore large black sunglasses and a sport coat with big shoulder pads, and his hair, which was thinning and red, oiled down and combed back. Paul would sometimes see him walking along Green Lane and would think about asking his driver to stop the car (a needlessly large SUV, actually) and give Chrismandu a lift. But Paul worried that it might embarrass his stand-in, so he never did.

Jimmy Mazzola had given Paul a pair of gold-framed prescription glasses for Cleveland Heep, and he gave Chrismandu the same glasses with clear lenses. Chrismandu would wear them all day long, even while eating breakfast and lunch. I asked him why, and he said, "It helps me stay in character." He was one of Night's believers.

Chrismandu's accent, as Pierce Brosnan said of Robin Williams in *Mrs. Doubtfire,* was a bit mottled, and that was because he was born and raised in northern England, in Sheffield, where his father worked in the Wilkinson Foundry, and he had spent his adulthood in Northeast Philadelphia, which had an accent all its own. He was also proud of his Mike Ditka imitation, and some of that was mixed in, too. He was dubbed Chrismandu in Sheffield while working as a courier. He made deliveries to a Pakistani restaurant where the owner said, "Christopher is too ordinary for you. From now on we call you . . . Chrismandu." Chrismandu had played a bookie in *Unbreakable* and a poker player on the TV show *Hack* and a street vendor in the movie *National Treasure* but was still looking for his first credited role, where his official Screen Actors Guild name would appear in the final credits right alongside all the other actors'.

When he found out he was in the running to be Paul Giamatti's stand-in, he could not believe his good luck. Paul had long been one of his favorite actors. "I seen Paul Giamatti first time as Pig Vomit in *Private Parts*, and I fell in love with him," he said. "The intensity he brought to it." Then he said something painfully true: "That Pig Vomit was a broken, broken man." Chrismandu drove his fellow stand-ins crazy at times with his talking, but amid all his jabbering there was poetry.

He knew most of Paul's roles long before he got the job on *Lady*. "My local Blockbuster video, they never had the *American Splendor* movie, and then one night I'm at our twenty-four-hour Save-A-Lot, and there it is, in the five-dollar bin. I just loved that movie. That Harvey Pekar, he's probably the quirkiest bastard on Planet Earth, and Paul just nailed him. I seen the real Harvey Pekar couple years ago, when he came to the library to give a talk. I ask him about Paul, and he says, 'Paul did a good job, but I didn't get enough money.'"

That Paul did not have the classical features of a leading man but was still getting regular acting work gave Chrismandu hope. He worked sometimes in children's theater in Philadelphia. One of his biggest jobs had been as the voice of the title bear in *The Adventures of Paddington Bear* at one of the city's lovely old theaters.

Weeks after he was hired as Paul's stand-in, Chrismandu had not met his subject. Then one day Paul was coming down one of the Cove's many cement staircases while Chrismandu was climbing up.

"Hey, man, I'm your stand-in," Chrismandu said.

"You're my stand-in?"

"Yeah!"

"Really. Well. Whoa. Wow. My stand-in. That's something."

The whole idea of a stand-in—a person whose sole job was to pretend to be you, in body, for several hours a day—didn't put Paul at ease. Still, he made steady eye contact with his stand-in as they talked, and that made an impression on Chrismandu. The stand-in said, "Well, it's good to meet you, sir," and saluted the actor. Paul liked that word, *sir*. His father had used it often. Paul saluted him back and said, "Good to meet *you*, sir."

Before long, Chrismandu began to wonder if he might be able to get regular work with Paul. Travel to wherever Paul was shooting. Stay in hotels. Get to know him and the other movie people around him. Paul's *Lady* stunt double—who, unlike Chrismandu, actually looked like Paul—had done stunts for Paul on other movies. Chrismandu was earning, as the SAG contract required, $17.50 an hour plus overtime, plus wet pay, an extra $14 per day for the days he had to work in the pool or stand in the rain. To paraphrase Billy Ray Valentine in *Trading Places,* he could hang with these people for a while. Paul stayed pretty well clear of him. He liked his Coach Ditka imitation, but he didn't want to create any false expectations.

The movie's lead actor knew something Chrismandu did not. Paul knew that if you stripped away all the extras—the hotel suite, the giant payday, the car and driver, the coddled life—there was no essential difference between what he was doing to make a living and what Chrismandu, so gratified by having his voice in a children's play, was doing. Every day, people were treating Paul like "Paul Giamatti," but in his mind, he and Chrismandu were more similar than different: two thirty-eight-year-old men, each with a wife and a young son at home, trying to make a living in a line of work that guaranteed nothing.

———

To prepare for her first big scene with Paul, the one in which Cleveland asks Young-Soon to look up the word *narf* for him, Cindy Cheung pulled out all the stops. She asked someone from production if she could have, in her elegant suite at the Ritz-Carlton, a replica of the poolside chaise Young-Soon would be lounging on during the scene, for practice. It showed up close to immediately. But life on a big-budget movie—that snap-your-fingers quality—didn't particularly impress her. She found daily housekeeping to be an intrusion, and living in a hotel was not part of her dream. She'd call her husband every night when he was off work. Like most novelists, he had a day job, as an editor for an online version of *Forbes*.

How was your day?

Boring—nothing happened.

No, tell me all about it. I really need to know.

Cindy had flown in an acting teacher she was close to from her San Francisco days at the American Conservatory Theater, Bonita Bradley. Cindy didn't tell Night about it. Maybe she knew how it would sound to him—like she didn't have faith in him as a director. Cindy put Bonita up in a room at the hotel and worked with her extensively for five days. To Cindy, it was an investment. They worked in Cindy's suite and ate at various Asian restaurants in Philadelphia. One night Cindy, Bonita, and June (Mrs. Choi in the movie) went to dinner at Porky & Porkie, a Korean restaurant with a Vietnamese owner. June told the owner, "She's the big star. I'm just the mother." June was convinced that Night really had died as a child, as a spoof documentary about Night on the Sci Fi Channel had once maintained. They shared auditioning war stories, and June scolded Cindy for telling Night and Doug Aibel her true age: "*Never* tell your age. Never, never, never." Cindy spied on the Korean diners and waitresses, looking for clues to Young-Soon. She paid close attention to the rounding-out vowel sound at the end of many Korean words. She started experimenting with scrunta and narfa.

In her hotel room, Cindy had Korean tapes, giving herself a crash course in a language she did not know. She had taught herself the Korean alphabet in a week, so she wouldn't have to learn her Korean lines from a transliteration. She also had videotapes of Paris Hilton and Jessica Simpson, which she and Bonita watched over and over. The teacher and student watched how the starlets played their stomachs, hips, bottoms, navels. "Even when they bow, they're saying, 'I rock,'" Cindy said. The Koreans Cindy watched didn't do that. For Young-Soon, Cindy would need some of each.

Bonita, fine-boned and wearing a pink pashmina, took notes on a legal pad and sat on a chair in the lotus position, barely moving. She had taught Annette Bening and Harry Hamlin and Denzel Washington and thousands of other actors whose names you probably don't know. Cindy could have been one of the latter group, but then Night had hired her. Bonita's specialty was something called character embodiment. To help Cindy find Young-Soon, Bonita asked her to embody various animals. Getting there was, as they say, a process.

"Go to your core, to the part of your body that is most Korean," Bonita said. Her voice was hypnotic.

They were in the suite's sitting room. Cindy was wearing khaki clamdiggers and a pink shirt with no shoes, no makeup, no jewelry. Her fingernails and toenails were painted pink. She started groaning loudly, with her eyes closed. She sounded like she needed a doctor.

"You are Korean," Bonita said softly.

Outside, it was a hot August day. Eight floors below, a parade of midday cars and cabs and trucks trudged north and south on Broad Street, but the traffic noises were muffled by the time they reached Cindy's open windows. Out at Bristol, *Lady in the Water* was in full swing. Cindy wasn't there because she had no scenes scheduled for that day. Most days she had no scenes. The only actor on the set every day was Paul. The only stand-in there every day was Chrismandu.

Cindy started moaning in Korean. She was rolling her head around and saying, "*Ching gu ga re keyau chaud deh yo*. Oh-ma, *oh*-ma!" Again and again. "Oh-*ma*! *Oh*-ma!" Before long she was shouting. A housekeeper armed with fresh towels made a quick entrance and exit.

"What animal comes to you?" Bonita asked.

Cindy went to the floor, supporting herself on her hands and knees. Her head was going crazy now, like a mad dog's. She made an exhaling noise that sounded like a horse sneezing. She made a muted groaning noise, like a dolphin underwater.

And then, without any instruction from Bonita, Cindy stood up and started dancing wildly, as if she were Young-Soon in her dance-club scene. Cindy twirled her hair and repeated one of her lines over and over: "What's up, baby? What's *up*, baby? What's up, bay-*be*." And then other lines from other scenes, but all the while dancing: "She wants to know who told you this word. Who told you this word? This word. This word. Who told you this word? A narf, the bedtime story says, is a sea nymph. A sea nymph. A sea nymph." She was growing quiet now. "A sea nymph. A sea nymph."

"Keep the animal inside you," Bonita said with urgency.

"Oh-ma! Oh-ma! O-o-oh-ma! She says she talk about it *a little bit*." Cindy sounded a little drunk.

Her real-life cell phone rang. Cindy checked it, put the phone down, and said, "Why can't you be more like your sister? She married a dentist." It was a line from the movie.

"You're two years old," Bonita said.

"She wants to know who showed you this word," Cindy said.

"Now use your legs," Bonita said.

Paul had a whole bit about actors using their legs, but it involved the elaborate crossing of legs in parlor-room murder mysteries. Cindy was jumping up and down.

"Use your feet," Bonita said.

Cindy continued jumping up and down.

"Feet," Bonita said quietly.

Cindy started running her toes through the thick carpet as if it were beach sand. She made a circle.

"Now you are the age when you first heard the story."

"It's an ancient bedtime story, Mr. Heep. An ancient *Eastern* bedtime story. My great-grandmother used to tell it. Ancient story, Mr. Heep. Ancient bedtime story. Ancient. Mista Hee-pa. Mista. Heepa."

When Cindy came out of her trance, if that's the right word, Bonita said to her, "I think it's helpful to think of animals when you're playing that scene, to help you go from one culture to another."

Cindy explained herself to Bonita. There was, it turned out, no mad dog or singing dolphin or sneezing horse in her work. Nothing like it. The only animals Cindy had in mind were a mink and a baby elephant. It was her secret with Bonita. Night would never know.

A couple of days later, Cindy was doing the "could you look up *narf* for me" scene with Paul. It had been nothing but hurdles, for Night when he was writing, for Cindy when she was auditioning, for Paul and Cindy when they were rehearsing. It was the one when the moviegoer would take a first step, or not, into the narf world. Cindy could make or break the movie right there. *How can you not know what a narf is? You know about Little Red Riding Hood, right?*

Cindy was sprawled out on the actual poolside chaise, in her bikini with the fluorescent yellow straps, a book on her lap and others at her side. She hadn't been expecting to do the scene that day, but Night, through one of his four assistant directors, had called her in. For all his planning, he could turn on a dime and often did. It helped him feel fresh and maybe a little dangerous. For Cindy, showtime came with no notice.

Night started shooting the big scene in an afternoon drizzle. There were tiny raindrops on Paul's glasses. Cindy found it distracting. She was supposed to be sunbathing. Bonita was nowhere in sight.

On the first take, Paul, unscripted, began the scene by saying, "Hey." Cindy was surprised, because if there's one thing she knew, it was that in an M. Night Shyamalan movie script, every word was there for a reason. It was not the decline of modern civilization as we know it, but it was pretty bad. And now, with one added *hey,* all bets were off. She made an unscripted grunt back. She went to hand Paul some books, as they had rehearsed, but now the books felt unbearably heavy. Cindy became terribly self-aware. She had one foot up, the other down. As Doyle was peering in on her, Cindy could feel her awkwardness. She could feel that she was clinging too much to what she had been working on with Bonita. She was not doing what she had done in rehearsals. She was not seizing the moment—the moment was seizing her.

Later, I asked Night how it went. He said, "It was like Cindy rehearsed it too much, overthought it. She didn't trust the moment, like she did in the audition. She wasn't trusting me as the director. It seemed like she had too much stuff in her head."

Night said that without knowing anything about the work Cindy had been doing with her old drama coach. Or maybe he did know, just not in the conventional sense.

———

They reshot the scene several days later. Before the cameras rolled, Night saw Cindy with her nose in her script. He told her to stop rehearsing. He said, "On the day, whatever happens, happens." He was telling her to do what she'd done at the audition. Steal the moment. Feel the weight of the shaving cream in your hand. Cindy found that direction liberating, the best acting advice she had ever received, really.

From the first take, Cindy nailed the reshoot. In the space of two minutes, she was funny, bratty, curious, seductive, kind, smart, dismissive, respectful, American, Korean. In the days to come, there were times when Night felt she was the *only* thing working. The whole salary negotiation thing, it wasn't even a footnote to him anymore. Night was looking for angels wherever he could find them. So far he had Paul, and now he had Cindy. He had his rides to Bristol with his cell phone off and Dylan on. Whenever he felt unsure about the script, a siren would go off in his head and remind him to do the damn work.

All through the set, and through the shoot, there was a Dylan thing going on. It was there from the beginning, at the read-through. Night had asked everybody to think of their own personal narf, and lean John Boyd, one of the smokers, had thought of the woman from Dylan's "Shelter from the Storm." That evening, at the Cuban restaurant where the cast congregated for dinner, Boyd and Paul, a Dylan fan, had compared notes. Labor Day came and went. School began. September turned into October. Some of the overnight shoots were cold and windy. All the while, the Dylan vibe got more and more intense. One morning Night went to Paul's trailer to discuss the movie but ended up talking mostly about Dylan. Night was discovering the singer then, but Paul had been listening to him for years, his interest in Dylan flowing from his interest in Woody Guthrie, guitar-strumming poet of the American worker, mid-twentieth century. In the fall of 2005, Dylan's *Chronicles* was a national best-seller, and the Martin Scorsese documentary on Dylan, *No Direction Home*, was getting a lot of attention. The regular reports of body counts from a troubling distant war made certain lyrics seem especially heartbreaking and urgent, even if all the symbols and imagery and attached meaning were, according to Dylan, a cosmic accident. Paul would sometimes go over to Boyd's cramped trailer with Dylan CDs, some of them rare, the '61 recordings from a Minnesota hotel room, stuff like that. Boyd was at the age when you still think you can figure lyrics out, and Paul had some of that in him, too, but his questions were more rhetorical. ("'Time is an ocean but it ends at the shore,'" Paul said, citing the "Oh, Sister" kicker. "What does it mean, what the fuck does it *mean*?")

Paul liked Boyd. Part of it was that Paul had worked with John Boyd's father, the actor Guy Boyd, when Paul was starting out. Most of it was that Paul saw Boyd doing a lot of good acting in a tiny role, moving his head in interesting ways. Before *Lady*, Boyd, guitar in hand, had auditioned for the director Todd Haynes to play Bob Dylan in a studio movie. He had the laconic quality you associate with Dylan, and he liked to ride trains. The director loved Boyd's audition, but the role went to an actor who was far more of a name, Christian Bale. That was one Boyd had wanted bad. He was not shy about playing and singing in public, and one evening Night stopped the golf cart he sometimes used to get around the set and listened to Boyd playing "Don't Think Twice, It's All Right." Paul walked by just then and said, "Get back to work, ya bunch of damn hippies." Near the end of the shoot, on a crisp fall night, Boyd played Dylan hits for an assortment of actors, extras, the guy playing the tartutic, a teamster, a dishwasher from catering, and a few others who happened by. Nineteen sixty-seven all over again. This congregation was an illustration of Night's point: There was something about Dylan that brought outsiders together, made them feel connected to something bigger than themselves. Night was trying to do the same thing in *Lady*. The characters in the movie were supposed to come together, and Night hoped the community of moviegoers would, too, even if the Disney CEO was predicting the demise of the theater experience. After *The Village*, when the Disney people were throwing their hands up, Night had told Nina, "You can't trust me—you don't know where I'm going." Dylan had spent his whole career saying that, and people followed him anyhow. It seemed like Dylan didn't care. Maybe it was an act, maybe it wasn't, there was no way to truly know.

Night was different. He did care, and he was up-front about it. He wanted to go any damn place he pleased, but he wanted you and me and everybody else to follow him there. It's an expensive decision, movie tickets costing what they do and free time being in such short supply.

When Franny drove him to the set, Night would sometimes listen to the bands under consideration for the party scene, the band that would play two Dylan covers. Night had two songs in mind, "Maggie's Farm" and "It Ain't Me, Babe." As he listened to the bands assembled by Sue Jacobs, the movie's musical supervisor, he had no idea what they looked like or where they were from. There were fifteen or more in the running. They were from all over the United States, and they were all obscure. There was one group that caught his ear, a heavy-metal band, all wailing guitars and frazzled nerves. Night heard something in their voices he hadn't heard in any of the other bands. They were true originals desperate to make the music their own. Night said to Sue, "Tell me about Silvertide." Of all the bands he was listening to, Silvertide turned out to be the only one from

Philadelphia: five young guys about three years out of high school, from Northeast Philadelphia, where Chrismandu lived. The band had opened for Mötley Crüe and Van Halen and Alice Cooper and had put out three records. Night was intrigued.

One night, after a thirteen-hour day on the set, Night went to a recording studio outside Philadelphia to hear Silvertide play "Maggie's Farm" and "It Ain't Me, Babe." The lead singer, Walt Lafty, a twig with long blond hair, was wearing a leather vest and no shirt and sort of pulling it off. The band had a presence. Their "Maggie's Farm" was a pure, sweaty screech, and Night rocked out listening to it.

But the band was playing "It Ain't Me, Babe" at Dylan's tempo and with Dylan's emphases. It wasn't what Night was looking for. He said, "They're playing it like a love song." He was wondering if the song could have a punk element to it. He liked the band Green Day.

Silvertide's producer, separated by a large window from the five band members, was sitting at a massive control panel. He said to Night, "Maybe you want something like this." He started smashing the heel of his heavy boot on the studio floor, and with each hit, he said, "Bop, bop, *bop;* bop, bop, *bop,*" hitting his chest with his chin on every third *bop.* "Something more English Beat," the producer said. "More of a Birmingham sound." The Birmingham in England, where the English Beat was formed.

The producer went into the band's room, said something briefly to Walt and the boys. The transformation was immediate. It was like Night giving Paul Giamatti a suggestion on how to deliver a line.

Walt—in a staccato way, with a pause between every word—started screaming, "But it ain't *me,* babe. No, no, *no,* it ain't *me,* babe. It ain't *me* you're looking for, *babe.*" Really fast and very, you know, Birmingham. If the song ever had any tenderness, Silvertide stripped it clean and turned it into something angry. There was nothing remotely sweet about it. Night was ecstatic.

One day Night tried out Youssou N'Dour's version of the Dylan song "Chimes of Freedom" on the five smokers and some others. Night was considering it for the closing credits. "Chimes of Freedom" is a powerful 1964 Dylan protest song that a really progressive college radio station might play once or twice a year. N'Dour is an amazing talent, like nothing you hear on commercial American radio. His voice is both tribal and melodic, and he sings in French, English, and Wolof, the language of Senegal, the West African country where he lives. But the combination, N'Dour singing Dylan, was strange and slightly annoying. Maybe not as annoying as the treacly 1985 do-gooder hit "We Are the World," featuring Bob Dylan and Michael Jackson and many other stars, but that gives you the idea. The smokers listened respectfully as Night played N'Dour's version of "Chimes," but they responded with silence and odd looks. Then Night said, "It's a family movie." The Cove's resident smokers responded as a chorus: "Oh. We get it now. Yeah. Right. Okay. A *family* movie." Still, it was a hard piece of music to fall in love with.

But it wasn't for Night, and that's the point. You had to see Night as he listened. N'Dour's "Chimes" was as sweet as the Silvertide version of "It Ain't Me, Babe" was angry, but Night was beaming and grooving, his head bopping up and down like a jackhammer. He had been transported. He completely believed in it. He believed in the enigmatic lyrics, in the African rhythms that would be so unfamiliar to white America, the whole thing. If he used it, it wouldn't be commercial and it wouldn't be calculated. Just the opposite. N'Dour singing Dylan was another version of Night's movie, outsiders coming together. It was Night listening to himself.

8.

Night was making dangerous moves. He was shooting very little coverage, movie filler that can be dropped in during editing to cover up glitches. After wrapping long, complicated scenes with multiple actors, various deputies would ask Night again and again if he wanted to shoot coverage. All directors shoot coverage. Without coverage, one actor with a momentary vacant stare can wipe out an otherwise perfect two-minute scene. The question was commonplace until the day Night said, "How many times do I have to say it? No coverage, no coverage, no coverage."

You heard that tone from him sometimes, a tone that suggested he was all alone. When those same deputies pointed out certain imperfections—Paul had an infected pimple on the back of his neck for a day—Night's answer sounded almost like a mantra: "The crooked nose on the beautiful girl makes her look more beautiful." It was weird. Within the realm of a fantasy, and that's what Night was making, he wanted something that looked and felt real. In moviemaking, real is a tightrope.

Night was shooting *Lady* dangerously dark. The darker you shoot, the harder it is to keep the camera in focus, a job that fell to Glenn Kaplan, the focus pull, who stood beside Chris Doyle on take after take with a focus dial in hand. Doyle was dwarfed by Glenn, an XXL barrel-chested Californian who often wore colorful beach shirts and a faded Red Sox cap. Glenn was awed by

Doyle's talent. "A great DP like Chris Doyle doesn't see the world the way ordinary people do," Glenn said one day after watching dailies. "For them, colors are richer, everything moves faster than for normal people. Chris Doyle is like Wayne Gretzky playing hockey, always knowing where the puck's gonna be next."

Watching dailies, Night saw that some of the takes—sometimes the best takes—were out of focus. One day during dailies, he said, "Are we *ever* gonna get this movie in focus?" After that, Glenn stopped coming into the screening room and instead stood with the operator in the cramped projection booth. Glenn thought the projector was part of the problem, and so did other people. He said to the projectionist one day, "You gotta get this projector in focus—my job's on the line here." Eventually, a new projector was brought in, but nothing changed. All the while, Glenn never complained about how darkly *Lady* was being shot, even though it made his job much harder. He was a proud man and had just come off another difficult show, *Jarhead*. "The two things you can't improve after you wrap a movie," Glenn told me, "are the actors' performance—and focus." The only person more aware of that than Glenn was Night.

One day after lunch, Glenn played some hoops with Night. The game seemed to be about more than basketball. Glenn wasn't a good shooter, but he outweighed Night by maybe a hundred pounds, and he killed Night under the backboard. Frustration was pouring out of him along with his sweat.

But the most dangerous decision Night made—more dangerous than shooting dark; more dangerous than forgoing coverage; more dangerous than casting himself or Paul or anybody else—was the hiring of Chris Doyle. During one take Night said to Chris, with rising urgency, "Stay on the actors, stay on the actors—the *actors!*" There were times when Super Chris seemed to be shooting another movie. Elaine—Doyle's assistant, driver, therapist, and surrogate mother, who was often on a search mission for her boss's misplaced cell phone or wallet (he had no keys)—believed he didn't really get drunk, that he just needed a sort of alcohol drip to keep functioning. But Night and others didn't buy her theory. Doyle's behavior was too erratic to support it. After a take that had gone especially awry, somebody on the crew said in a stage whisper, "He *might* be drinking."

Doyle had an office in the old 3M warehouse building that he had decorated with red Japanese lanterns, Chinese murals, votive candles. There were shelves crammed with photography books and works of literature that he carted around the world in shabby suitcases. Late one evening, Night said to Brick and me, "Come here, you gotta check this out." Night sounded like a fourteen-year-old sneaking around. We slipped into Super Chris's office, and Night asked, "What does it smell like?" The office had no windows, and the air in it was heavy and musky and foreign. Doyle's den reeked of . . . Doyle himself.

Jeff Robinov, the Warner Bros. production chief, didn't come to the set at all during the forty-five days of shooting. Alan Horn, the president of Warners (as Night finally took to calling his new studio), came once. There was general nervousness about Horn's visit. Franny, Night's unflappable driver, replaced his usual shorts with pressed black slacks to pick Horn up at the airport.

When Night introduced Horn to his director of photography, he was prepared for anything. One of Doyle's specialties was the first impression. Upon meeting Night's parents, the doctors Shyamalan, Doyle said, "Save me—I'm incurable." Upon meeting Cindy Cheung's mother, he said, "You can't be the mother, you must be the sister," and started playfully hitting on her. During a party scene loaded with extras drinking fake beer from real bottles, Doyle walked up to a group of kids in for the day and said, "Heinekens all around?" But when he met Horn, Doyle did little more than bow while Night shrugged and said, "He's the best we could do."

Horn went into Cleveland Heep's bungalow to watch Paul do a solo scene. Horn was dressed with a studied casualness, wearing loose Levi's and an elegant lightweight sweater, the sleeves pushed up to nearly the elbows. Still, he looked like the boss. He took a piece of paper off Cleveland's desk to make notes to himself. When the scene wrapped, he mimed clapping.

He complimented Paul on his work, and Paul thanked him but did nothing to extend the conversation, as you would expect. Horn picked up on Paul's uneasiness, wished him well on the rest of the shoot, and Paul trundled off to his trailer. Night took Horn to his trailer to have a conversation about the state of the movie. A small army remained in the bungalow to set up the next shot, rearranging the furniture and the camera and the lights. It was hot and crowded in the bungalow: There were three prop people, maybe eight gaffers and grips, a couple of stand-ins, including Chrismandu, some hair and makeup people, maybe fifteen people in all. Everybody was aware that the boss was around for the day, and some were wondering wryly if Jimbo's would open that night. There was no chance.

With no provocation, Doyle announced, "Okay, people, why not, already?" He sounded like a schoolteacher addressing an inattentive class.

And then, in one fell swoop, he dropped his beltless lightweight cotton pants to his ankles. To the question boxers or briefs, the answer was neither.

People whooped and one person said in a voice filled with mock pain, "Oh, dude—why?"

Doyle, beaming in the crowded bungalow, did a pirouette and said, "Why not? Why not?"

One of the hair ladies screeched, "He's got a small butt!"

John Rusk—the movie's assistant director, a droll bearded man—said, "That's not all that's small."

After lunch, the regulars filed into the screening room to watch dailies. Super Chris was often the last one in, when he came at all, but on this day he was early, standing in the back row as the seats and steps filled up. Two seats were left open, for Night and Alan Horn. John Rusk stood outside the entrance. He could see Horn and Night approaching. There was some shrieking, and John Rusk popped his head in. In the back of the screening room, Doyle had dropped his pants again, this time for an audience double in size.

Lady was Rusk's fifth movie with Night, and he had an intuitive loyalty to the director. His job was to make sure the trains ran on time, and they did. When he said, "Quiet on the set, please," there was immediate silence. Rusk knew if Horn walked into the screening room and saw the movie's cinematographer standing with his pants around his ankles, it might not inspire confidence in the whole Bristol operation. But he let it play out. He couldn't try to manage Doyle. Nobody could, not even Night. The movie's DP did another dance, naked to the *Lady* world, and then pulled up his pants. About a second later, no more than two, Horn entered the screening room. The sober-looking Warner Bros. boss took his seat, and the director of *Lady in the Water*—a $140 million business, the production and marketing budget combined—sat beside him. The dailies were shown, and they were good. There were no focus issues. Horn clapped again and spread some praise around. Night was running a tight ship. Horn was pleased.

Night heard about his cinematographer's public displays of nakedness soon enough—the minute Horn went off to make a call. Night thought it was funny. More than that: He understood it. "Chris has a need to create excitement for himself, to be unconventional, to feel dangerous," Night said. "He needs to see excitement in other people's eyes. It's what keeps him alive."

Night, really, was the same way. He forever needed another person responding to him, to the words he said, to the ideas he had, to the movies he made. He had to be inspiring, and he had to win you over. When it went well—when that first live audience devoured *The Sixth Sense;* when he cast a magic spell on the Burch guests that balmy April evening—it left Night feeling euphoric. When Night's connection to other people was muted or nonexistent—his inability to engage the mother and her young actor son in that elevator in New York; the public's jumbled response to *The Village*—he would get sullen. You could see his excitement if there was somebody new around, a fresh subject to convert. But if the only people within earshot were Brick Mason or Maddie or Betsy from wardrobe, he was happy to work them over again, too. The biggest difference between Night and Chris Doyle was that Doyle had a need to deaden life's pains. (Alcohol helped Doyle feel more like Super Chris.) Pain inspired Night.

Night loved working with Doyle. To Night, he was an artist version of Allen Iverson, the star guard for the Philadelphia 76ers, "hugely talented, but not willing to do what the team needs him to do to win." The challenge to Night was to see if he could inspire Doyle to be something other than what he was.

Night didn't see anything unusual in the timing, how Doyle was pulling his pants up as Horn was coming in.

"He's just lucky," Night said.

It was surprising, to hear that from Night. He was usually so dismissive of luck. A few days earlier, he had gone on a tirade about an uncle who claimed his young son would now pulverize Night in one-on-one because the boy had suddenly shot up to six-two. "That's *completely* the wrong message to send him, that he'll win because he has height," Night had said. "What's height? Genetic luck. Tell me when he's taken over one hundred thousand shots in his life, like I have, then I'll be worried." Night was actually angry. He didn't want his cousin to turn into another soft, affluent American who felt he was owed basketball success merely because he was tall.

Had Horn seen Super Chris naked, the cinematographer certainly would have been fired. The stakes were high that day. The stakes were high every day, yet Doyle was getting it done, getting Night what he needed, making him feel uncomfortable, as he wanted to feel.

"That's it?" I asked Night. "Just luck?"

"Look," Night said, "give Chris ten takes. Nine of them, he's focusing on a flowerpot or some other insanely wrong thing. But one of them he nails. Every time. He's lucky."

"I thought your thing is you make your own luck."

"For me, yes," Night said. "Chris Doyle is different."

A few weeks later, Paul was swimming in Story's underwater cave, ingeniously dropped into the industrial plant's fifty-foot-high circular water tank. Paul was a good swimmer, and his submerged acting was photographed by a team with a specialty in underwater photography. "It's amazing how in focus you guys get everything, even though you're shooting underwater," Night told them. Doyle and Glenn had nothing to do with the shot.

Nobody was paying any particular attention to Doyle until he stripped down once again and paraded for a long moment at the top of the tank. The shock factor was gone by now, but four or five people dutifully raised their cell-phone cameras to record the moment anyhow. Bhavna was visiting that day, and Night comically shielded his wife's eyes from the action as

Doyle dived in. Once in the water, the skinny-dipping DP at-tached himself to the movie's lead actor. Between gasps for air, Paul could be heard shouting, "This is unholy!"

The dozens of men and women working the movie—the crew Night had assembled—represented, collectively, over a thou-sand years of filmmaking experience. Some were more willing to share than others. Jimmy Mazzola, the prop man, was the most willing of all. Night picked up stuff from him all the time. When he saw Jimmy each day, he'd say, "My man!" Jimmy and Night were on the same wavelength, even though Jimmy was as blue-collar as Night was highbrow. To Jimmy, his vast collec-tion of mechanical butterflies, real butterflies, underwater pens, oversize glasses, and all the rest were the tools of his trade. To Night, they were talismans.

One day Jimmy said, "Something you'll never hear, like from an ordinary guy who just goes to the movies, is somebody talking about the way a movie's photographed. I only heard it this one time in all my life."

He then told about working on the movie *The Pick-up Artist,* in Brooklyn in the mid-1980s. It was being shot by Gor-don Willis, the director of photography for *The Godfather.* A New York mobster made arrangements to visit the set, not to see Molly Ringwald in action or to hang out with Danny Aiello in his trailer or to check in with one of the teamsters but to meet one person: Gordon Willis. "The wiseguy says to Gordy, 'The way you shot *The Godfather,* that was something beautiful, never seen a movie better lit in all my life.' "

But it was obvious from watching dailies that *Lady in the Water* wasn't being shot like your ordinary mainstream Holly-wood movie. Amid his drinking and stomach-kissing and flash-ing, Doyle was doing luscious work. He often needed a lot of help to get there—especially from Bill O'Leary, the lighting chief—but he got there.

The photography looked timeless. You couldn't tell what time of day it was, or even the year. Except for the cell phones and Young-Soon's low-slung jeans, there was nothing modern about the movie. It might as well have been set in the Summer of Love. (Many of the wardrobe choices were bound to the late 1960s, not for psychedelia but for earth tones.) There was something gentle, sexual, and portentous coming through Doyle's work, like the dune scenes in *Summer of '42*. There were days when Night actually felt okay about the movie. One day in dailies, he said, "All right, Maddie—you can call off Roger." It was an inside joke that everybody got: Night would not need to make an emergency call to bring back Roger Deakins, the toothpick-chewing DP who had shot *The Village* so well.

Technically, Super Chris was a manager. He oversaw the "camera department," a group of a half-dozen people he worked closely with and quaintly referred to as "my team." (Doyle complained that he had only one "yellow" on his team, Yen Nguyen, the camera loader, short, dark, beautiful, and very quiet.) When a scene was being shot, there were two people right beside Doyle. One was Glenn Kaplan, and the other was Ronald "Red" Burke, the dolly grip, who moved the camera as the film rolled. The job requires assured hands, a keen sense of awareness, and ESP. To have the camera in the right place at the right time, the dolly grip has to know what the actors are doing, what the DP is seeing, and what the director is thinking. Night was pleased by how often Red knew exactly where to be. Night, working with Red for the first time, could see why there were movie people who regarded him as the best dolly grip on the East Coast and maybe in the country.

Red, a lifelong Brooklynite, was the old pro of *Lady in the Water*. His first movie job had been on *The Godfather*, working under

Gordon Willis himself. Sam Mercer liked to say, "Red came in on *The Godfather*, and he's going out on Silvertide," the movie's high-decibel Dylan cover band. Red had worked on nearly two dozen Woody Allen movies, most of them with Gordon Willis and Jimmy Mazzola, and by the summer of *Lady*, he had fluffy white hair and a slightly stooped back. Doyle's nickname for Red was "One Hundred Years of Cinema." Occasionally, after a good take, Doyle would hug Red and kiss the top of his head through hair that hadn't been red in years. Still, there was something boyish about Red. When lunch was called, he'd get on a bike with a basket and race over to the food tent, a few hundred yards away, to beat the line. He knew the tricks of his trade.

One day they were shooting a scene in which Paul and Bryce were sitting on a bed. The scene was quiet and intimate and long, and it required Bryce to cry. Night wanted to start the scene with the camera close to the actors and gradually pull away from them—a pullback shot. Night, of course, had no plans to shoot coverage. (No coverage, no coverage, no coverage.) For the scene to work, he'd need perfect performances from five people: the two leads, plus Super Chris, Glenn, and Red. Doyle had to move the camera back and forth subtly between the two actors. Red had to push the camera, with Chris sitting behind it, down a fifteen-foot-long train track at a precise, ever-changing speed. And Glenn had to adjust the camera's focus over the course of the take.

Doyle spent an hour or more setting up the shot, with Chrismandu and Jacqueline standing in for the two leads. It was being shot inside a warehouse that was dark, dead, and stuffy, except for the chilly patches where cold air was piped in through a giant hose. The catering table looked tired, with the cap off the peanut butter jar and a knife stuck in it. Plastic water bottles, their labels peeling off, were floating in a bucket of half-melted ice. Doyle was in his own world, seemingly obsessed with placing

Chrismandu's head in a certain position so that Cleveland Heep's shadow would fall on Story's delicate face, even though it would be there in only a few frames. But the big thing, the pull-back part of the shot, Doyle never rehearsed.

When he finally had the shadows and light where he wanted them, the actors and Night were called in. Night didn't want to rehearse with Paul and Bryce. He knew he would get the most emotion in the first or second take. They knew what to do—they had practiced the scene well in the basement re-hearsal room. Night was worried about wearing them out. And when it came time to roll film for the first take, Paul and Bryce hit all their notes. But Night felt that Doyle's camera work was jerky, and Red's pace, uncharacteristically, was too fast. "I'm not feeling the love," Night said. He felt no love on the second and third takes, either. And then the takes started getting bad.

Red was either too slow or too fast; he paused too long in the middle or not long enough. Sometimes he knew things weren't working—in the middle of one take, he mouthed an "Oh, shit." On other takes, Night told him. Doyle wasn't making things eas-ier, panning too far left and too far right, as if the actors' ears were the most important things in the shot. (Whether the shots were in focus—Glenn's work—Night wouldn't know until he saw dailies.) In between takes, Red was watching replays on a monitor to see what the camera was seeing, with Night next to him shaking his head in a slow burn. Red was off his game on a shot that would normally be second nature to him.

By the ninth take, Paul was fighting boredom, and Bryce was looking cried out. Night, with some hostility, said to Doyle, "You go so far right and so far left, you lose the entire mood of the scene—why don't you just lock it down?" Lock the camera in place, with the two faces in the frame, and do no panning at all.

Super Chris looked emasculated. This time somebody else had denuded him. He walked away for several minutes. When he returned, he refused to make eye contact with Night or to respond to anything he said. When Night, desperate, resorted to the language of wooing, Super Chris, dead serious, said, "Aren't I allowed to be quiet?"

They shot an eleventh take, a twelfth take, a thirteenth take. The actors were getting more and more tired, though between takes, with the tension swelling like a bad sprain, Paul watched intently. Red, the old pro, was white-faced and unnerved. None of Night's usual charms were working. For once, his spectacular vitality seemed manufactured. He'd say, "Cut!" "Great!" "Awesome!" "Let's do another one right away! Fast, fast, fast!" But it didn't seem like anyone was feeling the love. At last, on professionalism alone, the takes improved, and Night felt he had something he could use. If there wasn't, he could reshoot, but Night regarded that strictly as a last resort.

The vision Night had for the scene hadn't played out. He had the shot in his mind and the shot on the storyboards, and then real life intervened. But what he had was okay. He could use it. More work would only make it worse. Night quietly called for lunch. Red, feeling defeated, slowly walked to the big white food tent.

At lunch, Red sat with Jimmy Mazzola, Bill O'Leary, and some of the other New Yorkers. Somebody said, "You did a good job in there."

"The director didn't think so," Red answered.

He wasn't using Night's name. He knew nothing about the success of *The Sixth Sense*, didn't know that Night had directed it. Red didn't go to movies, he only worked on them. Red said the problem with the pullback scene was that the mechanics of it should have been figured out in rehearsals, either with the stand-ins or with the actual actors. Either way, he would have learned what mark to hit on what word. "Bad planning—that was the whole problem," Red said. The director had embarrassed him. He wasn't used to that.

He considered himself a mechanic, even if others did not. He believed most of moviemaking was mechanical. "For the life of me, I can't understand how he's using Chris Doyle," Red said. There was Brooklyn in his voice. His hands were folded placidly on the lunch table. He believed Doyle could be a DP who orchestrated the setup of the shots without actually operating the camera. Red had seen that done on other shows, and Night had, too. On *The Sixth Sense*, Tak Fujimoto was the cinematographer, and Kyle Rudolph operated the camera for him.

"Chris is really a very sweet guy with a very good eye," Red said. "But he's killing himself with the drinking, and he can't handle the camera. And the director's got the single best camera operator in New York already working the movie. He could call him right in." Red was referring to Pat Capone, who was operating the B camera, the shots that involved no actors—doormats, clouds passing overhead, extras walking down a corridor, things like that. It was Pat Capone who had picked up a piece of Red's finger off a New York street one day during the Steve Martin remake of *The Pink Panther* after a camera mount had sliced it off. (Red sat in a hospital waiting room for hours, but the tip was a goner.) But Red wasn't praising Pat out of loyalty. He had the movie in mind, a movie he would likely never see. He cared about a thing being done right.

Red said there was one thing saving the show: the actors, Paul and Bryce in particular. "Two pros," Red said. It was his highest praise.

Barbara Tulliver, the editor, was worried about how Bryce was coming across in dailies. "It seems like every time she's on the screen, she's crying," the editor said. She and Night were sitting in the screening room after another day of a crying Story. Everybody else had left. The room was dark. Barbara always had a pen in her hand, a notebook on her lap, and her hair often up in a bun. She was wearing a crisp, tight button-front shirt, her usual uniform; there was something schoolteacherish about her. Some days Night was ready to hear what she had to say, and some days he was not. In the Bristol version of *The Wizard of Oz*, Jimmy would have been the Tin Man, after he gets a heart; Doyle, the Lion, after he gets courage; and Barbara, the Scarecrow, after he gets a brain. (Paul Giamatti had traces of all three—plus, humor.) Barbara was Night's intellectual alter ego, and sometimes Night didn't feel like fighting with himself.

"If people see her face and expect her to cry, that's not good," Barbara said. She wasn't faulting Bryce's performance but how Night was using her. She knew it was tricky, criticizing Night. She had learned that during *Signs* and relearned it at the read-through. To have a successful relationship with Night, you had to manage him, and that was nearly impossible. Disney had discovered that.

"It's one note," Night said. He was speaking of Bryce's performance, but he could have been speaking of his direction of her.

Barbara said nothing. She knew when to quit.

Night went into a slow, long, rhythmic nod. The silence was striking. The implications of Barbara's observation were significant, both for what had already been shot and for what was still to come. Bryce was such an exquisite crier, you could shoot it all day long. Her eyes filled up and the tears rolled due south, straight down her high cheekbones, shooting off as if they were ski jumps, then landing on Cleveland Heep's drab work shirt or whatever she was wearing.

Bryce was the most earnest actor on *Lady*. (Chrismandu,

Paul's stand-in, was a close second.) The crew loved her and compared her favorably to another actress who had grown up in the business, Gwyneth Paltrow. Bryce took nothing for granted. She was polite, Night sometimes felt, almost to the point of being unreal.

One day Bryce was sitting on the Cove's industrial cement steps. They were between takes, and there was a gaggle of *Lady* people around: extras, stand-ins, actors, crew members, hairstylists, makeup artists—the usual suspects. Night was within earshot. Bryce had just seen *In Her Shoes,* the Cameron Diaz movie that had been shot in Philadelphia.

"How was it?" a woman asked.

"It was . . . good."

"We need more," another woman said. They wanted not just Bryce's take on the movie but her review of the costumes and the makeup and the set decoration. They wanted to know how Cameron Diaz looked and how the *Shoes* crew made her look.

"I'd rather not get too specific," Bryce said. "I'm sure there are a lot of people here who worked on it."

So polite.

Bryce analyzed everything. She was like Night that way. But she didn't pontificate. She was far more comfortable posing questions.

One mellow summer night, Bryce was sitting on the steps of her trailer. Inside her trailer were pictures of Albert Einstein and Audrey Hepburn and Martin Luther King, Jr., among other heroes. She had Joseph Campbell's *The Power of Myth* in her hands. Keith Jarrett was in the air, drifting out of Paul's camper. When Paul stepped outside, Bryce asked if he had read any Joseph Campbell. Paul nodded.

"Isn't he amazing?" Bryce said.

"Bunch of bullshit!" Paul answered. "Don't believe a thing he says!"

Bryce laughed, but nothing would deter her. She was on a spiritual quest, in some postmodernist way. She was planning her wedding during the *Lady* shoot and looking for a combination rabbi–Buddhist monk–physicist to officiate. On her off days, she was writing a script that had an Einstein role. She treated Night as if he had the answers to the great riddles of the universe. It didn't make him comfortable.

After the cry alert from Barbara, Night had several long conversations with Bryce about her performance. When they were alone, her inherent awkwardness came back, and Night was relieved to see it. To Night, *that* was the real Bryce, the one who never knew the right thing to say. For a long while during the shoot, Night had felt she was coming off like any other young good-looking actress telling smooth stories on some second-rate late-night TV show. ("Actors turn me off; human beings turn me on," Night would sometimes say.) Night wanted to strip her of artifice, find a way to get back the rawness he'd felt from her on a New York stage. That was who she'd been in *The Village*. That's who he needed for *Lady in the Water*.

The return of Bryce was gradual. One evening Night was mocking the vampish poses young starlets, like Bryce, assume for their red-carpet shots. He had the whole thing down: left toe touching right heel, hands on hips, spinal slouch, chin on shoulder. Bryce laughed, at Night and at herself, and Night knew he would eventually get her back.

Some days later, they were shooting a scene where Story is dragged by a scrunt over long wet grass. The scene had been worked out carefully by Jeff Habberstad, the stunt coordinator. Bryce was placed in a harness that was supposed to protect her as she was dragged through the grass. But the mechanical scrunt's speed was so great that Bryce was rolling all over the place, as if on a carnival ride gone wild. Her legs were getting nicked by twigs and plants and the heavy, coarse grass. But she told nobody about it. In between takes, she wore a long robe so nobody could see.

Night took safety on the set seriously. When he saw Bryce's welts and scratches, he was upset.

"This shouldn't happen," he said.

"I'm sorry," Bryce said.

"I'm going to call Jeff on this."

"Please don't. *Please* don't. It's not his fault."

"You don't realize: This is not about you. This is about the movie. I can't have my lead with welts all over her legs. Now, what about the scenes where you *don't* have welts all over your legs?" In the craft of making movies, this is known as a continuity problem. Mary Cybulski, the movie's meticulous script supervisor—the "script girl," Red's old-school phrase—was always on guard for continuity problems.

"We could maybe put makeup on them?" Bryce suggested.

Night wondered if he should call in the nurse on the set.

"I can't have a reputation as a director who doesn't protect his actors," he said.

But all the while, he was considering Bryce, her scratched legs, her mangy wet hair, her pale facial makeup, her ebullient eyes. Night could see how happy she was with her welts and her bruises, how pleased she was to take one for the team. It confirmed what he thought he'd known. Bryce was a believer: in the script, in Night, in the message of the movie. She helped give Night faith that the whole crazy thing made sense. She helped keep Nina out of Night's head. Nothing could get Nina out completely, but Bryce was helping.

Prior to his gig as Paul Giamatti's stand-in, Chrismandu's biggest movie job was his uncredited role playing a bookie on *Unbreakable*. Chrismandu said that *Lady in the Water* had a completely different vibe. Then Night had been coming off *The Sixth Sense* and feeling invincible. Many of the *Unbreakable* locations were in the path of everyday Philadelphia life—Franklin Field on the University of Pennsylvania campus—and there were thousands of extras and hundreds of people with their noses in a fence. Night and the crew and the actors were all over the city. There were two big stars around, Bruce Willis and Samuel L. Jackson. Traffic was snarled. There were police officers and security people everywhere, and some days there were helicopters carrying photographers with long lenses. It was as if the whole world wanted to know what Night was doing. He was it.

"This shoot is like family," Chrismandu said. He was wearing his Cleveland Heep glasses and still working on his reddish beard, determined to look more like Paul. Night noted what Chrismandu was doing. He noted effort from wherever it came, whether it was from Red, Bryce, Chrismandu, or the young man who made the morning smoothies. You could see what Chrismandu meant, making the comparison to family: meals together, daily inquiries about health, hidden secrets and eccentricities, a dynamic father figure in Night.

All the while, Night was a father at home, too. There was one day during the shoot when Franny got Night home at three-thirty A.M., and Night got himself up four hours later for a performance at his daughters' school. Some days the girls were in the driveway when Night left for work, waving goodbye. When they came to the set, they watched the mechanical green scrunt and its scary orange eyes with fear and awe, fingers half over their own dark eyes. You could see they thought their father was magical, a mad scientist, an important person. They understood that the movie he was making had been their story first.

"It's tough to go from Clark Kent to Superman," Night said one day when we were driving to the set.

"Where are you Clark Kent?" I asked. "At home or on the set?"

"That's the thing," Night said. "I don't know."

On the set, Night had to be the answer man in times of confusion, and the rest of the time he had to give the impression that if everybody followed his instructions, things would be fine. Paul had signed on for that. His attitude was, when in doubt, do what the director wants. But Paul had his moments of doubt, and everybody else did, too. In the shoot's background soundtrack—Night's cackling laugh—there was the hint of hysteria.

There was a scene in which Paul was having milk and cookies with Young-Soon and Mrs. Choi in the Choi apartment. Night had Paul sitting on the floor, childlike. At the end of every take, Paul would let the milk dribble down his bearded chin, and Night would laugh in uncontrollable bursts. Cindy Cheung didn't get what was so funny, but she laughed anyhow, not wanting to be the person to break the mood. Chris Doyle was comfortable on the outside. He didn't like how the milk-and-cookies scene was framed or lit, and by way of protest, he was muttering about it ("Looks like a fucking TV shot"). There were times Night wanted to say something similar but didn't. He couldn't afford to go under his breath like that. He couldn't afford to set himself apart or show doubt. There were too many people depending on him to lead, too many people watching his every move.

He was overloaded every day. He was trying to keep Nina out of his head and the spirit of Dylan in it. He was trying to find peace. In every take, he was trying to get the crew and the actors and the Warners people to see the story as he did. And when that didn't happen, his disappointment turned into frustration, and every so often he said things with the candor and anger that people use when they're in their own house, sur-rounded by family. So Night asked Glenn Kaplan when the movie would finally get in focus. And Night told Chris Doyle to simply lock down the camera, because given a long leash, Night felt the DP would at times make choices for himself and not for the movie. And Night told Red Burke—One Hundred Years of Cinema himself—that he was going too fast or too slow, even though it meant embarrassing the movie's old pro. They were rare, these mini-tantrums. He didn't even raise his voice to deliver them, which made them more deadly. But Night felt they were necessary, in the name of moviemaking.

Night was good at keeping his frustration in check. For his first big scene playing Vick, the frozen writer, the hair ladies made him look like he was ready to deliver the six o'clock news. But Night was the emperor in his new clothes, and even though there was murmuring in the peanut gallery about his hair, nobody was willing to say something directly to the boss, except for Jose. Night took a look in the mirror with fresh eyes and saw how poufed and smooth and ridiculous his hair was. He headed toward the hair-and-makeup trailer to see the hair ladies. Marching over in his heavy black work boots, he said, "I'm gonna read them the riot act!" He sat himself down in one of the swivel chairs, all masculine. There was enough hair product in the trailer to open a salon, and the air smelled of baked hair. Night looked at himself in the mirror and said, "You know, maybe we see the character of Vick in different ways, but this is what I have in mind—tell me what you think." Some riot act.

Chris Murphy was the video supervisor. When Red went to look at a replay of a pullback shot, Murphy made that happen. It was routine for Night to say into an intercom, "Chris Murphy, last little bit of that last take," and it would instantly appear on the monitor beside Night's director's chair. Murphy had worked on all of Night's movies since *The Sixth Sense*. He was personable and opinionated, kind of a gadfly, a student of Night's methods and manners. Night liked him.

Murphy performed his job with the nonchalance of a pro who knows what he's doing, and Night was okay with that as long as the work was good. Then came the day Night was shooting his most delicate scene with Bryce, in which Story tells Vick his future. It was Night's close-up. Night had told Bryce to think of herself as a nurse who has to tell a patient whether he has AIDS. It was wrenching. Night shot a take and walked over to the monitor to have a look at himself and the scene.

The moment the take started playing, Night began shaking his head.

He said, "For once, Chris Murphy, could you get it in synch?"

The gaps between sound and picture were so minute that a person with ordinary eyes and ears never would have picked up on them.

Night watched through the end of the take and said into the intercom, "This is the main reason you're on this movie, to have this scene in synch. And it's not. *You have failed.*"

I had never heard Night be so hurtful and cold. In the nurturing environment he had created, his words were so unexpected, direct, and cruel that they were a shock to hear. There were a dozen people standing around Night, and there was no sense of schadenfreude. People were just disturbed, feeling not only for Chris Murphy but for Night, too. Night didn't do things like that, become emotionally unhinged, not when everybody could see him, when everybody was expecting him to lead.

Murphy later told me that whenever a movie is shot on film, with sound recorded separately, it is impossible to get a

perfect matchup of sound and picture in an instant video replay. He said sound always had to be marginally ahead of or behind the picture. Night felt that was not the case.

But Night's outburst wasn't about mechanics. Night saw
something on the monitor he did not like, and in that moment
Chris Murphy became Nina Jacobson and Oren Aviv and Dick
Cook. Murphy became Harvey Weinstein during *Wide Awake*
and the computer graphics people who Night felt didn't get the
space invader to work at the end of *Signs*. He was Paul Giamatti
not reading the script right away, Cindy Cheung not accepting
the SAG minimum, Jose having doubts about Night's teaser. At
that moment Chris Murphy was everybody who could not be
inspired by Night's vision. The mechanical problem with the
replay rekindled Night's feelings of loneliness, and it triggered
a public panic attack. It was as if the theme of his movie—
becoming part of something bigger than yourself on faith
alone—was proving false in real life. Chris Murphy's true failure, to Night, was that he was not as committed to *Lady in the
Water* as Night was. Nobody could be, but Night didn't know that.

To others, the incident with Chris Murphy was much simpler.
It was a systems glitch, a staple of modern life, as anybody who
owns a printer knows. If you were there, you could feel Chris
Murphy's hot cheeks, his humiliation, his pain.

As for Night, everyone just figured he was nervous about
his performance, uptight, in a crap mood, in need of a full
night's sleep. Anybody could get like that now and again.

Night regretted criticizing Red during the pullback shot. Red
was a pro. He was making the movie better every day. Night had
berated the wrong man that day. Preparing the shot correctly fell

to Chris Doyle, and, as Night was an expert on Chris Doyle's limitations, monitoring him ultimately fell to Night. Night saw Red crossing a parking lot, stopped him, and said he was sorry for what had happened. He got almost no response from his dolly grip. Red was pissed.

The next day Night tried again. The problem with the pull-back shot could have been avoided had Doyle rehearsed with the stand-ins, he told Red. "It's not your fault, man. Cool?" He was apologizing again, and Red still wasn't accepting it.

Later that day, Red told me, "Public humiliation, private apology," and made the international symbol for male mastur-bation. Red had standards from another era. Everything was *not* cool. For Red, his craft was his life, or at least a big part of it. He still wasn't using Night's name. Every time Red said *the director,* his eyebrows went up.

Several nights later, Jimbo's was open, and Red was stand-ing in a circle with some of the other New Yorkers. Red wasn't a party person or a drinker. For him, it was one drink and back to his room. On *Mona Lisa Smile,* Julia Roberts had told Red she was going to send a limo to make sure he came to the wrap party. He told her not to bother.

Night was at Jimbo's that evening with Bhavna. Despite the Ping-Pong table and the tiki decorations and the bean-bag chairs, Jimbo's felt like a union hall. Night was at home there. People were telling Chris Doyle stories, overtime-pay stories, *Unbreakable* stories. There were people smoking cigarettes who never smoked during regular working hours. It's a stress-ful business, and the green tint to the light in Jimbo's helped people relax. Night saw Red and walked over to him. He knew on ESP alone that Red had not accepted his earlier apologies, and it was bothering him.

Night introduced Red to his wife and said to her, "This is the guy I yelled at, and I shouldn't have."

Red was impressed; the director had obviously told his wife about the incident. This apology was public. To Red, that changed everything. He accepted Night's apology. Night was relieved. He needed Red, and he needed Red to believe in him.

Paul was an avid reader of obituaries, and one of his favorite phrases was "Ends are never pretty." I tried to offer some rebuttals—Nelson Rockefeller, for example—but Paul was certain: Ends were always bad.

Paul was fatalistic and practical, bound to no religion, formal or otherwise. The ease with which Night spoke about faith was foreign to Paul. But they got along famously on the set every day (often to the exclusion of the other actors). They knew each other's cultural reference points. The guy who played the stiff in *Weekend at Bernie's*. How Al Pacino worked with directors (*Let's fucking try it! That was fucking stupid!*). The Scientologists and their penchant for crisp blue dress shirts. Night was the ideal audience member for Paul's improv, for his fake titles and invented dialogue. Night loved Paul's title for the porn version of the movie: *LADIES in the Water*. Later, Paul came up with this dialogue for Young-Soon and Cleveland.

Young-Soon: Mr. Heep, Mr. Heep—you got time for a quickie?

Cleveland: Not now, Young-Soon. But tell me: Could you look up the word *narf* for me?

Night and Paul were both verbal and quick in the extreme, but so different. With Night, everything meant something. Paul used the word *strange* as often as Night used the word *meaning*. Paul could see the irony in anything, and Night didn't want to. Paul read the obit for Joe Bauman, who had hit seventy-two home runs as a minor-leaguer in 1954 and had died in Roswell, New Mexico, the U.S. capital for UFO sightings. He saw the movie possibilities immediately: the minor-league slugger whose body is invaded by a space alien. But coming up with the idea didn't mean he was going to actually *write* it. There was no way. Why would he write when people paid him good money just to read lines and make faces?

Night had more ambition for Paul than the actor had for himself. Paul, with prodding, told Night about his upcoming roles, as a heavy, doing a voice-over, some funny stuff, some independent stuff, a mix.

"Dude, what are you doing?" Night said. "C'mon—you're a leading man!"

Paul shrugged. "I hear ya."

"You gotta take only leading-man roles."

"Yeah."

"I want you to go home tonight, look in the mirror, and say, 'I am *the* man, I am the *man!*'"

Paul was more likely to go to his temporary home (a suite at the Rittenhouse), turn on the TV, and click his way across the universe, looking for news, of a certain kind. One *Lady* night, after the death of the great Don Adams, Paul stopped for every clip that showed Maxwell Smart talking on his shoe phone or using the cones of silence or fighting Chaos.

One day Chrismandu nominated an exception to Paul's rule about ends. Jackie Gleason, he said, had gone out well.

"Really?" I asked. "Why do you say that?"

"He ate what he wanted to eat, and he did what he wanted to do," he explained. "He died young, but he never suffered. Nobody ever knifed him or nothing like that. He made people laugh, he had plenty of money, then he died. My father loved him."

I told Paul what Chrismandu had said.

"Jackie Gleason," Paul said. "That's good. That's really good. Jackie Gleason. Pretty end. Wow."

Some weeks later, Paul did something out of character. Paul asked Chrismandu for his telephone number and address, so that if a producer was ever looking for a stand-in for him, he could suggest Chrismandu. It wasn't like Paul to enter into another person's life, to take initiative that way. He didn't want people entering his life unannounced. But what Chrismandu had said was true: The odd congregation Night had assembled really was like family, at least for a few months.

Jim Gaffigan, an actor and comedian, heavyset and balding, had one day of work on the movie, playing a pool maintenance man. He had a two-minute scene with Paul in which they examine long strands of red hair that have been clogging up the Cove's community pool. In a rehearsal, Gaffigan held up the red hair and, in the cadence of his actual line, said, "I don't know whose hair this is, but whoever it is, she's related to Ron Howard." Paul, for a change, was laughing at somebody else's joke.

"You'd never see two character guys in one scene in an episode of *CSI*," Gaffigan said between takes. He and Paul were the same age, and Paul knew his act. Gaffigan was huge and he towered over Paul.

"You're right," Paul said. "They'd be like, 'Two character guys too many.' "

Gaffigan gave Night exactly what Night wanted right away, first take, first shot of the morning, but they kept going because everyone was having so much fun. It was an easy scene for a change. After one take, Gaffigan looked up at the camera and, in the voice of a TV reporter covering a hurricane's devastation, said, "Never has there been so much male-pattern baldness in one scene."

Night was worried that Gaffigan was offending Paul by treating him as an equal, but the opposite was happening. Gaffigan was putting Paul at ease. Being singled out, as he'd been by Horn, made Paul nervous. He had true humility.

Night looked at Paul and saw the next Gene Hackman, the next Tom Hanks. He imagined more for Paul than Paul was willing to imagine for himself. Either he really didn't get Paul, despite all their time together, or he knew Paul better than Paul knew himself.

During shooting, Night called the emotional climax of the script "the mailroom scene," the "life and death" scene from Cindy's audition. It brought together all the principals and one actor, Tom Mardirosian, who had little more than a bit part. Tom played Mr. Bubchik, a Jewish man beyond middle age who is mostly an off-camera voice, stuck in his apartment bathroom dealing with gastrointestinal issues. On the other side of the door is his wife, Mrs. Bubchik, played by Tovah Feldshuh, a theater legend for her one-woman show as Golda Meir. The Bubchik apartment was done in extreme Miami Beach—gold everything, with some silver accents. During an afternoon of shooting in the apartment, Night rubbed his temples and said to himself, "I can't *think* in here." Tovah was a saucy, gum-chewing trip, loud and fun and warm, wearing a Pat Nixon beehive hairdo for her character. Night's direction for her could not have been more direct: "Halve it. Halve it again. Tone it down from there." Tovah and Paul, working one simple scene with Mr. Bubchik groaning from the bathroom, ate up *sixteen* takes. At one point, tape was put on the floor, marks for the actors. Paul's was green and Tovah's was pink. "Pink," Paul said, "for the lady." Tom Mardirosian did not have marks. His character, working for part of one day, never left the bathroom.

Until weeks later, when Mr. Bubchik reemerged for the biggest scene in the movie, the mailroom scene, the life-and-death scene. Tom had been hired after the read-through, so he was meeting most of the other actors for the first time that day. His costume was pajamas and slippers, as if he had come straight from the loo. Everybody else was dressed, and Tom couldn't understand why he was not. He'd never been given a script.

The mailroom scene was complicated in every way. Tom, in a voice of comedic manic worry, kept saying to the other actors, "What the hell is going on here? What's this whole thing about? What the fuck am I supposed to be doing? Am I supposed to just wander around in these goddamn slippers?" The whole thing was one big mystery to him. He didn't have a single line in the mailroom scene. Yet there he was with all the heavy hitters:

Mr. Paul Giamatti (Cleveland Heep)
Miss Bryce Dallas Howard (Story)
Ms. Cindy Cheung (Young-Soon Choi)
Ms. Sarita Choudhury (Anna Ran)
Mr. Bill Irwin (Mr. Leeds)
Ms. Mary Beth Hurt (Mrs. Bell)
Mr. Jeffrey Wright (Mr. Drury)
Master Noah Gray-Cabey (Joey Drury)
The Rev. M. Night Shyamalan (writer, director,
    Vick Ran)
Also:
The five Perez de la Torre sisters
The five smokers

Night gathered the twenty actors in the mailroom and gave a pep talk. It was uncharacteristically brief. "This scene," Night said, "is all about saving this guy." He meant Paul. It was an insight. From the script, you would have said the scene was all about trying to save Story.

For a while, Cindy had been looking for something from Night, some sort of direction, direction he was usually happy to give. Then she realized she was getting it, in Night's silence. She had what she needed, and now was the time to execute. He had laid it out weeks earlier: *You know your lines. You know the role. On the day, whatever happens, happens. Trust yourself.* She was ready to do exactly that. Night had faith in Cindy. Now it was her turn to show she had faith in Night, and in herself.

Several days before the mailroom scene, Night didn't know if he could have Chris Doyle shoot the movie's most important scene. All along, Night had planned to have Doyle shoot the scene using a small, lightweight handheld camera, the kind often used in documentaries. It would lend a semblance of reality to a fantastical scene. The mailroom would be crowded, and Doyle, so tiny, could move easily and intimately among the actors, who revered him. The act of photography was something like sex for him, and it showed. The actors appreciated his crazy love.

But working a handheld camera requires a rock-steady hand, and in the excitement of the day, Night didn't know if the camera would be too wobbly in Doyle's fingers; Night didn't know if Chris would point the camera in the right place at the right time. It was the kind of scene in which you had to make every take count, and Night could not know which Chris Doyle would show up that day. The scene would be emotionally draining, especially for Paul. There were only so many times you could ask him to get completely worked up about the interior life of Cleveland Heep. In the language of the movie, and in everyday life, Night had doubts. The voices were kicking in.

You can never rid yourself of all doubt. You found that out when you were playing Vick. If you don't think Doyle can give you what you need, bring somebody else in.

Chris got you this far. Stay with him.

It's too risky. You can't count on him getting lucky, not this time.

But what kind of message does it send if you don't let him shoot it?

That life's imperfect.

"What would you think about a Steadicam shot for the mailroom scene?" Night said to Chris.

A Steadicam is like a handheld on a much bigger scale. It helps create intimacy; not as much as a handheld, but it's sturdier. Doyle hadn't operated a Steadicam on *Lady*. It requires considerable physical strength.

Had Night just taken the shot away from him and brought in Pat Capone or somebody else to work a handheld, Doyle might have walked away from the movie and not returned. He could have had a tantrum or gone into a funk. He might have tried to talk Night out of it. But because it was a Steadicam, Night knew Chris would accept the idea. It wasn't an affront.

Now Night was doing something out of character. He had said at the start that he would be ruthless, and you have to be to make the movie you want to make. People are always going to get hurt along the way. From the first day of shooting, Night couldn't possibly keep the slo-mo Lick-Slap Kenny in the movie. The boy would be hurt by being cut, but the movie would be better. There was no debate. But now, late in the shoot, Night put Chris Doyle's state of mind ahead of the movie's technical needs. He ditched the handheld and went for the Steadicam shot, to spare Chris. Night knew good karma would serve his movie best of all as the end neared.

———

Night never explained to the actors why Doyle wasn't shooting the scene. They were surprised to see a new man there, Kyle Rudolph, tall and broad, with a no-nonsense manner. It was Kyle's camera that Bhavna had blessed years earlier on the first day of shooting *Wide Awake,* and he had worked in different capacities on each of Night's movies. Doyle was on the set for the mailroom scene, bopping around on the edges, so the actors assumed Kyle was someone the DP had brought in to work a specialty shot, like the scuba crew shooting the pool shots. Beyond that, they didn't think about it too much. They had other things on their minds.

Kyle was like Mr. Bubchik. He had no idea what was going on. He had been called at the last minute, and all Night had told him was that he would be shooting the most important scene of the movie. Beyond that, nothing. It bothered Kyle, but Night didn't want to overexplain it. He thought too much information would bog Kyle down.

On the day, Night felt like he had on the morning of the read-through. His stomach was in such a roil, he could have been playing Mr. Bubchik with his GI issues. He was popping TUMS and fighting a headache the whole day.

The scene was all about faith. Faith in the power of a family, a tribe, a guild, groups of all sorts. Faith in our ability to heal others and ourselves. Faith in storytelling in all its forms: biblical storytelling; "the Hindu tradition of storytelling," as Night's father put it; the storytelling parents do with their children, easing them into their nighttime dreams.

Kyle was moving through the mailroom, his T-shirt soaked with sweat, recording shots he wasn't given the chance to understand. He was a hired hand, and he was annoyed at Night, but none of that really mattered. In its own way, even what Kyle was doing was an act of faith. That was how Night saw it. Kyle was honoring his craft and earning his pay, but he was also helping Night get the shots—if the whole thing worked—that would make you think about the movie weeks and months and years after you saw it.

The scene required Paul to let go of grief, Cleveland Heep's grief, and likely his real-life grief, too. It wasn't actually a "life and death" scene but the other way around. By way of greeting that day, Paul had said to me, "Nipsey Russell!" The obit had been in the *Times* that morning: the rhyming Nipsey Russell, game-show host and comic, a talk-show regular in Paul's boyhood, the Tin Man in *The Wiz*, the all-black version of *The Wizard of Oz*. Paul was different that day, wandering off to remote places in the warehouse between takes, keeping to himself. No routines. One line, spoken through sobbing, was "I can't, can't, can't." He can't let it go. Paul's face was red, and he was trembling. Watching Paul at work, I thought of his father, gone at fifty-one, his mother left to carry on alone. I thought how devastated I would have been, had I lost my father when I was newly out of college and starting out. When you see the movie, if you see it, you may also think of someone gone too soon. That's part of Paul's skill, to get you to feel those things. It's why Night had cast him. It's what Night was seeing, the day at the restaurant, when he glimpsed the shoe.

Night had written a powerful and beautiful scene, and now he was directing it, but he no longer owned it. He had turned it over to Paul in his trembling, to Tom Mardirosian in his slippers and pajamas, to Kyle Rudolph strapped to his Steadicam, to all the others. For the first time, after months of shooting and rehearsals, Paul was not saying, "Yeah, sure, fine." Paul was acting from his heart, and Night was directing from his brain. Night had already worked through the emotion of it, and now he was addressing the technical side of it. He wanted Paul to be in certain places on certain words, and Paul was somewhere else, someplace unfinished and deeply sad. He was doing well just to get the words out. Night's driving force—*it can always be better!*—doesn't work for everybody, or anything close to it. There was a hint of frustration on both their parts. Night had nothing to cackle about. The evening of the death-and-life scene, Night was trying to let go, but it wasn't easy. It's not an easy thing for any father to do.

Paul was on the floor of the mailroom, as the script instructed him to be, surrounded by the "seven sisters," the five Perez de la Torre sisters plus Anna and Young-Soon. They were there to heal him. The scene had been inspired by a ceremony Night had first seen at a cousin's Hindu wedding, just as he had seen the young boy talking to himself at a family funeral. The voices had told Night to use a Hindu wedding ritual as a centerpiece of a mainstream, made-in-America movie, and that was what he was doing.

Cindy placed her hand on Paul's back, spread her fingers, and closed her eyes. His body was warm and his shirt moist. She could feel his flesh. He was taking full breaths, his back heaving gently, rising and falling, rising and falling. The hands of the other sisters were placed on him one by one, and now there were seven hands on him and everybody had their eyes closed. Cindy was suddenly aware of how *alive* Paul was, like a sleeping animal in the woods, warming the earth with its body. She could feel everything in the room, in her darkness. She could feel her fellow actors breathing, lights burning, eyes welling, film rolling, sweat rising, Night watching. She had never felt more alive in all her life.

9.

In late October, after Night wrapped the movie, I flew to Los Angeles to see Nina Jacobson. She had a sleek office at the Team Disney building in Burbank, on a spotless campus that felt like a sprawling, high-end psychiatric center. There were some homey touches in her office—family pictures, children's art—and she had a remote-control device to close her door.

The president of Disney's legendary film company had short hair and John Lennon glasses. She was wearing a chic suit of fine wool and leather work boots that could have stomped anything. She was a few years older than Night.

M. Night Shyamalan was a pivotal figure in her life—*The Sixth Sense* helped make her career—and she had a lot to say about him.

You could see immediately how she and Night would have gotten along famously, and how they would have battled. They both had enough words and phrases and analogies to turn you around on anything. When I heard her speak, I realized that Night, as with his Johnnie Cochran imitation, had Nina down cold. He could do her voice, intense, scratchy, somewhat whiny, but also authoritative. She seemed sure of herself. She had a penchant for sweeping statements: "Night captures that moment between the sacred and the profane." I had no idea what that meant, but it sounded awfully good.

When I told her about the oval head shots—Nina and Dick

Cook and Oren Aviv, the We Don't Get It Trio, drifting in and out of Night's crowded head—she seemed surprised. In Nina's mind, she was the jilted one, and she offered proof: During the breakup dinner at Lacroix, Dick Cook had pleaded with Night to make *Lady* for Disney. It was Night who had said goodbye. Nina was left feeling broken. He was the one who got away.

"When we got back to the hotel, Dick said to me, 'You've got to realize in these relationships, you're going to give more love than you get,' " Nina said, recounting an event now nine months old. "And he's right. That's how it's always been: The patron gives the love, and the artist receives it." She didn't see it from Night's side: When the patron rejects the art, the artist is left feeling all alone, no matter how much success he's had.

But Nina's play-by-play of the dinner was mostly consistent with Night's version. She, too, remembered numerous petite courses; tables too close together; Night talking about Harriet Beecher Stowe; a tense dinner that went on forever. But she said Night was wrong if he thought that Nina and her boss and her marketing man had come to the dinner without a plan. Their goal was to tell Night the script needed more work, and that maybe it should be shelved in favor of writing or directing something else. "I said to Night, 'This script is like the pregnant woman looking at her ultrasound and seeing an embryo at four months,' " Nina recalled. "And Night said, 'Are you saying the script needs five more months?' "

Nina said that if they couldn't get Night to abandon *Lady,* they were prepared to let him make it, but with a smaller budget than he had for *The Village.* They never expected Night to walk. What Night said to Cook at the elevator—"I thought we were going to ride into the sunset together"—Nina could have said to Night.

She did not believe, as Night did, that Disney had turned into a soulless, vacuous corporation wanting Night to make nothing but supernatural thrillers that would satisfy the fan base, open big, do $200 million in domestic and $100 million more with international, DVD sales, and everything else. But what was she going to say? *Yep, he nailed it; that's who we are to-day?* She was a Disney employee. She had a big high-paying job with stock options and all the rest. You'd see her name near the top of those lists of the most powerful women in Hollywood. Anyway, she didn't think the Disney movie division was in such dire shape. *The Chronicles of Narnia,* for instance, looked promising.

We talked a lot about *The Village.* If *Signs* had been a three-run home run, *The Village* was a one-run double. But *The Village's* numbers had no influence on how she'd read the *Lady* script. "Our assumption was that we were going to love it," Nina said. She was drinking unsweetened cranberry juice out of a plastic water bottle and fidgeting. She was in constant motion without ever leaving her chair. "We all had a lot of excitement about reading it." *Excitement.* One of Paula's favorite Hollywood words.

Nina said that when Night's longtime assistant had made her L.A. rounds that Sunday afternoon in February to hand-deliver the script to the troika, there was nothing to read into Paula's three awkward encounters. I asked if Disney had wanted to reassert control of the relationship, starting with Night's rules for the way his new scripts would be read, but Nina said that was not the case.

"It was a ritual for us, a Nightism," Nina said of the Sunday afternoon deliveries. "He loves good drama. The only reason I was late for Paula was because I had to take my son to a birthday party. The priority for me is family first, then job. We're not people who delegate our child care."

That sounded reasonable—parenting first, work second. (It was a mark of affluence to be able to order things that way.) My Disney visitor's badge—bar-coded, with the telephone number for security below a picture of Mickey—was stamped October

31, 2005, and Nina was making arrangements to get Halloween costumes from wardrobe: a Cinderella dress; a belly-dancer outfit in the style of *I Dream of Jeannie*. Another perk of a big job.

Night, like Nina, tried to keep his weekends clear to be with his family. But he didn't put his life in boxes: writer here, director there, father here, husband there. He saw his own childhood in his two girls. When one drew a Halloween pumpkin with blood dripping down its cheeks, Night was delighted. *Lady* had begun with his girls. They had visited the set often, with Bhavna. For Night, his various roles blurred together into his *life*. That was why he didn't know where he was Clark Kent and where he was Superman; it was changing all the time. There were Sunday afternoons when he had to write, or make a call, or watch audition tapes. Bhavna and the girls would wander in and out.

To Night, the three Disney executives should have treated the reading of his new script at the appointed time on the appointed Sunday as part of the fun. If Nina had really been on board, she would have left the party a half hour earlier and kept her date with Paula, and with Night's script. It would have been a symbol, nothing more, that she actually *was* excited. But Paula was on time and Nina was not, and on that Sunday evening, Night went to bed (or tried to) without knowing what Nina thought of the script. Sometime between *The Sixth Sense* and that Sunday afternoon, Night had lost Nina. He no longer inspired her.

"Any guilt I might have felt over Night's anxiety on that Sunday night was lessened for me by my knowing that my children know that they come first," Nina said.

They were in different places. When you're the writer and director, you own the script, financially and emotionally. Night had no boss except himself and his standards. He had no money worries. He was freed up in a way few people are.

Nina was an executive, with layers of bosses and a pay-check that kept her in low-carb soups and children's birthday presents and all the many expensive things demanded by modern life in tony Brentwood. She'd been drawn to the business by her love of movies, then lured to Disney by the promise of *The Sixth Sense*. But that was seven years and many movies ago. Things had changed. When *The Sixth Sense* was in movie theaters, Disney was a $40 stock. By the time of *The Village*, it was a $23 stock. Nina's job was to make movies that made money, the more money the better. Lately, there hadn't been much profit to report. *The Wall Street Journal* had been writing that story for a while.

I asked Nina if she was frustrated that Night hadn't taken more of her suggestions on *The Village*. Maybe the movie would have made more money if he had. "All in a day's work," she said. "The chief requirement in hiring a director is not compliance." I couldn't tell if that was a yes or a no.

My interview with Nina kept returning to the night of the Lacroix dinner, to the breakup. "I remember Night saying, 'I feel like you don't have faith in me,'" Nina told me. "And I said, 'We're not talking about our regard for you.'" It sounded like faith and regard were the same things to Nina. They were not to Night.

They were both still hurting. Nina wanted to know how the shoot had gone; Night, helping the girls sort through their candy at home, wanted to know what Nina was saying. In their search for peace, they were both stuck.

Without Night in the room to debate her, Nina's most important point sounded logical: "What was I supposed to do when I read the script and didn't get it? Lie to him? When he was writing, he talked about this script with me more than any of his others. He said, 'This could be my *E.T.*' I was prepared to love it. And I didn't."

If Night had been there, he would have come out swinging: *You should have given me the space I've earned. You didn't even try to understand it. You're too scared to take a chance.* But in his absence, Nina's simple declaration made sense. In a way, what she did was brave. The easy thing to do would have been to say yes to a director who always made you money.

I asked Nina about the news stories in the trades, the ones Night had read when leaving the Hotel Bel-Air that February morning, the ones announcing that Night was leaving Disney for Warner Bros. She knew that the mention of creative differences had set Night off, that he felt the Disney side had violated the terms of the divorce.

"It was honest," Nina said. "We did have creative differences. We agreed that we would treat each other with respect and kindness. We kept silent so Night could sell the script elsewhere. I feel we acted very honorably."

I asked what she thought about Night taking *Lady* to Warner Bros.

"I thought that would happen," she said. "I knew how much Alan Horn loved *The Village.*"

In February I spoke to Nina again, on the phone. She asked if I'd seen the movie yet. I hadn't. Night and Barbara Tulliver and a team of editors were editing every day, and all there was to see so far was a rough cut. Night wanted me to see something much closer to finished, and that was at least a month away. Nina asked if I'd read the review of *Lady* on a website called Ain't It Cool News. I hadn't heard of the website, knew nothing of the review, and couldn't imagine how it even existed. Night had been showing the unfinished version—no music, uncorrected color, extra scenes, rudimentary sound—only to handpicked groups, looking for feedback.

"The reviewer had the same problems I had," Nina said. She started to describe the points made in the review—too many rules, too many peculiar words—and suddenly stopped herself short. Maybe she heard her own tone: *I told you so.*

Nina didn't know who had written the review. Evidently, it was unsigned. The significant thing to her, it seemed to me, was that the first review was negative.

It was sad, really, to hear a woman of Nina's intelligence finding validation from an anonymous reviewer critiquing an unfinished movie that had been made—if nothing else—with integrity. If *Lady in the Water* turned out to be a failure—and Night knew that was a possibility—it would fail honestly.

I couldn't find the review. It had been removed from the website. When I asked Night about it, I imagined he'd be furious every which way: at the reviewer, at the review, at the website that had posted it. *Furious* turned out not to be the right word.

"We screened a rough cut in the screening room in the barn," Night said, falling immediately into the tone of storyteller. "A friend brought a friend, a kid who goes to NYU who wants to be a director. The second I heard about the review, I figured it must have been this kid. He was the only one we didn't know. So we called him. At first he denied it, and then he admitted it was him."

Next you might have expected, *And I read him the riot act.* That was one of Night's regular phrases. He went another way.

"I wanted to meet him, face-to-face. I was going to New York anyhow, so I arranged to see him at some little dark place downtown, near NYU, like a small restaurant-bar.

"When the kid first came in, he was like *I'm the big man*

here. Very arrogant. First he gets all this attention for the review, now the director wants to meet him, that whole thing.

"The first thing I said to him was 'Let's leave aside how *completely* wrong it is to come to a screening like the one you came to, where I tell you the movie's unfinished, that what you're about to watch is a rough cut, that it still needs a lot of work, and that you can all be helpful to me by telling me what you think, and then you go out and write a public review about a private experience. I find all that unbelievably troubling, but that's not even on my radar screen compared to what I'm about to tell you.'

"And by this point the kid is trembling. He has no idea what's coming next.

"Then I say, 'I can find anybody who will come watch a rough cut and say, "It was good—I like how you used the butterflies," or whatever. That doesn't do shit for me.

" 'But you come in and you have real opinions and real criticisms. You're the kind of person who can help me make the movie better. Because I'm going to use every last second I have to make this movie as good as I possibly can make it, and I'm going to listen and see what I can learn from you.'

"And by this point the kid's apologizing, saying he's sorry and he should never have done it and all that. But that's not what this meeting is about. He had very valid criticisms and he cared about movies.

"I say to him, 'Do you know Francis Ford Coppola added one hour to *The Godfather* from the time he first started showing the rough cut until the time the movie was released? One hour. It would never have been *The Godfather* without that hour. But Coppola couldn't work that way today, because somebody would sneak into a screening of the rough cut, post a review on a website, say that the movie's just another gangster picture, the studio would lose faith, and that would be the end of it.'

"Now the kid's locked in with me. I say, 'Do you want to be the director of *Dukes of Hazzard VIII*? Do you want to be part of the generation that supports only movies like that? Or do you want to have an original voice?'

"He says, 'Original voice.'

" 'That's what I'm trying to do, too—have an original voice. Say something new. I'm trying to take a chance. And someone like you can help me. And you actually did. Even though you did it in the forum that you did, and as wrong as it was for you to do it that way, I still learned something from your review, and I still want to thank you because you're going to help me make my movie better.' And he was all wide-eyed.

" 'But if you're ever in that situation again, be a man and say it to the director's face. Say it to *my* face. Say it artist to artist.'

"And now he looks like he's gonna cry. I say to him, 'Someday you'll be editing your movie, trying to make it better before it goes out to the world, and I hope I can do for you what you did for me. We need more African-American directors. We need more points of view. But as directors, we all need the space to find our voices, where we can take chances, see what works and what doesn't, and that's what editing is all about. They spent a year editing *The Exorcist*, you know? That's why I'm showing rough cuts, to get responses before I go out to the world. All right? Cool?'

"We hugged. He got the website to remove the review. He wanted to do that. We were together for a long time, close to two hours. And I had all sorts of shit going on, but I felt this was the most important thing I could be doing. For myself and for him. It actually was very, very cool."

That was Night's response to a would-be director who had trespassed on his property, real and intellectual. But Night didn't see him as a trespasser. Well, at first he did. At first he *was* furious.

But not by the time he met him. By then Night saw him as another person he could turn around, another person who was lost, another person he could inspire. Along the way, the kid—the anonymous before-the-start-gun reviewer who helped validate the opinions of one of the most powerful women in Hollywood—did Night more of a favor than he could ever know.

Night left the NYU student, the would-be director, on a sidewalk in lower Manhattan, and went back to work in a mixing studio. As he walked down the sidewalk, in the brisk winter wind, a powerful feeling washed over him. The episode was so unexpected—reading the review, meeting the reviewer, the different emotions the whole thing had wrought: anger, denial, forgiveness, acceptance. Night practically ran to the studio, the strap of his backpack bouncing off his shoulder with every step. He was ready for whatever was next.

Regarding the movie, Night knew the kid was correct. It had serious problems. Night had a month to try to improve it, to find his voice, the director's own voice, amid all the other ones in the movie. At that late hour, it wasn't there yet.

When he was done with his work, the kid would like the movie. That was Night's goal.

April 18, 2006

Night had a quiet and peculiar day at the farm on a gorgeous weekday in mid-April nearly half a year after shooting wrapped.

I know there's something I should be doing now, but what is it?

At seven P.M. that evening, Night would be screening *Lady in the Water* for a group of strangers, forty of them, scorecards in their hands. Civilians, Night called them. The people for whom Night made movies.

After shooting had wrapped in late October, Night went into hibernation with Barbara and her team. For most people, editing would be a study in tedium, but it's a productive outlet for a certain strain of obsessives, Night being Exhibit A. Night had blocked off November and December 2005 and January and February in the new year for editing. His job now was to pull the right parts from the right takes and order them the right way. His job was to turn his Bristol footage into a movie. Every so often, looking for feedback, he'd show a rough cut of the picture, or parts of it, to small groups of hand-picked people. That's how the kid from NYU, slipping through the cracks, got to see it. The would-be director from Night's alma mater said publicly what a lot of the others were saying to Night in the safety of the barn: They didn't get it. If they knew Night, they might be afraid to say it to his face. It didn't matter. Night could tell what they thought by the positions of their heads while watching the movie, or through their facial expressions afterward. They weren't laughing, they weren't startled, they weren't moved. Night *knew* he had something. The actors' read-through had gone so well. The mock teaser—with Brick Mason's simple storyboard pictures and the snippet of opera—was so beautiful. The dailies were strong. But it wasn't coming together as a movie. Night felt like a hamster in a tiny cage, furiously going nowhere.

Night devoted one afternoon to the scene in which Paul asks Cindy to look up the word *narf* for him. Night watched different takes of it at least a hundred times. Finally, against all previously stated logic, Night chose the first take from the first time he shot it, when Paul went AWOL from the script and opened the scene with an impromptu "Hey." Yes, there were water droplets on Paul's glasses and Cindy felt confused and Night felt he had lost her. But that was then, *on the day.* Five months later, in the editing room, at the end of a long day, Night saw it differently. He *loved* what Cindy had done. In it went. He thought about it all night. The next morning, it was out.

His desperation was showing up in unexpected ways. In the dead of winter, and in the middle of editing, Night left *Lady* and went to New York for a few days to direct a two-minute spot for American Express, part of a series called "My life. My card." Night dreaded leaving the *Lady* editing room, but knew the break could only help him, and that the campaign would generate interest in *Lady*—if he ever actually completed the movie. Tiger Woods was in the series, and so was the actress Kate Winslet and Mike Lazaridis, the inventor of the Black-Berry. Night wrote his own spot and in the kicker says, "My life is about finding time to dream." You see him trying to find a restaurant where he can do nothing but fall into the lives of the strangers around him. He imagined saying, *My life is about finding time to think.* Editing *Lady* had been an assault on his senses. All through editing, he felt like he did that day in the gold-and-silver Bubchik apartment—he couldn't clear his head.

There was a print component to the series, with an Annie Leibovitz photograph and a questionnaire, filled out by the ad's subject. Each subject listed on dotted lines his or her first job or last purchase or wildest dream. For "alarm clock," Tiger Woods had written "5:00 A.M. sharp!!" Night, in cramped schoolboy print, wrote, "Preoccupation." For "biggest challenge," Tiger had written, "How can I become a better person tomorrow?" Night wrote, "Not letting work make me unhappy." But his work *was* making him unhappy. How could it not? He was trying to make the most important and personal movie of his life for a new studio that would be spending $140 million on it, and the people who were watching early versions were leaning the backs of their heads into Night's well-upholstered screening-room seats, bewildered or bored or both. Be a better person tomorrow? Night was just trying to *get* to tomorrow. He tried to contain his desperation. He kept up appearances.

When the spot was all set to go and not before, Night told his mother about the American Express campaign.

"It's not like an ad," Night said. "It's more like a two-minute movie. It's going to premiere during the Oscar telecast. Millions of people will see it, all over the world. The print part's going to be everywhere. It'll be in *The New Yorker!*"

He was assuming the role of needy son, still trying to impress his parents, still looking for praise. He knew from experience it wasn't easily done.

"Then maybe something good will come out of it!" Night's mother said cheerfully.

In late February, after working on editing the movie for four months, Night flew to Los Angeles and in a screening room on the Warners lot showed *Lady* to Alan Horn and Jeff

Robinov, along with other studio executives and *Lady* crew members. After four months, the movie should have been pretty close to done, but Horn and Robinov had a muted response. They said encouraging things, but Night could tell they were worried. They knew it wasn't there yet, and Night did, too. Listening to the responses of the group during the movie, and to what was said afterward, Night felt he had discovered the movie's fundamental flaw: *Lady* was coming across more like a play—where words trump action—than a movie.

"I think I need more time with it," Night said to Horn. He wanted them to consider what they had just seen as a rough cut, even though, by the look of it, it was way beyond that by then. Night knew if he had another month he could come back with something much better. Among hundreds of other things, he wanted to make the scrunt scarier. He wanted you to feel what peril Story and Cleveland were in. Night was nervous as he asked for more time. They were still getting used to each other.

"Then you should take the time," Horn said.

No hesitancy, no doubt, no second-guessing. Night was not accustomed to that from a studio executive.

"Really?"

"Of course. If there's anything I can do to help, call."

By saying everything with almost nothing, Horn had inspired Night. His spirits lifted. Horn was saying to Night what Night had said to Cindy Cheung: You know what you're doing, and if you don't, I'm here to help.

The voices kicked in.

You've been screaming in the wind for years and finally someone has heard you.

Horn?

Yep.

Alan Horn, karate expert and reserved studio boss?

Yes!

In Night's head, there was a beat.

Maybe.

Still, Night left the Warners lot relieved. He felt like a student facing expulsion, saved by a professor's extension. Leaving the Warners lot that day, even though his movie was a mess, Night had a feeling of assuredness. Somebody believed in him! He suddenly felt seized by the need to see . . . *Nina Jacobson.* All through the *Lady* shoot, he had wanted to chase the oval picture of her out of his head, but he was never able to do it. For the nine weeks of shooting, he never found his peace. But now, with a new lease on life extended to him by Horn, Night realized something he didn't know during the shoot, that Nina was *not* the enemy. She had made Night better—as a writer, as a director, as a boss. In their years working together, Night had wondered if he would always be a child to her, but now he had figured out that she had actually helped him grow up. He wanted her to know that he'd pull her out of a burning building. It was the old Night mojo talking, out of nowhere, odd, half-crazy and inspiring. It was the same thing he'd wanted to tell the stewardess, the same thing he wanted to tell Chris Doyle, the same thing he did tell Cindy Cheung that day in the audition room. He quickly set up a breakfast date with her.

They met at the Hotel Bel-Air. It was nothing like the breakup dinner at Lacroix. Night ate huge pieces of French toast, and there was no fighting. They talked about *Lady,* and about other movies, too. Night now knew things he hadn't known before: It wasn't Nina's fault that she didn't "get" the original *Lady* sale script; it was Night's fault. And now, after all the script revisions, after all the shooting, after four months of editing, there had to be a movie in there somewhere, if Night had enough game to find it. And none of that had anything to do with Nina. All Nina did was dismiss a flawed script. Sure, she could have seen beyond the flaw, or shown faith. But she didn't, and that's what led Night to Horn. It worked out. Or it could, if Night could do his job. It was all on Night, and he liked it that way. It was late in the day, but he had found his peace.

He had a month of work ahead of him. A month to make *Lady* a picture people would want to see, his *E.T.* One month until he would return to the Warners lot and show the movie again to Alan Horn and prove to him that his faith in him was justified. Night knew how minute changes had ripple effects throughout any movie. *E.T.* had proved that to him. He saw the movie when it first came out, in the summer of 1982, shortly before he turned twelve. The movie transported him. Twenty years later, he took his older daughter to see it when it was re-released. There were added scenes, changes in the score, the beats were different. The movie they watched had no impact on his daughter, and did nothing for Night. Night felt like a piece of his childhood had been robbed from him. He couldn't figure out the problem. Had he changed in a fundamental way, or had the movie? He ordered a DVD of the original version and, when he was working on *Lady*, showed it to his younger daughter and a group of her friends in the screening room at the barn. Everything came flooding back to him, the magic and fantasy and dream of the 1982 movie. The young girls loved it, too. Night was convinced: It was all in the editing.

March was all fury. He made hundreds of changes. I'd tell you about them, but I didn't know much about what he did myself. Night and I were talking regularly, but I wasn't over his shoulder during editing. He wanted me to see the movie when it was closer to complete. He wanted me to see it with fresh eyes, like an ordinary moviegoer. The main thing he wanted to do to *Lady* then was to drive the play—the theatricality—out of it.

At the end of March, Night returned to the Warners lot, to watch it with a few dozen people, mostly Warner Bros. executives and Night's crew members. Bryce was there with her fiancé. (I had wanted to come to this screening, and Night was fine with that, but Horn wouldn't allow it.) Night felt the movie was ready for Bhavna to see, and she and Night sat together, off by themselves. As Bhavna watched *Lady in the Water* for the first time, Night spent the entire movie reading her, noting when she squeezed his arm, when she laughed, when she cried, when she held her breath.

When they had married, there was no promise of professional success for Night. There were a million aspiring screenwriters and directors on the NYU campus in the early 1990s, or so it seemed. The only thing they both knew was that Night would work hard. Night's in-laws, at first, were dubious about his ability to make a living in his chosen field. What he did didn't seem like proper work. In the early months of their marriage, Bhavna and Night lived with Night's parents, the doctors Shyamalan. *They* had proper professions. And now Bhavna was sitting in an opulent screening room in the company of the Warners president, watching a movie written and directed by her husband and inspired by a story he had told their two daughters, a movie that would open on thousands of screens across the world, supported by a $70 million marketing campaign—if he could finish it. Night was like Vick, the author character he played in the movie. Vick couldn't finish either.

Bryce loved the movie and the crew was praising it and Horn and Robinov were talking about how they would market the movie and what it would do overseas. Everybody was looking ahead, except Night. He knew the movie had not made progress. In fact, over the course of a month, it had gone backward. He could tell by Bhavna alone. She had said to him, "I love it, but it's not your most important movie." Bhavna knew him better than anybody in the world, loved him more and supported him more, and even *she* wasn't seeing the movie.

Night blamed himself. If he really had made the movie he
wanted to make, it would have been obvious that *Lady*—by far—
was the most important movie he had ever made. He felt completely alone. The voices returned.

It's not Horn.

*No, it is Horn. You've been praying for somebody to hear you
and now someone finally is and it's Mr. Alan Horn!*

*I wish it were that easy. It's not. It's not Horn. It's not Chris
Doyle. It's not Paul Giamatti or Cindy Cheung. It's not Nina. It's
not the stewardess on the Warner Bros. jet. It's not the kid from
NYU. It's not Bhavna.*

Why? Why must it always be so complicated?

What I'm trying to do, you do alone.

You're not alone. You're surrounded by people who help you.

Without them, I'd be lonelier still.

In early April, when Night returned from Los Angeles, I got to
see the movie, nearly four months before its release date. At
Night's invitation, my wife, Christine, joined me. We had met
Night nearly two years earlier, on that balmy evening when his
energy invigorated an entire dinner party. As I got to know
him, I found him to be only more invigorating. I never got
tired of listening to him or watching him in action, spinning
his rings and laughing crazily, tying his boots while spewing
words faster than his listeners could absorb them. I was learning from him all the time, about storytelling, about reading
people, about working hard. He became more than a subject
for me. In ways, he became an ideal.

I'd come to see what Bhavna had known for a long time:
Beneath Night's zeal were great reserves of sadness and desperation. His outsized ambition and determination made him
crazy, but they also kept him sane. He really did want to make

art for the masses, not just profitable filmed entertainment, and he was suffering for it. That may sound pretentious, but it's the truth. Night, generally, was agonizingly honest whenever he examined himself, which was often. During takes he'd sometimes say, out loud and to himself, "Why can't I get this to work?" I was rooting for him and his movie. Maybe that sounds like the writer getting too close to his subject, but to me, honest reporting is you dig as deep as you can and you write what you find, and what you feel.

When Christine and I arrived at the farm, in very late afternoon, the air was cool and windy. Maddie escorted us to the barn. Any other time I would have just walked there myself, but this was an event. Night greeted us warmly. He was still - jet-weary from his Los Angeles trip, and from everything else. He walked us into the screening room. It was half past five. He gave—most atypically—just a few words of instruction, pointed to the projectionist, and he was gone.

The yellowish overhead light dimmed slowly. Our anticipation was exquisite: Christine and I were on a movie date, our grandest one ever. We had left our cell phones in the car, along with our everyday lives. First came the company credits, the Blinding Edge Pictures logo of the diving man. And then, with no warning, Paul Giamatti's bearded face and bold eyes filled the screen. He was looking to squash a bug. Behind him was the movie's chorus, the Perez de la Torre sisters. They were screaming. We laughed. We were off.

The screening room had forty seats, but we were the only people in it. At one point, the plan had been for us to watch it with a test audience, to watch it with forty civilians, forty people unknown to Night. They would have been given scorecards and Night would have analyzed their results. But Night had canceled the test screening. He knew the movie wasn't there from Bhavna's response alone. Still, he screened the movie for

267

Christine and me. Forty responses from strangers might overwhelm him, but one or two from people he knew was different. Maybe we could help.

Night and I had spent a lot of time together. He liked being examined. When I didn't know what he was talking about, he'd figure out another way to explain himself. I could not imagine a more emotionally available subject. Night, to me, was Andre, from *My Dinner with Andre*, a movie Night watched on my suggestion. All the movie shows is two people engaged in a dinner conversation in an elegant restaurant. Except at the beginning and end, Andre, a theater director, does nearly all the talking. He describes to Wally his trip to a forest in Poland with forty strangers just to see what happens, and the other desperate things he does to get out of his comfort zone. I have always felt like Wally, who lives on the hope that today might be the day his agent calls with good news about one of his plays and in the meantime he's comforted by home delivery of *The New York Times* and other simple pleasures. (Paul Giamatti has a lot of that in him: Happiness is being in a Vietnamese restaurant, reading an Ian Fleming novel while a steaming bowl of egg noodles warms your face, nobody bothering you. To me, Paul was as familiar as Night was exotic.) In *My Dinner with Andre*, Andre is inspiring and Wally is inspirable. That played out for Night and me. I think of optimism as a form of prayer, and maybe it is, but Night made me realize that hope is not enough. To him, positive thinking was a single brick in the foundation and nothing more. I never heard him begin a sentence with the words "I hope." He didn't confuse *hope* with *faith*. Faith was born in effort.

Watching *Lady in the Water*—the version I saw of it—was a devastating experience. By far the biggest obstacle for me was that I couldn't figure out Story. I didn't know if she was a human being or a mermaid or what. The idea of her as a narf, a sort of angel, went right over my head. Story—and here I must detach Story from the lovely real-life Bryce—cried too much. She spent a lot of time in the shower and I didn't know why. It wasn't like she had to stay wet. I didn't know anything about Story's life. She felt too abstract, and that made the movie feel abstract. Where did she come from? Where was she going? Why should I care?

There were good things. The whole look of the movie—Chris Doyle's photography in particular—was sumptuous. Night was natural in his role as Vick Ran, writer in despair, wanting to save the world; the role fit him. Paul did an excellent job. He gets to do more in *Lady* than in any other movie he'd been in: He's angry, he's droll, he cries, he carries Story while running from a scrunt, he's on the screen for two hours, and he's good the whole time. (As Night's mother would say, maybe something good will come out of it for him!) Sarita was outstanding as Night's sister, Anna Ran. Their relationship was, for me, one of the most believable things in the movie, and I saw the movie more through her eyes than anybody else's.

In fact, late in the day, when Anna stands in the mailroom with Young-Soon and the five Perez de la Torre girls as one of the seven sisters, *Lady in the Water* became the movie I had hoped it would be. From that point on, I was swept away. It became, for me, about Cleveland, and not Story, and that made all the difference. I still didn't care about Story, but I wanted to know if Cleveland would be healed. In the last fifteen minutes, I finally had a rooting interest. It was soaring. It wasn't too little, but it was too late.

The closing credits came. I wondered if my parents would like it. They like esoteric movies. I waited to hear Youssou N'Dour singing Dylan's "Chimes of Freedom." But it never came.

By prearrangement, Night was not there when the screening concluded, and I was relieved. Christine and I left the barn in stunned silence. I knew she felt as I did. We stepped out through doors designed for horses and were surprised to see how much light was still in the sky. We walked down a minor hill and to our car, drove through Wyeth country, found a restaurant, and over dinner compared our similar notes.

"What are you going to tell Night?" Christine asked.

"He's gonna want to know what we thought of the movie."

"Are you sure?"

The next morning Night called me before I could call him. Night knew what I did not, that *Lady* was not a movie yet. Once, I had anticipated a celebratory conversation, but now I was dreading it.

"I'm not the intended audience for this movie," I told him.

"You didn't dig it," he said.

"You loved *E.T.* I didn't. Maybe I'm not qualified to be discussing this movie. Maybe my tastes are too earthbound for it."

"Where did it lose you?"

There are artists who can't take criticism from anybody. Night can't *not* take criticism. At Night's invitation, I laid out everything. So much of what we say in our everyday conversation is dressed-up bullshit—trying to get people to like us, trying to keep our jobs—it felt good to be able to speak to somebody who felt he needed to hear what he didn't want to hear. Night knew he could make the movie better. That's why he was listening to me, just as he would have listened to forty different voices, had he been ready to fill the screening room with strangers that afternoon. The ability to hear voices—internal voices; external voices; voices that have language; voices that don't—we all have it, Night said, but you have to make yourself available to them.

After that phone call, I saw Night in even more heroic terms. I didn't "dig" an early version of Night's movie. So what? I'm one viewer, watching a movie that was still in editing, just like the kid from NYU. What drew me to Night in the first place was his energy at the Burch party and what awed me about Night was his effort, his endurance, his willingness to struggle.

He wasn't Bob Dylan. When Dylan played electric and the old folkies booed him, Dylan knew he was doing something right. Night would never be happy willfully alienating people. He had never completely buried Manoj. But the originality of Dylan was a true inspiration for Night, and making *Lady* was a giant step for him. By risking his career on a fairy tale, he was making the rest of his moviemaking life possible. He was making good on what he told Nina after *The Village*, that he didn't want his audience to know where he was going next. He wasn't going to let the success of *The Sixth Sense* define the rest of his career.

The following morning, Night called again. This time he was all revved-up. He said he was going to begin the movie with a voiceover that would explain the legend behind Story, so that the moviegoer is ahead of the movie's characters, and the driving tension is to see if the actors will catch up. That sounded interesting. It sounded like *Columbo*, the old Peter Falk detective show, where we know things that Lieutenant Columbo does not, and we watch to see if he'll figure it out, even though we know he will. Night was going back to one of his earliest script drafts, when he had opened the movie with an explanatory voiceover, but he had abandoned it along the way. It came back to him when he and Bhavna, both fans of horror movies, watched a screamfest, *Hostel*, in their hotel room on their March trip to Los Angeles. The movie opens with a murderer cleaning his bloody tools. "That one image," Night said, "made me stay with the movie." Night's idea was that you would hear the voiceover at the start of *Lady* while looking at pictures—paintings—of Story's underwater world. "If you make the right tonal change it can infect the entire movie," Night said. "It could be really beautiful. Cool, right?"

My contribution was minor, like seconding a motion. There were many others. There was the kid reviewer from NYU. There was Barbara Tulliver. There was Bhavna, the person most open to Night's movies, who told her husband, maybe inadvertently, that even she couldn't tell what Night was trying to do. There was Alan Horn, giving Night the time he needed, another way of saying that the movie was not there yet. Most significantly, there was Nina, Night's most critical reader. Night had placed our *Lady* problems on a scale and now the scale had reached its tipping point. In his desperation, Night was finally in his comfort zone. Now was his chance to be Michael—Michael Jordan—and get off a two-pointer in traffic at the buzzer, with Team Jordan down by one.

As a tester, I was now spoiled. Night disagreed. "You haven't even seen the movie yet!" he said, but I knew I'd need a long time before I'd be able to see *Lady* with fresh eyes. I see movies in movie theaters, and only once, typically. Night sees movies again and again. He had seen *Lady* dozens of times, more than that, tinkering all the while. He was looking for one more thing. He said, "I'm like a scientist now, mixing all these chemicals together. You can put in a hundred chemicals, and you get nothing. But if you add one more, and it's the right one, the whole thing goes *poof!*"

The next two weeks were a blur.

———

It seemed like seven P.M. was never going to come, and then it did. By Night's calendar, *Lady in the Water* made its debut in front of forty strangers in his screening room at the barn at seven P.M. on the third Tuesday in April 2006. Its scheduled public premiere was three months and three days away. As the civilians came in, parking their cars and minivans and SUVs by a stone wall off an old farm work road, Night watched discreetly from the porch of the farmhouse. It had been a peculiar day for him, a day with no *Lady* work to do, just the long wait for seven o'clock. Night was wearing a T-shirt one of the smokers had worn in the movie, stenciled with the words FLUORIDE IS MIND CONTROL. He wore jeans, as he did every day, but he had given his daily work boots a day off. He had on sneakers, Vans, the kind skateboarders wear. He was never too far from his boyhood.

Franny, Night's driver, in his dress-up pressed slacks, picked up Alan Horn and Jeff Robinov at the airport and drove them to the farm. Sam Mercer came in. So did Jeremy Zimmer and Peter Benedek, Night's agents. Jose Rodriguez was there, of course. They would all be standing, or sitting on the floor or on folding chairs. The forty seats were for the forty guinea pigs. As they came in, Maddie and a new assistant, April, had them sign confidentiality agreements, a promise that they wouldn't go out and review the movie on the Ain't It Cool website or anything like that. At the end of the screening, each person would be given an off-white heavy-stock card with a series of multiple-choice questions about the movie, then the chance to comment on it. Barbara Tulliver made brief introductory remarks, and the movie began. April waved to Night, a signal to him that the lights were down and he could now slip in. He got in just before the new two-minute voiceover—read by David Ogden Stiers, Major Winchester on the TV version of *M*A*S*H*. As the detached booming voice delivered the legend of Story, moody pictures of her world filled the screen. There was complete silence and stillness among the civilians, and a deep thrill came over Night. *This is the way the movie needs to begin!* Then Paul's bearded face filled the screen as he looked to squash a bug, and behind him the Perez de la Torre sisters screamed, as they always did. There was a communal laugh in the screening room. Night had 'em. Now he had to keep them. He listened and watched, to see if the audience would make the moves he needed them to make, from humor to suspense to fantasy to tenderness. Intellectually, he had thought it out every which way, but it wasn't an exercise anymore. He watched a young girl, maybe eight, cover her eyes and turn her head to the side when she sensed the scrunt was going to attack. He could see her terror. Night was delighted.

Before the screening, Night had told me that he just wanted to feel like Rocky Balboa when the final credits played. "If I'm standing, that'll be a victory," he said. Nothing he'd ever worked on had required so much effort, or brought him so much doubt. If he was hearing the collective silent voices of the forty movie-goers correctly, the first screening was coming off like a repeat of the actors' read-through on that hot August day in the cold hotel ballroom. In the audience's laughing, crying, screaming, and silence, Night heard a craving for a message they had buried a long time ago, that magic can happen, if you believe. Who's talking about things like that anymore? Nobody. Almost nobody.

When the movie was over, Night slipped out as quickly as he had come in and went over to the farmhouse. The civilians filled out their cards and headed to their cars. Horn and Robinov and Sam and the others came into the farmhouse, like athletes returning to the sanctuary of the clubhouse after a game. Robinov said, "Can you believe how it played in there? Amazing." Horn looked at Night in a way that said, *What did you do these past two weeks?* The old farmhouse was vibrating.

April came in with the scorecards and handed them to

Night. His heart was racing. A few people had suggested to Night that a screening at the director's own converted bucolic barn, a million miles away from the sticky floors and mushy chairs of a mall multiplex, would skew the results, but Night dismissed that. He had shown test screenings for *The Village* at the barn, and those results told him what hundreds of thousands of people told him shortly after its national premiere: The movie confused them.

Night retreated into the cramped copying room. There were many places he could have gone, but that's where he went. Fourteen months earlier, on a Saturday night, he had handed Paula a disk with the sale script for Disney, and Paula had dutifully made copies, on a machine that could handle only twenty pages at a time, for the Disney troika. Night put the forty cards on the copier and thumbed through them one by one. His daughters were home in bed and Bhavna was in India on a philanthropic mission. *Lady in the Water* had been like an affair for Night, but now he was ready for it to end. He needed it to end. He was spent. He studied the cards and read the comments and tallied the scores. He could feel the blood coursing through his veins, the sweat on his neck, the thin MIND CONTROL T-shirt clinging to his body. He had been looking for a person to hear him for years. He knew who it wasn't. It wasn't Nina. For all his decency, it wasn't Horn. It wasn't Chris Doyle or Paul or Cindy. The answer was in the cards. It was us. We go to his movies—the more, the better—and then Night has his proof: We hear him.

Night did the math. He could turn anything into a number, and now he had nothing but numbers in front of him. He checked the math again, to make sure it was correct. He couldn't believe the result. He was stunned. None of his movies had ever scored higher. It matched the best test scores *The Sixth Sense* had received, right before its release.

Carefully, one by one, out loud and to himself, Night went through the cards, reading the responses to the question, "What would you tell a friend about this movie?" The civilians said the movie was suspenseful, scary, funny, unexpected, different, spiritual. In perfect Palmer script and little-child print, in full sentences and ungrammatical fragments, the message was the same: They liked the movie. One woman who checked off the twenty-one to twenty-four age box said, "That it's a bizarre mix of comedy, fantasy, action, scary—suspenseful—yet works—kind of like it didn't make up its mind in a good way." Thirty-nine cards were positive or better. One card was negative. One person did not like it. Night wondered what he had done wrong.

There's the power of one person's faith, and there's the power of a group. *Lady in the Water* had some of both. Night with his cousins, trying to get the cup on the table to move, had some of both. So did Night in Bristol, with the actors and the crew. Night had created a village, and the village made him feel less alone and helped him make his movie. People bought into it. Paul Giamatti put Chrismandu's name and telephone number in his wallet! That was something.

I had less than a bit role at Bristol—guy with notebook—but I felt the pull of village life. One day during preproduction my car conked out on the Brooklyn-Queens Expressway; over the phone, Jimmy Mazzola gave me a *Who's Who* of mechanics in his borough plus an invitation to his house for a recuperative meal.

Near the end of the shoot, I went to the California desert for my day job, to cover Michelle Wie's first golf tournament as a professional. In the third round, I saw her take what looked to me like an incorrect drop. The correct drop would have had her backswing impeded by a bush. Reporting the story—the way I felt was the right way to report it (talk to the subject first and the rules official second)—led to her being disqualified. If you want to do something unpopular, get a pretty, talented, likable sixteen-year-old girl golfer disqualified from her pro debut. I got bombarded. One caller to my house said my head should be severed, stuck between a sliced hamburger bun, and crammed into a microwave. Returning to Bristol, to the village Night had created there, was a relief.

Paul Giamatti understood the weird spot I was in in a way almost no one else could, even though the stakes in his father's situation with Pete Rose had been incomparably higher. Paul gave me the advice he follows himself: *Who gives a fuck what a bunch of strangers think?* In his own way, Paul was warm about the whole thing, warmer than I knew he could be. About seven people understood what I was trying to do, and he was one of them. You might think it was a coincidence, that I was around Paul just then. I don't.

At a Halloween wrap party for the movie, Yen Nguyen, the beautiful camera loader, came carrying a golf club and dressed as Michelle Wie. We had never spoken during the shoot, but that evening she said to me, "How do you like my costume, Mike?"

"Funny," I said.

Night knew I was lying. He said later, "She doesn't know you well enough to be making that joke."

He had his own take on the golf incident. "Michelle Wie's your subject, you're looking for moments when she reveals her character, and the moment she took that drop in front of that bush, she did. She was taking a shortcut. I'll bet Tiger has never taken a shortcut in his life." Night didn't even know what had made me watch the drop so intently in the first place. All during the drop, Wie's experienced, professional caddie,

I thought, had looked nervous. I don't know what he was thinking—our true thoughts are our last great privacy—but I do know what his face was saying to me: *This is going too fast.* In a completely different circumstance, when Paul's shoe spoke to Night, it must have been nearly the same thing. So far, listening to voices had done nothing but get me in trouble, but what the hell. There was no denying their power.

During the shoot, *The Philadelphia Inquirer* ran a story about how people complete a sentence that begins, "I believe . . ." I found it interesting and polled various *Lady* people on the subject. Cindy Cheung said, "I believe that imagination is our greatest power." Chris Doyle said, "I believe all the world is a little mad except you and me and even you are a little strange." Bryce said, "I believe in the power of the individual to alter the destiny of humanity." Paul said, "I believe there is no way Shakespeare wrote those fucking plays, no way in hell."

Night said, "I believe."

"Right," I said. "But how do you complete it?"

"It's complete," he said.

We were driving to work. It seemed like Night was always driving to work, even when he was driving home.

"I believe. Period."

He was already working on the next one.

Author's Note

This book is nonfiction. The scenes and names are all real. Many of the quotes have been edited, as spoken language doesn't always work on paper, but no liberties in meaning were taken. If a conversation was recounted by others, I used it only if the source was trustworthy. I found Night to be more trustworthy than most.

Night read the book in manuscript form and made numerous suggestions, many of which I took him up on. His main note was to cut out the boring parts, which I have tried to do. He made no suggestions to make himself look better, which is part of his dazzling oddness. I think I know now the meaning of *counterintuitive*.

Readers may want to know, among other things, how I got in Bryce's trailer (she invited me) or Sarita's handbag (she told me what was in it) or, to the degree I did, Night's head (ditto). You are welcome to write and if I can tell you I will. (Modernists may use mbamberger0224@aol.com.) Please, though, do not ask me to get your ideas to Night. For that I suggest mental telepathy.

Michael Bamberger
April 25, 2006
Philadelphia

13   CONTINUED: 13

K M/W CLEV   B - CU CLEV   M/W STORY

13D   13D   13E

CLEVELAND
6 You know you're not allowed to swim
7 in that pool. It's for tenants
8 only.

He stares at her. She looks back. He looks away.   *

CLEVELAND
9 And you need to wear a swimsuit.

Beat. She is gazing at him with beautiful eyes.

CLEVELAND
10 Where are you from?

WOMAN
11 The Blue World.

Beat.

CLEVELAND
12 Is that an apartment?   _END 3_

She does not understand his question. Beat.

WOMAN
13 Do you feel an awakening?

CLEVELAND
14 I'm sorry?

WOMAN
15 It will feel like pins and needles.
16 Inside.

She points at her chest. Beat. He stares at her.

WOMAN
17 It is not you,
(beat)
18 Do not feel bad.

She goes quiet. There is an awkward silence in the bungalow.

CLEVELAND
19 I won't get you in trouble okay.   *
(I'm not going to get you in   *
trouble, okay? You can go.)   *

WOMAN
20 Thank you.   *